Hearing God's Voice

Thom Linders

Copyright © *Thom Linders,* 2025

All Rights Reserved

This book is subject to the condition that no part of this book is to be reproduced, transmitted in any form or means; electronic or mechanical, stored in a retrieval system, photocopied, recorded, scanned, or otherwise. Any of these actions require the proper written permission of the author.

Table of Contents

Introduction 1
Chapter 1 GENESIS 5
Chapter 2: EXODUS 59
Chapter 3: LEVITICUS 113
Chapter 4: NUMBERS 146
Chapter 5: DEUTERONOMY 197
Chapter 6: JOSHUA 239
Chapter 7: JUDGES 259
Chapter 8: RUTH 289
Chapter 9: 1 SAMUEL 295
Chapter 10: 2 SAMUEL 337
Chapter 11: 1 KINGS 374
Chapter 12: 2 KINGS 411
Chapter 13: 1 CHRONICLES 443
Chapter 14: 2 CHRONICLES 477
Chapter 15: EZRA 513
Chapter 16: NEHEMIAH 528
Chapter 17: ESTHER 543
A Final Word 551
Final Bibliography 552
Answer Key 556
Appendix: Daily Bible Reading Plan 566

Introduction

Christianity is not a religion. I have heard it said that religion is man's attempt at reaching God. God's ways are too high for us. We will never possess the ability to reach Him.

Remember the legend of Icarus, whose father had invented wax wings? He tried to fly to the heavens, and when he was too close to the sun, the wings melted, and the child plummeted to his death.

We read in Genesis 11:1-9 of how the people of Babel attempted to build a tower to reach God. Punishment and the confusion of language and the scattering of people through the earth result. Why? God did not intend for man to reach Him.

Humanity's purpose is to glorify God. That is the beauty of the Gospel message. Even though God knew man would sin and be separated from Him, He still created man. Before the foundation of the world, He had provided a way for man to be redeemed to Himself through Jesus Christ.

According to Wikipedia, there are over 10,000 distinct religions in the world.[1] But there is only one way for man to connect to God.

Jesus said: "I am the way, and the truth, and the life. No man comes to the Father but by me." (John 14:6)

Why would such a powerful and awe-inspiring deity create such a restrictive process? Because He is Holy. Holy is perfect. Why would there need to be alternative ways when the one that exists is perfect?

Many view Christianity as one of the world's great religions. Approaching it as such is a mistake which some denominations make. Christianity should be a relationship with God through His son, Jesus Christ.

Communication

With any relationship, communication is the key. When communication ceases, marriages dissolve, companies fail, and peace shatters. It is vital for both sides to communicate with each other.

God wants to hear our prayers. Like a parent, He wants us to open our hearts and minds and let Him know how we're doing. He wants to hear our concerns, comfort us in our sorrows, and rejoice in our victories.

Daniel praying in front of his window three times a day is a good example (Daniel 6:10-28).

But in truth, we should live our lives in a state of constant prayer (1 Thessalonians 5:16-17).

All of this is a good start to developing that close relationship which God wants to have with us.

Reciprocity

But any proper relationship is more than one party talking to the other. We possess two ears and one mouth; therefore, we ought to listen more than speak. How do we hear God talk?

I have felt the presence of Jesus many times in my life, but I have never heard an audible voice. We are told in John 10:27 that if we are His sheep, we will hear His voice. But how does God speak to us?

That is through His Word, the Bible.

When I first became serious about being a Christian, I needed to understand what it was I was believing in. I was determined to read through the entire Bible. Not just academically, I did that in high school. But prayerfully, asking God to reveal Himself to me.

I started in Genesis and ended in Revelation. At times, I could not put the Bible down. It was transformative.

Since then, I have read the Bible many times. After a while, it becomes a chore. OK, I have to read my Bible today.

You realize you are not hearing from God; you are just reading words on pages.

In this book, I am inviting my readers to go on what I hope will be a life-changing journey. Begin by praying for God to reveal Himself through the reading of His Word, but then each day read approximately eighty-five verses (see the calendar).

Ask yourself what those verses are saying to you. Not what they mean. As much as I encourage deep Bible study to understand scripture, here I want you to listen. What is God saying to your soul?

To help illustrate this, I will share a daily devotional of sorts. This is how the verses for that day spoke to my heart.

I take a moment to research the commentaries to make sure I am not passing along some heresy. But it isn't about understanding the hermeneutics and imagery. It is about being intentional to hear God's voice as you read.

Please join me here each day as I will share my experience, which should differ from yours, with you. I would encourage you to share with us your experience. May God bless all who join us in this journey.

Every day you will see a listing of approximately eighty-five verses (full chapters) to read. I encourage you to read those chapters and to help you focus on what those chapters are saying to you.

I have read those same chapters and will share what my thoughts are. I haven't researched these thoughts about the chapters, but they are a response to how God spoke to my heart while reading them. This usually relates to something in the scriptures.

I have found that journaling what my emotions are from those chapters helps me remain more focused as I read. Not just trying to get through my verses. I wanted to hear the voice of God.

My process is that I pray, "Lord Jesus, as I read, show me what you need me to see today." It's that simple, and you can use whatever process works for you.

My goal at my website, www.thomlinders.com is to build a community of believers who will interact with each other while reading the Bible and encouraging each other to keep reading throughout the year.

Chapter 1:
GENESIS

Day 1: Genesis 1-3: Separating Waters

I didn't get far into today's reading, which was chapters 1-3 in Genesis. Chapter 1, verse 6, tells us that God separated the waters from the waters.

The Fog

Remember, there was no land yet. The earth wasn't even a globe yet. He had created the waters, and there were two waters, so He separated them. Were these two worlds the one we live in and another we aspire to? I don't think so.

I once lived in McKinleyville, CA, and spent a summer launching fishing boats at a place north of Eureka called Trinidad. Every morning, I would drive through the thick fog of the Northern California coast through the giant redwood trees, towering three hundred feet with trunks so broad you can drive a car through them.

We secured the boats on their trailers at the boat launch, lifted them, and then lowered them by winch onto a railroad car, which we would lower into the harbor.

The fog was so heavy that your clothing would become wet. I would often ride on the cart down to the water so that I could communicate by radio to the person operating the winch; otherwise, they would not know when the boat had reached the water.

As the morning moved along, the darkness that was prevalent around us would fade. You could look out toward the sea, and there was no separation between the heavy wet fog above and the ebbing tide below.

I would watch as the running lights on each fishing boat disappeared into the mist.

The Light

Then, almost magically, I would watch a small cushion of air form and separate the fog from the waters. You could then see boats out on the horizon.

As the morning progressed, the jagged rocks would appear, and you could feel the warmth as the sun would break through.

To me, that is the scene we have here in Genesis. The mist was hovering over the water, and they were inseparable.

Then, as the light came into the world, they parted, leaving that layer of atmosphere which would contain carbon dioxide, which the plants God would speak into existence would need to thrive.

The Order

Without creating the plants first, they could not turn the carbon dioxide into oxygen and provide the environment needed for man and beast to survive.

I love how magnificently God had planned every detail out. There is so much order in everything He created.

I also see a parallel in this imagery of my transformation. I was just that cold, silent morning. There were waves pulsing within me, and you could hear them washing on the shoreline.

But I could not see through the darkness. My own beliefs in science blinded me.

Then God separated those waters, and the light came into me. He gave me the ability to experience life.

Warmed by the sun and surrounded by beauty, I sometimes forget the eeriness that preceded it.

I recall the effort I exerted on the job, but I overlook God's lifting of the darkness from my life.

May we always remember to humble ourselves and spend time with God so that our hearts may never grow weary?

The Joy

Later, as I ate lunch on the pier, I would watch sea otters playfully cavorting upon the boats anchored in the bay. They would swim through the water, propel themselves out of it to land upon the tarps that covered the boats, slide across, and then shoot off into the water again.

Little did I know that years later, I would tell my son about those playful otters.

I didn't know what God had in store for me because I was just beginning to see the beauty He had created.

How much more splendid will heaven be when our eyes can grasp all that God has created for us?

Tomorrow, we will read Genesis 4-6.

Day 2: Genesis 4-6: Patterns and Second Chances

I like to read many versions of the Bible. Though there are some I find cumbersome and others with translation challenges, most have good qualities as well. I often read a verse or even a book in four or five different versions to get the full meaning of the text.

This year, I will read the NIV for the sake of this book.

Making Love

In this translation, I read something interesting. This translation mentions many childbirths but describes only three as the result of "making love."

First was Cain, who should have been the rightful heir. But, of course, he was corrupted by evil and killed Abel.

Cain's banishment and Abel's death left Adam and Eve without an heir.

We later read that Cain made love and brought forth Enoch. This was the child of one already corrupted.

The name Enoch means "trained" or "dedicated."

Cain had departed from God and was not training his children in righteousness, but in battle. This is where the mighty Nephilim will probably come from.

These sons, trained in battle, would later take the daughters of Seth and further corrupt humanity. Invariably, sin's influence will expand its control once it has entered our world.

The third time the term "making love" results in a child is with Adam and Eve, who give birth to the true heir, Seth.

The Pattern

This sets a pattern we see later when Abram has a son with Hagar, Ishmael. His heir is the second son, Isaac.

Then again, with Isaac when Esau sells his birthright for a bowl of stew to Jacob.

This foreshadows the replacement of the first covenant (the Law given to Moses) with the righteous second covenant: that of faith in Jesus Christ.

It is important to recognize patterns in Scripture because they guide us in our own selfdiscovery.

We begin life by being taught to be good. We inevitably fail, as no one is truly good except God.

It does, however, establish the basis that there is good, and conversely, there is evil. Without one, we would not recognize the other.

It is the dichotomy that exists between them that magnifies their significance.

As we struggle with the challenges of life, we come to realize how wretched we are. Long before I knew Jesus, I knew I needed, or at least desperately wanted, a mulligan. A second chance.

We love, we make mistakes, and lose that love. We want it back. It is that feeling of belonging that matters, even if not always with the same person. That connection with another person.

After multiple tries, we realize we are not getting any better at it. With each relationship, we continue to make new mistakes. How many chances will we get?

Desperation sometimes sets in; we fear continued strikeouts will lead to the coach benching us. So, we compromise and settle for something that feels acceptable.

Transformation

Perhaps it is not the fairytale romance we had dreamed of, but it seems like something we could live with.

Fortunately, just as when Jesus turned water into wine in Cana in the second chapter of John, the best was saved for last.

When we come to that place where we realize we will never be good enough, and we place our only hope in Jesus, He gives us a perfect salvation.

Jesus gives us redemption that surpasses all else and enables us to even understand what love truly is.

Our feeble attempts at being good, which always falter, are replaced with Jesus' righteousness, which never fails. We get off that hamster wheel of trying and failing and can instead rest in the arms of our Savior.

Sure, we continue to sin and struggle with the personal dissatisfaction of our actions. But we know that Christ Jesus has already forgiven even those sins, and we can move forward knowing that we remain in Him.

Tomorrow, we will read Genesis 7-10.

Day 3: Genesis 7-10: 150 Days

This morning, because they are a little shorter, we will read through Chapter 10 of Genesis.

There is a lot happening in every chapter of the Bible, and these contain the story of Noah and the flood. I read through many commentaries about these verses on Biblehub.org, and there will never be enough days for me to dig into all that there is.

Solitude

What I found interesting was that only one of the commentaries Keil and Delitzsch Biblical Commentary on the Old Testament mentioned the 150 days.[2] That timeline struck a note with me.

Can you imagine the emotional turmoil that had to be going on within each of the members of Noah's family that was on that ark?

First, although they knew what water was, they had rivers, there were wells to draw from, and they had never seen it fall from the sky.

God tells Noah to build an ark, in the middle of the desert, and that He is going to send a flood.

The wells bubble up, the rivers breach, tides from the seas encroach upon the land. Suddenly, the skies even open up, and for six solid weeks, they continue to pour out on the land.

The inhabitants of this boat are living with the smells of all these animals while floating upon the waters.

Then the rain stopped. They bobbed along, being tossed about as the winds moved them.

Knowing that everyone and everything they ever knew was now gone, they looked out at the horizon.

Patience

Would this be it? Would they spend the rest of their lives aboard this floating zoo?

Days turned into weeks, weeks into months. Now, five months had passed. Would they have been better off to have drowned with their friends?

I'm sure they loved each other, but imagine a life where all you have to look forward to is another day of caring for the animals.

In the early 1980s, I moved to McKinleyville, California, with a girlfriend; her grandfather would take me fishing in Trinidad Harbor.

As you leave the bay, you can see the shoreline, but only for a while. Soon, every direction looks the same. It is easy to become disoriented since everywhere you look is just the gentle slope of the earth falling away into more water.

Sky and sea to the left, sky and sea to the right. In front of you and behind. As the days went by, I often grew tired because of the monotony. The occasional challenge of catching a fish would revive me.

Now imagine that same scene for 150 days.

God had told Noah that He would send rain for 40 days, and He had. We do not read that He told him how long he would be adrift. Was this his fate?

Purpose

Even in our daily grind, we can experience this sense of pointlessness. We wake up every day to shower, eat some breakfast, go to work, and then relax with the family and go to sleep, only to repeat it all the next day.

We can sense that there has to be more to life, but have no reasonable expectation of what that is.

We become anesthetized by the surrounding wonders, bored in a world of marvels that would have blown the minds of our ancestors. For us, it is just so mundane. We have 180 channels with nothing on worth watching, so we watch reruns from the 90s.

If that is how we feel, can you imagine what seeing water in all directions for 150 days, with no expectation of anything changing, would be like?

Noah had to have a steadfast faith that God would not have saved him for this. We also believe that God has a purpose for each of us. God's purpose for us continues if we still breathe.

I look forward with eager anticipation to the day when the Lord says I am finished and can come home. Every day until then, we must ask ourselves, "What is God doing today that I can take part in?"

We know that a day approaches when God will rescue all the savable and then end this world.

But each morning, I awaken and ask myself, "What remains to be done?" Maybe I can't even leave the ship that I am on.

I have to do the same tasks I did yesterday, but there must be details I have not noticed that will guide me to where God needs me to engage.

Do not grow weary that we are still in the battle of life; instead, seek God's will on how you can glorify Him.

Tomorrow, we will read Genesis 11-14.

Day 4: Genesis 11-14: Towering Ambition

Once again, today, we read three chapters of Genesis (11-14).

Foolishness of Pride

Quickly, we read how foolish men are. After leaving Eden, the people begin to multiply and decide they want to repeat the sin that caused Satan to be cast out of heaven.

In Isaiah 14:12-14, Satan's claim to make his head higher than God's led to his expulsion. Now, here is another attempt by men to make a tower so high it would be above God.

This time, a confusion of languages scatters men across the globe.

Then we see a half dozen generations, long though they be, pass, and we have kings banding together to increase their strength. The result is Sodom and Gomorrah being places of such great sin, and they would become historical references for places deserving of God's wrath.

Ingratitude of Greed

If Adam and Eve had been content with paradise, they could have lived with God in His glorious presence, walking with Him in the garden.

Peaceful and perfect, the garden was a haven of life and prosperity. They could have spent eternity there with Him.

But they wanted more. They wanted to be like God. Therefore, their punishment followed.

Then, men wanted to be higher than God, so He scattered and confused their language. Their ambition to be more powerful pushed them to form an unlikely alliance.

Idolatry of Self

Today, we want to make ourselves gods again. We create our own version of who God is and worship that image we have construed.

God did not let Adam go unpunished. He did not allow the people in Babel to escape unscathed, and He destroyed Sodom.

From the time of Abram to the present day, historical records document many great and powerful empires that attempted to dominate their people. Every time, the result has been the same.

Yet here we are again. Believing that the god we made up will not punish us for repeating the same mistakes they had.

Arrogance leads to the idolatry of self, the religion of me, and to destroying all.

Promises

Melchizedek, priest of the God Most High, comes along. He reminds them it is God that has provided everything.

Abram pays tribute, and God performs a miracle, fulfilling His promise to make him a powerful nation.

This 99-year-old man and his 90-year-old barren wife had given up on the promise of a child, but with God, all things are possible.

We see how Abram lies about Sarai being his sister - but God still keeps His promise.

God's character does not depend on us keeping His commandments or doing our part. He keeps His word because His word is true.

We are to emulate Jesus and let our character reflect the God who dwells in us. Loving others the way He loves us. Forgiving them as He forgave us. Showing His character even when others betray us, the way we betray Him.

Just like the people in the days of Abram, we get to choose whom we will serve.

Will it be the god of our own creation? I can assure you of disappointment because that idol has no power. He came from our own imagination and could do nothing.

God supremely deserves our complete devotion.

Tomorrow, we will read Genesis 15-18.

Day 5: Genesis 15-18: The Reward of Faith

We read chapters 15-18 in Genesis today, and from the very first verse, we hear the Lord is our shield and our reward.

Protection

So often have I bowed before the Lord, seeking His protection. Asking Him to put a hedge around me without acknowledging that He is the shield. He is the only protection any of us need. But we must think about how a shield works. We must position the shield in front of or above us. I think we often suffer harm because we place the Lord, our shield, beneath us. We sit upon it as if it were some sort of child's sled. A toy that we show no reverence for.

When we are not keeping the Lord in His appointed position, it is not unusual for the shield to not protect us from the incoming dangers of this life.

The Reward

So, we struggle, and then we return to the Lord, asking Him to provide us with a reward. A reward? My first question is—why do we deserve a reward?

We are an unfaithful, immoral group who deserve punishment but receive grace. Yet we presume upon the Lord that we somehow deserve a reward?

We mistakenly expect that this reward will be some material gain, a victory, or increased power. These are idols we have created in our own minds.

This opening verse tells us God is the reward. We do not deserve Him, but He assures us He is our reward.

When we have God, we need nothing else. There is nothing more.

Faith

In verse 6, we read Abram believed in the Lord. Faith is our righteousness.

It is not our works. We could do no works if God had not provided us the ability to do them. We are measured by our faith. Yet we are often like Sarah in verse 18:15 in that even though we do wrong against the Lord; we think somehow He doesn't know. We try to lie about what we did. Upon discovery of our lies, we, like Abraham, attempt to bargain with God. We must negotiate with ourselves.

God has given us the most lenient of offers. All He asks for is our faith. We claim we have faith but continue to trust in our bank accounts, our employers, and our doctors to provide us with safety and security.

For over fifteen years, I took a statin drug to avoid having a heart attack. I still had one. None of these things means anything to the Lord. Genuine faith is trusting only in the Lord for His provision and protection.

Passions

When we do this, we have no reason to lie to Him. He knows our passions.

When our hearts are not fully trusting in God, we wear ourselves out trusting in our own labors.

People may ask why we are not taking part in worship or ministries, and we claim we don't have the capacity with our schedules.

This is like Sarah laughing at God.

He knows how much time we have and that the only reason we are too busy is that we have failed to trust His word.

Tomorrow, we will read Genesis 19-21.

Day 6: Genesis 19-21: Distorted Priorities

This morning, we read chapters 19-21 in Genesis.

Not the Way God Made Us

We can see that in the times since Lot dwelt in Sodom until now, the priorities of man have changed, in some ways, and the sins of man remain the same.

First, we read about how the lusts of the flesh cause the men throughout Sodom to want to defile the angels who were staying in Lot's house.

We see angels sleep as they had entered his house to do so.

Homosexuality was a sin in those days, as it is now. God does not change. Cultural acceptance does not dictate what is right. The people in Sodom throughout the city felt this was acceptable, but it was still a sin, and for it, they were all punished.

God's mercy spared Lot and his family from the wrath he poured out on those cities.

Lot's wife looked back, and God turned her into a pillar of salt.

Like the cool kids

This reminds me of when I gave up smoking. I began smoking when I was ten years old. My parents smoked; therefore, cigarettes were always lying on the table.

In those days, commercials on TV and billboards made smoking seem sexy. You wanted to be the Marlboro Man. You knew rugged men would walk a mile for a Camel.

Even facing death by coughing, looking cool was too irresistible to pass up. So, you kept doing it until you got good at it.

We didn't smoke any of those wimpy menthol cigarettes, either. It was Winston because they were the sponsors of NASCAR, Marlboro, or Camel.

I would go through two to three packs a day, though some of that was while I was tending bar, and I would light a lot more than I would smoke.

In those days, not only could we light up at work, but in a bar, the air was so thick with smoke that you were going to be inhaling it, anyway.

Never Again

They had to do a tracheostomy on me when I had my accident, and I watched the respiratory technician suction the fluid from my lungs.

It was a mixture of blood, mucus, and tar. Black disgusting-looking sap being extracted through the clear tube. I remember thinking I would never smoke again.

Within a year of leaving the hospital, I was back up to a pack, then two packs a day. It was comforting. I knew it was not good for me. I didn't care.

Taken by God

After turning my life over to the Lord, I was working through some tough financial struggles, trying to keep my magazine alive. I was praying for the Lord's help, and I realized I was asking for financial help while spending money on these foolish sticks that I was no longer enjoying.

So, I prayed, Lord Jesus, please take this sin away from me. Let me be a better steward of the resources you have provided.

I have not smoked since, that was over two decades ago. Not saying I haven't watched as other people in my life have lit up and I wanted to. But the Lord has given me the resolve not to pursue this sin.

I am not saying smoking is a sin for everyone. The Bible doesn't address it. Because I had made it into something important, for me, it was.

Sin is Easy

Getting back to today's chapters, it is all about how we prioritize things in our life. In these verses, we see Lot will give his virgin daughters to the men to be raped. Their safety and purity were less valuable than protecting these angels, or perhaps than permitting the sin of sodomy.

We see this disturbing situation in chapter 20, where Lot's daughters get their father drunk, have incestuous relations with him, and become pregnant. This should be unthinkable today.

We see Abraham lie again about Sarah being his sister, so Abimelech takes her for his wife. Thankfully, in that situation, God intervenes and prevents her from being defiled.

Then, compare this sexual deviation to the value of a well, for which Abraham will give seven ewe-lambs to signify a binding agreement on whose they are. Granted, in a desert, water is life. We see with Hagar and her son how important water is.

Without water, life does not exist.

But the dichotomy between how little they valued the safety of their children, the virtue of their daughters, the sanctity of their marriage versus the rights to a well makes me question some things we elevate to great importance in our own lives.

Are we willing to follow God's will for our life? What if that might compromise our income?

Would it matter if that required, we forego our favorite pastimes and leisure activities?

I often warn against the idolatry of self; what are you placing above your commitment to the Lord today?

Ask Him to remove it, and if you will repent, watch what God can do. For those who want to see God at work, this is an intimate way to see Him.

Tomorrow, we will read Genesis 22-24.

Day 7: Genesis 22-24: Blind Faith

This morning, we read chapters 22-24.

Family Matters

The emphasis within these three chapters is faith. Blind faith.

First, we see Abraham, who had waited his entire life to have children. He sends his firstborn away because it was with his servant Hagar and not his wife.

Now, at one hundred years old, he has Isaac, and he loves him. But the Lord tells him to sacrifice the boy. Isaac is a foreshadowing of Jesus, God's only son, who He sacrificed for us. Much like Jesus had to carry His cross, Isaac had to carry the wood that became the altar on which Abraham was prepared to offer him as a sacrifice.

I would imagine Abraham was moving slowly, giving the Lord plenty of time to provide the offering. But he was still willing to obey the Lord.

We read at 22:7, where Isaac was noticing something a little strange as he carried the wood up the hill. He asks his father where the offering is.

Did he know his father would tie him to the altar?

What thoughts ran through his mind when his father tied him to the altar?

How about when Abraham stood over him holding the knife?

Provision

But he survived because God provided the ram. God always provides. He demands our obedience, but He is not merciless. When we obey, He will not cause us to suffer.

Consider how that affected the relationship between father and son. Was Isaac impressed with his father's faithfulness or appalled that he would sacrifice his only son?

Later, Abraham sends out this servant to get Isaac a wife. Customs in those days differed from ours today. I can only imagine Isaac wondering - this man who would have killed me had not God intervened, is going to have his servant pick out a wife for me?

Rebekah had to have an equal amount of faith. Here is this servant who she allows to put a ring on her nose and bracelets on her wrist. She goes off to a foreign land to marry a man she had never seen. But for both, this worked out very well.

Based on Trust

There are many lessons we can take from this section of scripture. May I suggest this one: that when we trust in the Lord, He is going to provide us with good things. He will not harm us, as we saw with Abraham on the mountain, and He will not give us terrible relationships.

Matthew 7:9-11 states: "Which of you, if your son asks for bread, will give him a stone?" Or if he asks for a fish, will he give him a snake? If you, then, though you are evil, know how to give good gifts to your children, how much more will your Father in heaven give good gifts to those who ask him! (NIV)

We see through the story of Isaac that we can trust God to provide us with the things we need and even those we want. Yet, how often do we run ahead of God and reject what He is giving us, thinking we can somehow do better on our own?

Even though my wife is the fourth woman I married, I have known she was the wife He gave me and that I would only bring troubles upon myself if I did not respond to God's command to love her every day (see Ephesians 5:25). Some days are harder than others, but I am sure even more so for her. We find happiness by obeying God.

Tomorrow, we will read Genesis 25-27.

Day 8: Genesis 25-27: Lies and Legacies

Thank you for continuing to take this journey with us today. After reading through chapter 27 today, I feel a need to ask you all to pray for each other.

Separation

We read how Abraham became the father of many nations, not only through his wife Sarah, who bore him Isaac, but also through Hagar, who bore him Ishmael. There was also Keturah, who gave birth to Zimran, Jokshan, Medan, Midian, Ishbak, and Shuah.

Ishmael, from the beginning, was a warrior and moved down near Egypt. The sons of Keturah moved to the east. This would have been the many tribes and nations which, to this day, struggle with the Israelites.

Later, Isaac had two sons, Esau and Jacob.

Esau carelessly treated his birthright and allowed himself to be tricked out of his blessing.

This is not to excuse Jacob or Rebekah for conceiving to deceive Isaac. I will leave that for another time. Instead, I think we should heed this as a warning.

We can all become blinded by our own desires.

Isaac's eyesight had grown dim, but even though he questioned twice if Jacob was his son, Esau, his desire for the food and to give his blessing drove him to overlook his gut instincts.

Twisting Scripture

This we also do. We try to be discerning, but not so much that it interferes with our plans. We know what we want to happen, and we try to justify that this is God's will for us. As a general rule, if it is not in the Bible, God did not say it.

We still will find the words in the Bible that will support our desire and twist the meaning of them toward our cause.

This is how Isaac falls victim to Jacob's deception. Satan was around to see that. He knows how it worked, and he will use that same gullibility to his advantage when we let him.

Therefore, we must approach all things in life, seeking God's will first. Then seeing if our plans fit within the scope of His. Not can we bend God's will to fit around our plans? It is a subtle difference, but an important one.

27:29 warns us to always bless Jacob (Israel), promising blessings to those who do so and curses to those who curse him.

Reunion

Moving on from there, I had a couple of other powerful impressions in these verses.

First, their deaths reunited Abraham and Ishmael with their people.

This instills in me hope I will see my mother and family, including my church family, in heaven. Death gathers us to our people.

The sense of community we build here holds eternal value beyond this life. I find encouragement in this.

Like most people, I believe there was much I failed to do while my mother was alive. Knowing that she won't just be a person in heaven but will be my people means I will have an opportunity to atone for those shortcomings.

No Way to Treat Our Wives.

And my final thought on today's verses is this: What is with these Jewish men lying about their wives?

I am not advocating for anyone to be jealous and controlling, but time after time, instead of standing up for and protecting their women, these guys lie and put their women up for play.

Their frequent exposure reveals that this is not Gcd's will for how a man should treat his wife.

For one thing, lying is always a sin. But a man should love his wife and be willing to lay down his life for her as Christ did for the church (See Eph 5:25).

Tomorrow, we will read Genesis 28-30.

Day 9: Genesis 28-30: Virtual Church, Real Faith

Good morning. We are nine days into this journey, and today, we read Genesis chapters 2830. I will share the three highlights that spoke to me.

Community

In 28:3, we read: May God Almighty bless you and make you fruitful and increase your numbers until you become a community of people. (Gen 28:3, NIV)

I have gained an understanding of the pressure a pastor faces when he is trying to build a church. The pressure to increase the size of your congregation is always there. Only by growing can you increase your resources.

When more people join your community, you have more people who God will lead to be teachers, greeters, join the praise team, and even add to your prayer group. These are all important to a growing community of faith.

Although we don't meet in a building, and I hope you all are members of a local church, my goal with these devotionals is to create a virtual church. A community of believers who will get to know each other and will encourage and pray for one another.

Our country, indeed, the world, can become more united in Jesus these days through the power of the internet. I have grown tired of this gift God gave us being used for vile purposes, and it is my intention to use it for His glory.

Just like in the local church, this only happens when members step out of their comfort zone and volunteer to help. I would encourage you all to introduce yourselves to each other, or to the group.

Tell us what you hope to gain from this community and what you believe your gift is. I believe we all know where our strength, or at least our passion, is. Along the way, I encourage each of you to share any thoughts, or needs, or concerns with me. My desire is for this to be a welcoming and inclusive place for all.

No manipulation

I don't want to be like Jacob in verse 28:20, however. Here, he is trying to bargain with, perhaps even manipulate, God. He says IF God will protect and provide, etc., then He will be his God. This is wrong.

God is God. He is my God, whether He gives me bread or a snake. He was my God when my back got broken as much as He was when my son was born.

I didn't even know Him at those times, but He still was and will always be. It is not within my, or any of ours, power to make Him God. He is God. As He Himself proclaimed, I am.

Fidelity

Most of the verses today dealt with this ancient ritual of polygamy. The text describes men receiving daughters as wages. Though jarring to modern sensibilities, we should feel thankful for our journey away from such viewpoints, a testament to our growth and God's grace.

That culture apparently did not value love highly. Jacob loved Rachel, and it would seem both she and Leah loved him. Both women believe that providing sons to Jacob will cause him to love them. We all need to be loved. Love should be unconditional, but not based on providing sons.

Leah's six boys were born out of her love for Jacob, or at least her desire for him to love her. Only Joseph was born from Jacob's love, which was always for Rachel. The rest of the sons were born because the servants were told to copulate with their master. We should keep that dynamic in view as we read through the history of how these tribes interact with each other.

Tomorrow, we will read Genesis 31-32.

Day 10: Genesis 31-32: Changed Attitudes and Unwavering Faith

Good morning. Today, we read only Chapters 31 & 32 of Genesis.

There are three things that stand out as I read through the Bible each morning. Today is no different.

Perception

First, in 31:2, we see that Laban's attitude toward Jacob had changed.

I know many people, including myself, who can be very stubborn. When someone has wronged us, real or perceived, we hold on to that grudge. We only harm ourselves when we do this.

Some say people don't change, and I am not sure I will disagree with them, on principle, but God can change a person's heart. I was a firm atheist and yet God came into my life and transformed me.

Whether a person changes, our perception of them or theirs of us can vary.

When I was younger, I hated President Ronald Reagan. I voted for President Jimmy Carter. Since my priorities have changed, I now recognize Reagan's strength as a leader and question my vote for Carter. Is it a change? Or is it growth? Maturation?

My point here is not political. It is dealing with how we lock in our minds an image of what someone is, and people are too complex to do that.

Just as we grow with experience in life, so do they. We cheat ourselves out of discovering who people are now when we prejudge them based on what we used to believe.

Availability

Second, in 31:11, an angel calls for Jacob, and I love his answer: "Here I am!" I ran from the Lord for much of my life.

Realizing my perception of Jesus was wrong crushed me, and I humbled myself. After I did, I felt Him calling on me to serve. This had to be a mistake. I was His enemy. How could He want me to serve Him?

God does not make mistakes. Empowered by him, I now have the words and courage to speak and write.

By removing barriers and providing resources, he has helped. Not because of any special quality in me, but because of who He is. He did this.

But, because my answer, and I honestly do not know why I responded this way, so I will attribute that to the Holy Spirit as well, was "Here I am."

I talk with people all the time about how they feel they should do this or that, and how they think certain things should be done.

When it involves service to the Lord, this is a sign that God is putting in your heart a desire to do something. The enemy is trying to interject fear so that you won't.

So, you may question if you have the time, the knowledge, or the ability to carry it out. Even though you believe someone should. That someone is you!

Stop listening to fear and take a chance. Next time you encounter that, say, "Here I am," and be amazed at what God can do through you.

Doubts

In chapter 32, we read how Jacob split his group into two camps out of fear. We read he felt unworthy. This is confirmation to me that we all struggle with these doubts.

Third, in response to those doubts, Jacob reminds God of His promises. God does not forget. Jacob did not remind God; instead, God guided Jacob to remember the promises and God's faithfulness.

He will not lead us into a path of destruction but will deliver us from those trails when we wander down them.

Thank you for reading along with us. You do not know how encouraging you all are to me.

May God bless you all.

Tomorrow, we will read Genesis 33-35.

Day 11: Genesis 33-35: Enough is Enough

Good morning. I hope you are all enjoying the daily devotionals. I wish I had more time every day to read God's Word. Just hearing His voice and letting it speak to my soul. Someday, I hope to retire and be able to devote all my time to reading and writing about my Savior.

For today, we will examine Genesis chapters 33-35. As usual, there were three things that really stood out to me.

Having plenty

First, in 33:9, Jacob is worried about how Esau will react to his return to Canaan, so he sends these lavish gifts ahead to soften his brother up. Esau's reaction, however, is, "I already have plenty, my brother. Keep what you have for yourself."

I know I am blessed more than many people. I have worked for a generous company for over two decades and we live frugally. This has enabled me to save and invest and, while far from being wealthy, I have long passed the point where we lived paycheck to paycheck.

This was not always our situation. I grew up very poor at some points. As you can read in my book, I even lived in my car a few times.

When my wife and I first started out, we had to juggle bills and scrimp to get by, and even then, it was only through God's mercy that we survived.

But we remained steadfast, served God, and over time, we gained the level of comfort we have.

Yet, at what point do we, any of us, say, "I already have plenty?" In America, that almost seems like a foreign mindset. We always want more.

Discontentment

Over the holidays, we had dinner with a friend who had a refrigerator and microwave from the 1970s that are still in everyday working condition. He maintained them, and the manufacturers built them to last.

The couple found contentment in their belongings, unfazed by modern advancements. It's rare for people to achieve the contentment advised in Hebrews 13:5.

Because of this discontent, we see what happens to Jacob and his family.

After this whole mess with Dinah being raped, Simeon and Levi slaughtered and plundered the Hivites for Shechem's actions, which were heinous.

Jacob told his household to "Get rid of the foreign gods you have with you." That results from discontentment. We read of it throughout the scriptures.

People want more, so they seek other gods who they believe will give them more than God has already provided.

It would be easy to fault them if we didn't do this, too. We make idols out of our jobs, our investments, and our bank balance. Struggling to make that grow so we can have more than what God has given us.

We bypass serving God to prioritize our financial and material wealth. In the end, we are materially wealthy, but spiritually bankrupt.

This was how sin resulting in rape and then murder had manifested itself in Jacob's household.

Change

This leads to the last point: in 35:10, God changes Jacob's name to Israel.

When we allow ourselves to be corrupted by this greed, we need to leave that part of ourselves in the past and become a new creation.

This is the picture of putting off the old man (see Eph 4:22-24) and being born again (see John 3:3).

Ecclesiastes 5:10 states that our wealth will never satisfy us.

Therefore, at some point, we all must adopt Esau's mindset and say, "I have enough." Let's invite God to transform us with contentment before the world taints us.

Tomorrow, we will read Genesis 36-38.

Day 12: Genesis 36-38: God's Plan, Our Resistance

Good morning. I hope you find a blessing in reading God's Word today. We read Chapters 36-38 in Genesis.

God's plan

The most prominent storyline in these chapters is Joseph and how he dreamed he would rule over his brothers and even his parents. Understandably, his family did not receive this well.

The underlying issue, however, is that God's ways are higher than our ways. Instead of realizing all blessings come from the Lord, we try to circumvent His plans.

This results in deceit, lies, and often death. This is not an isolated incident, and you would expect that after seeing it play out this way enough times, we would learn. But we never learn that lesson.

Resistance

Even today in America, resistance greets anyone with a plan that doesn't match the status quo, even when the status quo is failing.

We will lie, cheat, prostitute ourselves, and even plot murder to elude God's will.

God's will always prevail. We will learn in the next few chapters that what his brothers had intended for evil, God used for good. That does not mean we don't fight it, often to our own demise.

The Plan

There is an established blueprint of how things are supposed to work in America. We send our children off to school; they are to learn to be like each other. They train us from a young age to be pawns in a game we have little control over.

This results in a large group of interchangeable human capital from which corporate America can draw. If one employee leaves, we can just replace them with another.

They were all trained by a system to play a role and perform a duty.

Irreplaceable

In his book Linchpin, Seth Godin describes this situation, pointing out how important it is for people to step out of this mold and distinguish themselves as a unique and needed entity.[3] We should all strive to be irreplaceable.

This was what God was doing with Joseph. His brothers resented him for being different, just like some coworkers resent those who stand out.

Today, we see how the establishment, or as the news refers to them, the swamp, is not favorable to an outsider wanting to mix things up.

They assume that since no one has done that before, it will be uncomfortable. So, they resist.

Moving the cheese

I know many people who don't like their cheese to be moved. They learn to navigate the maze we call modern life, and by doing the same pattern, they always get their cheese. When someone moves it, they panic because they get to the end of the path, and it's not there!

It may be better cheese they would find by learning a different route. Perhaps even a great quantity of cheese.

That does not matter since it would require an additional effort for them to discover it.

Jacob's sons would rather kill or sell into slavery, their brother than accept change.

Fortunately, God knows our foolishness, and His plans are always much greater than our feeble minds can conceive.

When a new leader emerges, we need to develop a mindset of exploring what God intends to do. Attempt to be led by the Spirit to support the change so that you can contribute to future success.

In these days of transition, Lord, I pray that we as a nation will bow down to your power. You appoint leaders, as you did with Joseph, and it is for our good and Your glory.

Give us a heart to join your plan so that you will get all the praise.

Tomorrow, we will read Genesis 39-41.

Day 13: Genesis 39-41: Foreshadowing Jesus

Good morning. Thank you all for working through Genesis. Today, we read chapters 39-41, which focuses on Joseph.

Outside actions

We had already read his story of being sold into slavery and ending up in Egypt.

As a young man, he attracted the interest of Potiphar's wife, which led to trouble.

Sometimes, other people's actions will affect us. It was not Joseph who was sinning. Instead, it is Potiphar's wife who lusts after the strapping young man, and she attempts to seduce him.

Filled by the Spirit, Joseph resists the temptation of the flesh. Her sins still ensnare him as she holds his cloak while he runs naked from her chamber.

Knowing she would have to explain the boots under the bed, so to speak, in this case, a man's clothing in her chamber, she invents this deceitful tale. It gets her out of trouble, but places Joseph in prison.

Extreme circumstances

Sometimes, it takes extreme circumstances for us to recognize a gift or talent the lord has given us. The first few times I preached, I had written sermons and had weeks to prepare them.

It was only because I could not dismiss them; I knew I had to push myself out of my comfort zone and stand before the congregation and preach.

After my third sermon, my pastor and his wife got sick with COVID while returning from a planned one-week vacation. The situation forced me to rely on the Holy Spirit for messages for two additional sermons with no lead time.

During this time, the power of God overwhelmed me, as I felt it working through me. I was hooked and knew I would need to continue to serve the Lord.

Later, when my pastor suffered a stroke, I had to step up and write sixteen sermons in eight weeks. From this, my first book, "Moving Ahead: How to Make America Godly Again," came to life.

Lessons in forgiveness

There are so many great lessons from the story of Joseph, but what spoke to me this morning was the foreshadowing of Jesus we see within the Cupbearer and the Baker.

Though the Cupbearer felt the weight of guilt, Joseph's understanding brought him absolution. He delivered the wine to the Pharaoh.

When we partake of the Lord's Supper, aka Communion, we share in the wine. It represents the blood of Jesus, which was shed for the remission of sin. Not Jesus' sin; He had none. But for our sins.

After three days, reminiscent of the three days Jesus spent in the tomb, Pharaoh forgave the Cupbearer, and they restored him to his position.

The Baker was not so fortunate. His guilt brought upon him the punishment he deserved. When we have Communion, the bread represents the Body of Christ, which was broken for us. They pierced him for our transgressions, as prophesied in Isaiah 53.

When I eat the cracker that represents his body, I can hear that breakage.

We need to be broken to come to Christ.

They do not forgive the Baker; they impale him, and he dies. He gets what he is due.

The difference

Both waited three days, so why were the outcomes so disparate?

Jesus offers forgiveness to all, and we all need it. Romans 3:23 assures us we are all sinners. Romans 6:23 tells us we all deserve the fate of the Baker.

I can only postulate that, being the first to hear Joseph's interpretation, the Cupbearer repented and sought the Lord's forgiveness. He put his faith in Joseph's words, and God credited it to him. He found salvation through grace.

If the baker then assumed he would get the same, he was callous and did not repent. He felt entitled to forgiveness rather than seeking it.

Life or death

No one owes us anything. There is no obligation for God to forgive any of us. God offers forgiveness only by His grace.

God is faithful, however, and assures us that if we trust in Jesus with all our heart, soul, and mind, He will forgive us.

We need to repent. Perhaps whatever the sin was that the Baker had committed was something he was not willing to turn from.

In this storyline, we see that there are always two outcomes to sin: life or death.

From scripture, we can trust we have the option to choose life.

Repentance is a gift from God. We must desire it more than the sin which imprisons us.

Today, I encourage each of you to ask what is holding you prisoner. Are you willing to seek repentance and trust in the Lord for forgiveness?

We see in these chapters that God will forgive us and set us free if we can move past our love of the sins that bind us.

Tomorrow, we will read Genesis 42-44.

Day 14: Genesis 42-44: Do Something, Recognize Faults, Seek Forgiveness

As we read through Chapter 44 in Genesis today, we see how God orchestrates our lives, even when we are oblivious to His works.

Do something

The first thing that caught my attention was the question asked at the very beginning of chapter 42. Jacob asked his sons, "Why do you just keep looking at each other?"

I see this in every area of life. At work, I have sales agents who wait for their customers to tell them what they want instead of displaying curiosity and exploring what the client needs.

A small group of individuals at churches worldwide overwork themselves, filling all the gaps while others wait for instructions.

Even in our government, we see so few who will lead. Being reactive gets the funding to get reelected. Therefore, they wait for a lobbyist to tell them what to pursue.

Those in power see a leader who takes initiative as a threat.

We all can see areas needing attention, but even speaking up about something will commit us to rectifying that need. So, we remain silent.

This must change. For our country to experience revival, it must start with us. We need to see where God is working and be determined to join the effort.

Recognition

When we do, we will see how God will not only use our strengths but also remove our weaknesses.

Then, in verse 42:8, we read how Joseph recognizes his brothers, but they don't recognize him.

This is typical of sin. We try to block from our minds the transgressions we commit.

Have you noticed how much easier it is to recognize the sin in others than ourselves?

It is also easier to remember those who have sinned against us than those we have wronged.

When we share in the Lord's Supper, we are told to remember our transgressions, and if there is anyone we need to ask forgiveness from, we are to do it before partaking. I try to think about who that might be, but my mind rarely comes up with anything.

I know this is not an accurate reflection of my life. There is no doubt that I harbor bad thoughts, or inappropriate ones anyway, against many people.

We see someone with a torn or dirty shirt on at church, and our initial thought is that they should have more reverence in coming to church in such a way. We fail to consider that this might be their only shirt or that their washing machine is broken.

Instead of having judgmental thoughts, we should have compassion and inquire if there is a need we can meet. We may even do that, but not before first having the inappropriate response.

Do we ever go up to them and seek forgiveness and ask if there is any way we could assist?

Seek forgiveness

In 42:17, Joseph puts them in custody for three days.

For our transgressions, Jesus put Himself in a tomb for three days. The blood of our Savior washes away all our sins.

The Bible states: "For if you forgive other people when they sin against you, your heavenly Father will also forgive you." (Matthew 6:14, NIV).

Therefore, we can know we will be forgiven if we reach out to our brothers and will forgive them.

Today, we need to ask ourselves. Are we reacting more like Joseph or his brothers? Joseph initiates trials and tests that unify his family. His brothers wait to do what they are told. This puts them in a compromising position throughout these chapters.

Because they are being so reactive, in verse 42:28, they ask, "What is this that God has done to us?" It is not God who has wronged them or brought about the perils they face.

It is because of their sin against their brother and their unwillingness to take responsibility for this action.

Tomorrow, we will read Genesis 45-47.

Day 15: Genesis 45-47: Forgiveness and Faith

We are halfway through the first month, and we only have two days left in the Book of Genesis. May God grant me the words, and may the pace of this reading be to your liking.

Today, we read chapters 45-47.

God has a plan

We've read how Joseph's brothers wanted to kill him but sold him into slavery. Through the incident with Potiphar's wife, he goes to prison, but this exposes the talent God had given him.

God always has a better plan for us than we do. We think small; our fears and insecurities limit us. Because of obligations and responsibilities, we hesitate.

Sometimes, God intervenes and forces our hand through outside factors because His will is immutable.

I'm all right with this. I begin every day seeking God's will for my life, even when I feel discouraged by what seems like a failure. Whatever happens, good or bad, is His will.

I can find peace, drawing from Joseph's story. Losing doesn't have to trouble me. It is God's will.

His will is always for me to prevail. I am His child. He may send me through a season but will always want good for me.

We should forgive

We see in 45:8 this attitude in Joseph. He told his brothers that he forgave them because they had not sent him to Egypt. It was all God's will.

What his brothers intended for evil, God used for good.

Faith in God continued to prevail in this family. We see in 46:2 that Israel responds to God.

Don't make excuses

When God calls you to serve, even when it seems contrary to your plans and desires, what is your answer? All too often, we respond with an excuse:

Sorry, we can't afford that right now. Our commitments lie elsewhere. We don't have the time. I don't feel qualified for that.

Israel responds, "Here I am."

This is not because God is glorifying Israel. He is a shepherd and, like everyone else in Canaan and throughout Egypt, he is suffering through the famine.

Shepherds are a lower class of citizen and are detestable to the Egyptians, it says in 46:34.

God gives each of us skills and roles that are suitable for the Kingdom of God. He has a plan that brings this all together for His glory, which we should always be seeking.

Be what God wants

We run into conflicts because we get swayed to thinking we should be something society deems better. We want to be one of the cool kids. Why be a shepherd? No one likes them.

In 47:3, Pharaoh asks Joseph's brothers what their occupation is, and they tell him.

Maybe, if we are blessed to be doctors, lawyers, or accountants, we might boast of our achievements.

Most of the people I know try to boast of the company we work for, not our own position.

For years, I was a sales agent for a Fortune 500 software company. I attached their preeminence in the market to my status.

Trust in God

We sell ourselves to these companies we deem greater than ourselves, which is like what we read in 47:19.

Instead of trusting in God for provision, even after He has been faithful, we put our hopes in the company.

Verse 21-22 says that this reduces the people to servitude. It does the same thing to us. We become servants, aka slaves, of the company.

Although we may not agree with the things our employer is doing, we get behind them because our hope is in their success. If they succeed, we get paid, and soon we are beholden to them and the income they provide.

Verse 47:25 describes how we place ourselves in bondage.

As chapter 47 ends, Israel is dying and wishes to be returned to the land of his fathers. Don't we all get to a point where we want to return to that place we once inhabited?

There was a time when I had little concern for my career. When I first became a Christian, my only focus was on God, and He blessed me with a successful career. That success caused me to put myself in bondage, and now, like Israel, I wish to return to that place where I was closest to God.

Tomorrow, we will read Genesis 48-50.

Day 16: Genesis 48-50: God Exceeds Expectations

Today, we conclude our study of Genesis. Thank you for reading along. I love being in God's Word, but some days I struggle with other commitments. Having you all here provides me with the encouragement and responsibility to always carve out that time.

When I don't and let the world encroach upon my time, I feel disconnected, and my life can get sidetracked.

What a powerful set of chapters to end this opening book with.

God exceeds

First, we read in Genesis 48:11, Joseph states a truth I know often: God not only meets our needs but also exceeds them.

Israel states, "I never expected to see your face again, and now God has allowed me to see your children, too." (Gen 48:11, NIV)

Many years ago, I was publishing Tucson Parent Magazine, and I had to close that down. Print advertising was being replaced by the internet and since that was our source of revenue, it was no longer sustainable.

God was letting me fail, even though I knew He was always with me. Instead, I have learned He was moving me to a company where I have ministered to others. He has supported me beyond any expectation I had for the magazine. I have grown in my relationship with Him for over two decades.

God always has something better in store for us than we can imagine.

Patterns

In 48:14, we read how Israel crossed his arms and blessed Ephraim instead of Manasseh. This follows a pattern we had seen earlier with Isaac and Jacob, of the firstborn not getting the blessing. This time, it was not through trickery as it had been before.

God gave us his first covenant. That is the Law, which we will learn more about in our next book, Exodus. But it was the second covenant, that of grace through Jesus, that is better.

In verses 18-19, Joseph challenges his father for doing this, and we learn it is the intended outcome. The second will be greater than the first.

Then, tying off this idea, we read in 49:8-10 that Judah will be the line to which the brothers will praise. Jesus descends from the line of Judah. He is the lion of Judah, which is reflected in these verses.

Deliverer

This is important for several reasons, including, as we see in 49:18, that they are looking for deliverance from the Lord. Jesus is our deliverer. Then, we read a comparative reference to Jesus and how his death atoned for our transgressions. In 50:20, Joseph forgives his brothers for trying to kill him and selling him into slavery.

He says what they intended for harm, God used for good. When Jesus died, the crowd thought they were stopping His ministry. Instead, He was laying down His life because He knew it was the only way He could deliver all of us.

Sin holds us all as slaves until we place our faith in that sacrifice Jesus made. This is all foreshadowed by this story of Joseph.

I pray you will recognize how often we have harm done to us. We need to forgive those people who intend harm to us, trusting that God will use that for His glory.

Tomorrow, we will read Exodus 1-4.

Conclusion of Genesis:

Now that you have read the first book of the Bible, take a moment to reflect. How have the events in Genesis mirrored lessons in your own life? Do you feel yourself growing in knowledge? Are you also growing in faith?

For fun, here are five questions I want you to answer (I will post some brief answers at the back of the book).

1. What caused Adam and Eve to be expelled from the Garden of Eden?

2. Describe the story of Noah's Ark. What was its purpose, and what was the outcome?

3. Who was Abraham, and what were some of God's promises to him?

4. Explain the story of Sodom and Gomorrah. Why did God destroy these cities?

5. Summarize the story of Joseph. How did his experiences show God's sovereignty?

Chapter 1: Footnotes

1. "List of Religions and Spiritual Traditions," Wikipedia, last modified June 30, 2025, https://en.wikipedia.org/wiki/List_of_religions_and_spiritual_traditions.

2. C. F. Keil and F. Delitzsch, *Commentary on the Old Testament*, vol. 1, *Genesis 7–8*, accessed via Bible Hub.

3. Seth Godin, *Linchpin: Are You Indispensable?* (New York: Portfolio, 2010).

Chapter 2:
EXODUS

Day 17: Exodus 1-4: The Call of Moses

Congratulations, if you had set a goal to read a book this year, you just finished the Book of Genesis. Let's start today by reading the first four chapters of Exodus.

God Breathed

This is the story of Moses, the author credited with writing the first five books of the Bible. I say credited because all Scripture is God-breathed.

God is the author. Take a minute to contemplate that reality.

I have written two books, many magazine articles, marketing campaigns, poems, and even songs, and each one required that I pour myself into the project.

That is why the Bible is so special. When we read it, we hear the very thoughts that came out of the mind of the Creator of the universe.

It takes a lot of time to write even one book, but God, after creating the heavens and earth and everything within them, populated His creation with people.

Then, as if that wasn't enough, He wrote them sixty-six books.

We are eternally indebted to God for His divine generosity.

Some things stood out to me as I read this morning:

A Warning

First, I see a warning in Ex. 1:7.

The Egyptians had allowed the Israelites to enjoy the best of their land, rightfully so. It was God's plan. But now they have continued to multiply and are overwhelming the land and becoming too powerful.

Throughout history, attackers have overthrown the indigenous people of almost every country, such as the Spaniards overthrowing the Aztecs, and the Aztecs overthrowing the Inca.

Or, through peaceful coexistence, they allowed people to grow within their borders until those people gained control through a coup, such as China in 1911, Germany in 1933, or Guatemala in 1954.

A nation must be careful to protect its sovereignty. Fortunately for Egypt, God had a plan to move the Israelites to their own land, which He had given their fathers. The Egyptians, previously gracious hosts, now anxiously relied on the Israelites' continued labor.

America faces a problem today that requires immediate action. As I state in the book Moving Ahead: How to Make America Godly Again, we must be cautious in how we deal with this issue.

It Is Not Sustainable

Like Egypt and many other countries, if we don't correct the overpopulation of foreigners within our borders, we will have a revolt, and it will have dire consequences.

We Must Be Compassionate

When we look at Ex. 1:11, the Egyptians enslaved the Israelites and then escalated their cruelty to oppress them.

God Hears Their Cries

We desperately need God's intervention to solve this problem. If not, the people, even if they took part in causing the problem, will become victims, and God will hear their cries. We cannot expect mercy if we are not merciful.

Moses Was Guilty

Moving into Ex. 2:12, we read Moses kills an Egyptian. Since the Law hadn't yet been given, perhaps killing wasn't a violation, but right is right, wrong is wrong, regardless of definition. Killing a human was wrong then, as it is now.

That Moses looked around before killing the Egyptian is proof. His subsequent guilt, upon the discovery of his actions, further supports this.

Pharaoh wanted to punish Moses for those actions, which is why he flees to Midian. In Midian, we see that nothing we do can stop God's plans, no matter how much we mess up our lives. God reaches out to Moses in Midian, and from the burning bush, He brings him into that plan.

God had told Abraham He would give him and his descendants the land, and God is always faithful. It was never a matter of if, only when.

That time arrived, and God instructed Moses to lead the Israelites out of Egypt.

Moses was like many of us. When God calls upon us to take part, we look for someone else to do the heavy lifting. Moses likely thought, great idea, let's get those people out of Egypt where they are suffering. But he thought it would be better if God chose someone else.

I have seen so many people come up to leaders in the church, leaders in my company, leaders in our government, and share their great ideas. When a leader then agrees and asks what they need to get that done, most people step back and look for someone else to run with their "great idea."

God shows Moses that He is behind that idea and even assures Moses that He will provide the resources. This isn't enough for Moses, so God then provides the assistance through Aaron.

Step up

We won't be talking to a burning bush, but there are many things going on all around us where we can see God working now.

When you see God at work, you recognize that it isn't just a chance sighting. God is showing you where He wants you to get involved.

Don't be like Moses and look for someone else when God is bringing it to your attention. If He is pulling on your heart, you need to step up.

Where do your passions lie? What do you see happening that irritates you daily, making you wish someone would do something about it?

Be that someone!

Tomorrow, we will read Exodus 5-8.

Day 18: Exodus 5-8: God's Plan and Our Excuses

Moving further into Exodus, we are now getting into Moses's interaction with Pharaoh. Today we read chapters 5 to 8.

Know the Lord

The first thing that struck me was Pharaoh's response in 5:2: "I do not know the Lord."

I don't like over-mentioning the fact that I was an atheist before the Lord reached out and brought me to Himself. The only reason I do so is to glorify God, that He would save His enemy.

Pharaoh's attitude toward God was very similar to my own. Why would I obey a God I did not know? How could I call Him Lord when I did not even recognize Him as my Savior?

Romans 6:20 points out, "When you were slaves to sin, you were free from the control of righteousness."

Pharaoh, and many of us, believe he can go on acting any way he chooses. Even when confronted with a direct command from the Almighty God, he thinks too highly of himself. Kings in Egypt thought of themselves as a deity. They wanted their people to worship them.

Have Your Priorities Right

Today, most of us work for companies that treat us much better than Pharaoh treated the Israelites, but there is still a similarity.

Our employers want to provide us with our income, our healthcare, even much of our leisure activity. They want us to make them the center of our lives.

As Pharaoh states in 5:9, they want us to be so busy with company stuff, even masquerading as off-hours recreation, that we are too busy to notice what God is saying to us.

To continue to grow, the company increases our goals and demands more effort.

It has been my job to help the agents I train become more efficient so that they can produce more output, like the bricks in Exodus 5, with no need to provide them with as much straw. If we can improve sales efficiency, we won't need to spend as much on marketing efforts.

I will devise new ways to approach the sales process and test them. When they show promise of increasing the results, we roll them out to the teams, and they must implement what we show them.

We call this enabling them, but what we end up doing is putting them under stress. They then are called into their managers' offices to find out why they are not reaching higher quotas.

I can almost hear them asking why I made them struggle in their performance.

God Has a Plan

God always has a bigger plan than we can see. In chapter 6, He assures them He is about to show Pharaoh His mighty hand.

Whenever we are going through a trial, we should try to figure out what God is doing.

We can trust Him, knowing it is for the greater glory. But because we may not understand it at first, it causes anxiety.

Even though I remind myself that I should cast all my cares on Him (1 Peter 5:7), it doesn't stop me from freaking out.

God is faithful, and He has provided me with a greater life than I could have imagined. He has given me much more than I need, while withholding the punishment I deserve.

Still, when those challenges seem insurmountable, I try to figure out if there is another way I can achieve the results I need.

Like Pharaoh having his magicians recreate the miracles that God is doing, I attempt to conjure up my own method.

That is when my life reeks like the Nile when it turns into blood.

We must have faith that God is at work, and He will deliver us, just as He delivered Israel.

Instead of seeking signs and wonders, we must seek the Lord and walk with Him, even when someone else, even someone in control of our lives like Pharaoh was in the days of Moses, is prohibiting us from moving.

If the Lord is telling us to go, why are we not moving?

What is God telling you? Are you feeling He is leading you to a ministry or to contribute to a program?

Are your excuses not to respond as powerful as the God that is leading you?

Tomorrow, we will read Exodus 9-11.

Day 19: Exodus 9-11: Choosing Life or Death

The Supremacy of God

Now we work through the plagues. These are such familiar stories that have been told in movies ranging from Cecil B. DeMille classics to children's animated cartoons.

Each plague represents one of the Egyptian gods or goddesses. God was showing the Egyptians His superiority.

But there is a larger goal to all this suffering.

First, as we see in Exodus 8:15, when a situation arises, we will reach out to the Lord. We submit ourselves, bargaining with God that if only He would deliver us from those conditions, we would serve Him.

Shortly after the Lord brings us through our trials, we return to our normal hedonistic living—unchanged by all that we witnessed and unwilling to keep our commitment.

Those around us will point out that we are heading toward danger, as with the magicians in 8:19, but we will not listen.

The Lord, through His Word, tells us this is the nature of the human heart. He is never wrong.

We Must Be Holy

He wants to consecrate us to Himself. We are to be holy, just as God is holy (1 Pet. 1:15-16). This is what we see in Exodus 8:23. God separates His people from the rest of the world.

Yet, because of our own hard hearts, we fail to carry through, much like Pharaoh.

We all must take that three-day journey, suffering with Jesus and sharing in His death, burial, and resurrection, as God commands (Ex. 8:27).

When we do this, the Lord will make us different from the rest of the population. The world will hate us because of this difference.

Share Your Testimony

Last week I did a few book signing events, and I watched as people, even some wearing shirts with religious sayings on them, avoided making eye contact with me. I would offer them a free bookmark, and they responded as if the price was too high.

At first, I felt demoralized. I took it personally.

After a six-hour day with three books sold, I sought answers from God and remembered that He told us the world would hate us because it hated Him (John 15:18-21).

I thought of the crowd that I watched parade past me all day and realized that if they had loved what I was trying to share with them, I would have more to worry about.

Any minister can tickle your ears and share a message you want to hear.

When you share the truth that sin is wrong and people need to repent, they will not like you.

I'm going to continue to put myself out there, even though I feel very vulnerable when I do, because I also realized that I could talk to over a dozen people about what God was doing in my life and in our country.

That is what God wants me to do.

Choose Eternal Life

He will bring to Himself those whom He wants to save. My job is to be out there sharing that eternal life is available.

While the rest of the world will suffer death, the believer is like the animals of the Israelites in 9:4; they will not die.

We just give the world a reason to inspect us, as Pharaoh did the Israelites in 9:7, to see that we have life within us.

Not all will recognize the Lord. We see in 9:21 that some will leave their slaves and livestock in the fields, and they will perish.

Others will choose the path demonstrated by Pharaoh in 9:27 of confessing their sins and trusting in the Lord.

We must be discerning, however, because many will say they have trusted God but still have no fear of the Lord (9:30).

Destructive Lifestyles

We read about destroying the flax and barley. This tells us the time of year was January-February; that is when the flax would be in blossom and the barley forming heads.

The significance is that God wanted to punish their lifestyles. Flax made their garments, and barley was for brewing intoxicating beverages and feeding livestock.

He did not wish to destroy the Egyptians, however, so He left the wheat and spelt, which were necessary for feeding them.

Many will ask why a merciful God would deal with people in such a cruel fashion. Why not just soften Pharaoh's heart and have him let the people go?

We need to remember how quickly we forget all that God has done for us. Every Christian I know can tell you of a time God has saved them. They have stories of when He protected and provided for them.

Yet, you see them living as if they don't have any fear of the Lord. They make themselves the lord of their own lives.

Had God just moved the Israelites out of Egypt; there would be no lasting effect upon the generations that followed. It is only because of the magnificence of His deliverance, and the punishment He pours out in Egypt, that His people would pass on these traditions to this day.

Some argued the atomic bombing of Hiroshima shortened the war and saved millions of lives.

This is a similar situation. By doing these mighty deeds that only God could do, not only were the people of Egypt and Israel taught a proper fear of the Lord, but so would people throughout the world for generations to come.

Step into the Light

Still, daily, don't we all struggle to follow His commands?

Verse 10:2 says He did these things so that we may know that He is Lord. Are we giving Him lordship over our lives?

Will we wait until our lives are in ruin, like Egypt was in verse 7?

In verse 21, there is a darkness that is described as felt. I would imagine this resembles the darkness that fell upon the earth while Jesus hung on the cross.

I also see a similarity to the darkness that is encroaching upon the hearts of man today. This is a sign that the Lord is coming soon.

In those days, darkness fell for three days. When we read Revelation, that darkness that is coming will be much greater.

The only way to avoid this darkness is to step into the Light. We must place our faith in Jesus and let Him be our Lord and Savior.

Have you done this?

Great! Who do you know that has not?

Tomorrow, we will read Exodus 12-14.

Day 20: Exodus 12-14: A Time for Praise and Caution

Leadership

Today, the United States of America swore Donald J. Trump back into the White House as the forty-seventh president. The implications sparked furious reactions from some. Others were thrilled.

We read Exodus 12-14 today, and we can see a similar situation.

God chose Moses to lead His people out of Egypt. He had Aaron do the talking, but it was through the signs and wonders we read about that Pharaoh drives the Israelites out.

Cleansing

First, we see the people of Israel are to use hyssop to put blood around their doorposts. This is very symbolic.

The hyssop is a plant that was used in those days for cleansing. People used it in exorcisms and other ritual cleansings.

Here it is used to paint the blood of the lamb. They are to slaughter lambs and put blood around the entries of their homes.

When a Christian confesses faith in Jesus, they have His blood—the Lamb of God's blood— covering their heart. The heart is the doorway to the soul.

We also see that soldiers used it at the crucifixion when they lifted a drink to Jesus on a hyssop branch.

Protection

In Exodus 12, we see they place it on their doors so that when God comes through to slay all the firstborn males in Egypt, He will see the blood and will pass by those houses.

God will judge you when you do not have the blood of Christ covering your heart, and the consequence of sin is death.

For the Israelite, not having the blood of the lamb on their threshold would mean death would come to their firstborn male child.

Even before God brings this great destruction into the land, He provides a way to avoid it. For everyone, He provided the way before establishing the world. The plan from the start was for salvation to be available for all who would believe.

Of course, the Egyptians don't know this, and they suffer a death in every house.

The Weight of Darkness

One of the saddest times I can recall in my lifetime was when COVID-19 first hit. Despite the inclusion of many flu and other disease deaths in the statistics, I know several members of my church died. My extended family included several more people.

I do not believe in the vaccine, but I know that over the last five years, I have lost more friends and associates than I ever had before.

There was a permeating depression hanging in the air throughout the year 2020. The prayer meetings at church were a constant reminder of our shared vulnerability and mortality.

I could not even imagine the darkness that must have engulfed Egypt, as every house suffered at least one death—adults, if they were the firstborn in their family, children, pets, and livestock.

So, they drove the Israelites from their land, hoping to rid themselves of this curse.

Misplaced Priorities

But then they realized that most of their labor force was leaving. So, they pursued them.

They say, if God brings you to something, He will bring you through it. There are a couple of ways we see that play out.

First, He leads the Israelites with a fire at night and a pillar of rain during the day.

How often do we seek God's will for our lives? Knowing there is something He wants us to do but feeling uncertainty. Oh, how magnificent simply following a guiding pillar would be! The Word of God is that pillar, but it needs interpreting. This leaves room for doubt.

Then, as the Egyptian army catches up to the two-three million Jews wandering toward the Red Sea, the pillar moves and places itself between them.

Even with that comfort, knowing that God was leading them and protecting them, some people responded with fear and anxiety.

Just like the people today. Many believe that God had protected and led Donald Trump to the victory he had in November. More than one assassination attempt failed. These people continue to follow him.

But many others are so inflamed that they are carrying on like the Israelites, who were questioning why Moses had taken them out to the wilderness to die.

I am not claiming Donald Trump is Moses, but I believe God is in control. I believe God appoints leaders. Therefore, I believe this was what God wants for America.

The problem is that throughout the Old Testament, we see God appoint rulers who did not walk in the ways of their fathers and did wrong in His sight. We all need to be praying that President Trump seeks God in all that He does.

These could be the best of times, or the worst. It all rests in God's hands. Let us all pray we find His favor.

Tomorrow, we will read Exodus 15-18.

Day 21: Exodus 15-18: Following God's Lead

We have been driven out of Egypt, crossed the Red Sea, and now we will read Exodus 1518.

I can see some direct parallels in the world today. Here we have been through five years of Covid affecting our communities. High inflation has stifled growth. The only real growth has been rehiring the jobs that were impacted by the shutdown.

What Happens Now?

We now have new leadership in the White House, and people are waiting to see what will happen next.

At this moment, conservatives are singing praise songs, thanking the Lord for His deliverance, much like Moses in the opening verses of chapter 15. The Lord has become our salvation, and this is a time we all should praise Him.

What we need to be watching for is how closely the new administration stays with God.

Dropping to verse 22, we read that after only three days in the desert, the people grumble against Moses. People demand instant and continuous results. It took a lot of promisemaking for President Trump to get elected. Now, if the people are not seeing America move back to the values he espoused, they will grumble.

We Must Obey God

Scripture assures us that if we listen to the Lord our God and do what is right in His eyes, He will protect and heal our country (Ex 15:26, NIV).

And the Lord gives us specific instructions throughout Scripture on what He wants from us; see 16:4 for an example. But as we read, the people are not always so good at following instructions, and when they don't, they are quick to grumble again.

There will be those who are greedy and want to take more than they need, and this will cause their demise. Just as those who tried to get ahead of the Lord and save some of the manna for the next day found maggots and stench, we too will find that not following the Lord's leading will backfire on us.

God must be wondering, "How long will you refuse to keep my commands and my instructions?" as He asks Moses in 16:28.

The people of Israel had seen God lead them by the pillar of fire and cloud. They had seen Him part the Red Sea, provide water from a rock, and feed them day after day. But they still would not trust Him. They always believed they should establish the rules themselves.

His Grace Is Sufficient

Perhaps, like us, they were having a hard time understanding why the Lord does the things He does. It is not because we deserve it. We have earned His wrath, yet He provides us with grace.

Moses directs Aaron to collect some manna and preserve it in a jar for generations to come (v 16:33).

If we are going to have a free America to pass on to our grandkids and beyond, we must protect that heritage.

God has blessed us with a rich culture that we are watching crumble as we allow sin to prevail throughout our society.

Just like the people in Ex 17:3 who grumble about water, asking if Moses had led them out of Egypt to die in the desert. We forget all that God has done for us and then have no faith. He will do it again.

They ask in verse 7, "Is the Lord among us or not?" Faith is knowing He will never leave us. He will continue to provide if we follow His commands and instructions, but we don't!

Get In the Game

Maybe we try, but we just get tired? Like Moses in 17:12, we get worn out and need our friends to come alongside us and help us hold up our hands. God provides the victory when we keep our end of the deal.

It is easier to stay on the sidelines, do whatever we feel is right for us, and then hope someone else will get the job done.

Throughout our society, there are so many spectators, and they are the ones who grumble loudly, who want someone else to make things happen.

Some will step up, but like Moses judging all the cases, they are soon overwhelmed and burn out. We all need to participate. Life is not a spectator sport. We all must be in the game, doing all we can to help our leaders bring the victory.

Tomorrow, we will read Exodus 19-22.

Day 22: Exodus 19-21: Approaching God

It's Time to Sacrifice Our Idols

Today, we read chapters 19-21 in Exodus. The setting is the base of Mt. Sinai.

Reminders

I live in Tucson, Arizona, and although our deserts and cacti are mostly what we're known for, the truth is Arizona boasts fantastic mountains. We have what are called the sky islands. They call them this because we have the desert, which has an elevation of 1000 - 2000 ft., and then these ranges that can ascend to 10,000 ft. or higher. This makes them beautiful to see, leads to great sunrises and sunsets, and plenty of diversity. We also have great hiking and even skiing trails.

Mt. Sinai has an elevation of just under 8,000 ft., but they were coming from the desert of Shur, which is flat and at sea level. From pictures of the area I have seen, there is a great similarity.

As Moses ascends the mountain, God reminds him of what He has already done to Egypt and for Israel.

This is the chosen person who is leading the nation of Israel out of bondage. He has invoked plagues, parted a sea, destroyed one of the mightiest armies of the day, and yet God feels the need to remind him of who He is.

I can take comfort knowing, when I resist God's will for my life, because of doubts I have— more about my abilities than His—that even Moses needed this reminder.

Obedience

God points out the whole earth is His, but that if the people obey Him, He will make them His treasured possession. Sadly, that is a big if. Unfortunately, none of us obey God.

Thankfully, God knew this all along. I believe it is why He used that word "if."

Of course, the people responded, "We will do everything the Lord has said," but as we read on, we see they don't. It is easy to criticize them for this failure. Only if we do, we accept that we fail Him daily as well.

Consecration

Then we have this sequence of events: Moses must consecrate them, wash them clean, and have them ready by the third day.

Moses is no longer alive.

Thankfully, Jesus is the one who consecrates us, washes us clean, and ever since that third day, when He arose from the tomb, has made us ready to meet God.

When we put our faith in Jesus, trusting that He did all that, we can see Him. He indwells us through the Holy Spirit so that we can know God's innermost thoughts. He is in our hearts so we can know Him the way He knows us.

Moses was told to tell the people not to follow him up the mountain. If anyone tried to force their way through, God tells him He will destroy them.

The High Priest

Before Jesus' death on the cross and the Holy Spirit's arrival to live within us, we could not approach God. It required an intercessor. This was the High Priest who offered a sacrifice.

Jesus was that High Priest who offered Himself as that sacrifice so that we could always come to Him.

God warns He will punish those who hate Him and worship idols, along with their descendants, for three or four generations. He then says He will show love to those who keep His commandments and their descendants for a thousand generations.

I only wish I could keep those commandments. None of us can, but through the shed blood of Jesus Christ, we are all cleansed and are as holy in God's eyes as our Savior is.

Idolatry

Of all the Ten Commandments, the two that I believe modern man struggles with the most are not to make idols and not to covet.

These are sins that hide in our hearts.

We make idols of everything.

An idol is anything we elevate to an importance that surpasses God.

When we spend more time making money than we do focusing on Jesus, that has become our idol.

If our obsession is a sports team, a musical group, or working out, etc., and we use those things as a reason not to be doing what God wants (i.e., "No, I can't go to prayer meeting tonight, we have tickets to…"), that is an idol.

If we are honest and we're to use a stopwatch, do we spend more time focused on God or our jobs? More time in front of the TV or in the Bible?

The idolatry of self has permeated our society.

Materialism

We're perfectly satisfied with our home, our car, and our spouse. But when we repeatedly wish our house was more like someone else's, or our car was as nice as someone else's, or we wish our spouse was like that, we are slipping into that area of sin called coveting.

The entire goal of the marketing industry is to make us believe we need something different from what we have. Even those who follow the Christian faith do this, ignoring the Bible's message about finding contentment in God's provisions.

We call perfect eyesight 20/20 vision. Ironically, Exodus 20:20 says God is going to test us so that we fear Him. It is that fear of God that keeps us from sinning.

Today, we feel we can flaunt our sinful lifestyles and expect God to accept us. We have lost any fear of God.

Perhaps we know of what He did in the past, but we shrug that off.

We rarely hear anyone share their testimony, which is important so that people can understand what God is still doing for them.

If we were more consistent at sharing that information, people would have a more vibrant fear of the Lord.

Authentic Worship

God wants that fear to be authentic. In 20:25, we read He does not want us to create altars with dressed stones.

We behave as if, by making a fancier altar, we can prove our worth. Only the blood of Jesus will deem us worthy. The fanciest sacrifice we can make is still a filthy rag in God's eyes (see Is 64:6).

Therefore, we build giant cathedrals to impress the Lord.

He points out that when we try to ascend the steps to those places, we are exposing our private parts to those who see us ascend to worship.

It is all for show. It is all lip service.

God wants a genuine commitment from us. He asks in 21:6 for His servants to have an awl pierce their ear to show they are servants for life.

God's Law

We spent the rest of our reading time on the laws today. God's law is perfect, but no one could ever keep that whole law.

You may think you have done well, but the Bible says none of us has done well enough. To claim we are holy is to call God a liar and to say Jesus did not need to die for us (see 1 John 1:10).

The way chapter 21 covers every potential objection is important. We will try to say, "I know I sinned, but it is because something special happened." Moses highlights the unavoidable weight of our guilt, regardless of the situation.

"All have sinned and fall short of the glory of God." (Rom 3:23) Tomorrow, we will read Exodus 22-24.

Day 23: Exodus 22-24: Compassion and Consequences

We continue to make our way through the Law of Moses. Today we read chapters 22–24.

I will not get into each of the laws. They are important. I encourage you all to know them. Galatians 3:10 tells us that even under grace, we must know the law and keep the law.

Grace is God telling us He knows we will fail, but that He will forgive us those transgressions if we have put our faith in Jesus Christ. We still must try to know and do the whole law.

I like how God spells out specific details of how much a person should pay if they steal or harm or kill, etc.

Fires

In 22:6, we read that if a fire breaks out and spreads into a field, the one who starts it must make restitution.

I question how one should judge a government unable to extinguish fires—especially on a day when citizens pay taxes and expect that protection. Would that not fall under the same guidelines?

If the authorities cannot provide protection, leading to deaths, wouldn't they be found guilty?

How do citizens of a state like that continue to support such a government?

Presence of Evil

These are the things that happen when we allow evil to exist within our population.

For many years, we have ignored sin and debauchery in our country. We have allowed worship of idols and even foreign gods. We have prostituted ourselves with the occult.

Verse 22:18 tells us not to allow a sorceress to live, yet they advertise their services on television—and even some people who call themselves Christians will pay for their services.

I used to love reading the horoscope, but when I became a Christian, the Spirit in me told me it was a sin against God. I never really believed in them, but now I will not even look at one.

A lady I know likes to play with tarot cards. She thinks it's fun and harmless, but allowing evil of any kind to entertain us always has a price.

Foreigners

The next point that I want to make is something I mentioned in my book, Moving Ahead: How to Make America Godly Again, and some people on the far right had issues with it.

In Exodus 22:21, we read we are to treat foreigners kindly because we were all foreigners at one time.

From a hermeneutic perspective, yes, this was speaking to the people of Israel who God had just brought out of a foreign land, so there were some specifics involved.

I also stated in the book that all nations must have secure borders and be sovereign.

We need to uphold the laws, and we must remove the influences of evil from our land. This would include many of the illegal migrants who recently infiltrated our country.

However, verse 22:23 says, "If you do and they cry out to me, I will certainly hear their cry." Which means if we are not as compassionate as we can be (see Ex. 22:27), God will not be merciful toward us.

It's a complex situation. There are some areas where cleansing is necessary, but many foreigners, even illegal foreigners, provide valuable and needed services to our country.

We must set up processes to make sure we don't throw the baby out with the bathwater.

Angels

My last point of interest in these verses was the mention of the angel in Exodus 23:20.

Some would say that God was promising to send a reward if they did the good works He commanded. Since they failed—almost immediately with the golden calf we are about to read about—God rescinded that promise.

Others say it was the Holy Spirit; that had we kept the commandments—again, we didn't— He would have sent the Holy Spirit to them to be their guide.

I can accept this more than the idea that the angel He was speaking of was Jesus.

They clearly did not keep the commandments. They immediately and repeatedly sinned. We all do, continuously. So, that angel would not be forthcoming.

Therefore, humanity exists with a wall of separation from God.

Therefore, Jesus came to "seek and save the lost" (Luke 19:10).

Until we placed our faith in Jesus, and the holy sacrifice He made for us, there was no reason for God to uphold this promise.

Since God forgave us who have faith in Jesus and applied His righteousness to us, we now can expect that angel to come and guide us.

So, the Holy Spirit came upon the people at Pentecost. We had finally achieved the atonement necessary for God to complete that promise.

Have you placed your faith in Jesus? Or are you living without that guidance that God offers?

Tomorrow, we will read Exodus 25-27.

Day 24: Exodus 25-27: A Tapestry

We All Must Contribute

There are no coincidences.

They say, "The devil is in the details". I would say obedience is in the details.

There were two themes that stuck with me this morning as I read Exodus chapters 25-27:

First, why does the Bible contain such detail about the size of the tabernacle, the materials used, the items to be given by the people, etc.?

I am sure there are great theologians who could explain the significance of each of the materials, and why it had to be those exact measurements. They would be correct in that knowledge. I think it misses the point.

God is telling Moses that there are many people in the tribe of Israel. Each person received unique talents and resources. This was not by random chance.

God had reasons for providing the skills and resources each had. He wants everyone, including you, to know that you matter. You have something unique that God has given you, which He wants you to give back, of your own free will, to Him.

Everything Has a Purpose

I have done every job a person could do without an advanced degree. I have never been a doctor or lawyer, etc. which require those degrees. Everything else a layperson could do, I have done, or at least within reason.

Before spending the last twenty-four years at my current employer, I had worked at over fifty other jobs, many concurrently. Working two or three jobs at a time was normal for me. If I am not working at something, I am asleep. My nature is to overbook myself.

I remember looking at my resume once, thinking that anyone reading it must think I am a complete flake, or that I must have gotten fired a lot. Truth be told, I excelled and advanced in my career, but I was always searching for new challenges.

Stability in God's Plan

When I gave my life to Jesus, He showed me where I should work, and I have been there for over two decades. As I have been working there, I have required the skills I learned from each of those previous occupations.

Instead of looking like a trash heap of instability, I realized God was making a finely crafted tapestry. All those pieces fit together.

That is what I saw in today's verses.

God had gifted each person with specific skills and resources. He plans for all His children to be involved.

He specifies everything He will need so that no one can say, "sorry, I don't have this", or "I'm not capable of doing that".

There is something everyone can do or provide.

I still see many people who come to church every day and, as my pastor says, sit and sour. They don't get involved and then later move to another church because they don't feel needed or fed by the church.

More Than Financial

Ownership of our situations is a must for all of us.

"I possess skills and materials," we should affirm, "and though I may be humble, God will use them if I present them to Him."

Financial gifts are what we consider offerings. Churches have bills to pay and require those materials too. If God has gifted you with financial resources, then finding a church that you can help with those may be what He intends for you to do.

But, if you are scraping by, you still have so much more than money that you can give.

When you give, He will bless that offering.

We all have a purpose

The second train of thought I had was running on a parallel track.

When I read a chapter that has all this detail of materials, and measurements, etc. I read through it quickly. My mental track is saying,

"OK, this is all just a bunch of details. I am not about to build a tabernacle, so I don't need to pay attention".

Wrong!

This is when we all must pay extra close attention, because God put all these details in the Bible for a reason.

He wanted the people working with Moses to follow those exact instructions to prove they could follow orders. He also wants to see if you are listening to His words. It is in those details that I heard Him saying I have more to offer than those surface things I had planned to commit.

In truth, He needs nothing. He is God and the provider of everything. The reason He involves us is that He wants each of us to realize He made us for a purpose. With some exceptions, I believe few of us are living up to that task.

Tell yourself this: "God made me for a reason; therefore, I matter."

Then ask for clarification, "What is that purpose?"

How can you apply yourself more to the glory of God?

Life likes to keep us all so busy that we brush that off with the thought, "I don't have the time."

God is also the one who gives us time.

If we give our resources, God will give us more. If we give our time, God will give us more.

Are you ready to dig a little deeper and bless God because He has blessed you?

Tomorrow, we will read Exodus 28-29.

Day 25: Protect Your Heart and Mind

Today, we read Exodus 28-29, and as usual there were three things that stood out to me:

Protect the Heart

God provides the details to Moses of what Aaron and his sons are to wear in 28:4. The first thing mentioned is the breast-piece.

What this tells me is that God wants us foremost to guard our hearts. Where our treasure is, there our heart will be (see Matthew 6:21). Therefore, we must be cautious about what we let into our hearts and what we treasure.

I'm like most guitar players I know, I like to play different guitars. My son and I would stop at a vintage guitar store on our way to football games when he was younger. We would spend an hour just trying out different guitars and basses.

Guitar stores allow people to come in and play their instruments because, in doing so, we find an instrument that feels so good in our hands that we obsess about it.

One afternoon I played a Parker Fly. My hands were moving so smoothly upon its neck that I could play at speeds I had never reached before.

I had to have a Parker!

I knew this was becoming coveting. That coveting was a sin. Yet, I had to figure out a way to own a Parker.

God tells us to protect our hearts.

I play a Parker guitar almost every Sunday at church. I use it to honor and worship the Lord. But, for a while, I was coveting, and that was a sin.

I guess you could say what started out as a sin, God used for His glory.

A Heart for Jesus

Whenever we are sitting around thinking about things that matter to us, we should think about all that God is doing in our lives. Think about what that cost Him. Obsess on His glory. We should not be Googling Parker guitars and calculating what we would have to do to get one.

Because God knows how easily our hearts sway, his first garment covers that heart. As He states in verse 15, "Fashion a breast-piece for making decisions".

He goes into detail on the jewels to place upon this breastplate, which in Hebrew is called Choshen Mishap.

According to an article at chabad.org, each of the jewels has a special significance, which would make sense. Ruby for Reuben, for instance, is a red stone that represents the shame he had for transposing the beds of his mother Leah and Jacob's concubine Bilhah.

Emerald represents the tribe of Judah, which Jesus descends from. Emerald is a symbol of royalty and leadership. It is also my wife's birthstone. Driven by my wife's insistence, we raised our son in a Christian church, which led me to hear the Gospel and be saved. So, this fits.

The Light and the Truth

Ex 28:30 states that the breastplate has Urim and Thummim over Aaron's heart. This is significant because Urim means light and Thummim means truth.

Jesus is the light of the world according to the John 8:12, and John 14:6 tells us Jesus is the truth.

So having Jesus covering Aaron's heart would be like a Christian having Jesus dwell in their heart.

Knowing that the heart is desperately wicked (see Jeremiah 17:9), we see the breastplate was to provide leadership through the truth and light.

Protect our Thoughts

Then, in verse 28:38 talks about what to place upon Aaron's forehead. Not only did God want to protect his heart, but also his mind.

We must be vigilant to protect what we allow into our minds. While we think looking at representations of evil, or unholy images, is just entertainment, we must not be so naïve. Anything we allow into our minds corrupts what we think and how we react to different situations throughout our lives.

The people performed these actions for Aaron's consecration; these actions also apply to all of us. We are to be holy, just as God is holy (1 Pet 1:16) Consecration took time as well, which we see in 29:35 when it says it takes seven days to ordain them.

Therefore, let each of us seek sanctification. The process of purification takes time; be patient with yourself. However, continuing to allow sin into our hearts and minds will hinder the process, so we must repent and ask the Lord to consecrate us.

Tomorrow, we will read Exodus 30-32.

Day 26: Exodus 30-32: The Fragility of Faith

Forty days. Think about that as we read Exodus chapters 30-32 today.

How Feeble is our Faith?

We are reading about people who knew what God had done to bring them out of bondage.

They had been following this pillar of fire and cloud and had walked through a parted sea. He had provided them with food and water.

They celebrated at the base of Mt. Sinai as Moses ascended and they trembled as the smoke and fire came upon the mountain. Just forty days have passed, and they have lost all faith.

They will give up their gold to have an idol made so that they may worship it.

I would mock them more if I had not seen people lose faith much faster than this myself.

We often see people come to church during a crisis. They learn to pray and walk and aisle and ask Jesus to save them.

Their life changes, and their focus on problems, not the Lord, prevents them from perceiving the connection.

Joy returned to their life, so they stopped going to church and went back to their old ways, unaffected by their recent experience.

Even our Leaders

What I find most disturbing about this story is the actions of Aaron.

Aaron was the one who had been speaking to Pharaoh. He stood next to his brother Moses while God unleashed the plagues. The congregation listened intently as he led them.

If the people give him their gold, he will make an idol and worship it with them.

It is said that all men have a price. What is your price?

How firm would you stand if the enemy tempted you?

Later this year, we will read how temptations tested Jesus in every way, but he remained sinless. But none of us can say the same. We all fall into temptations.

Where was His Support?

The Levites will go through the camp and kill three thousand people (Ex 32:28), but where were they when Aaron was making this idol?

Why were they not standing with him and counseling him to resist the crowd?

All preachers need the support of the congregation. Yet, it can be a lonely pursuit.

We read at least six times in these chapters the words "Then the Lord said to Moses...". Moses had gone before God to seek His will for the people.

When I am preparing a sermon, writing this blog, or working on my next book, I present myself before the Lord and pray for His guidance. He gives me knowledge and words to write that I had not perceived.

My goal is to help others know about the love of Jesus.

Still, the first weekend I did book signings, I sat at a market for six hours and only signed three books. As I offered people a free bookmark, they looked at me with contempt.

My dejection and discouragement lasted until the Lord reminded me that the world would hate me because it hated Him (John 15:18-21).

Then I realized I would have more to worry about if the world embraced me. This would have been a sign that I was catering to the flesh, not the Spirit.

My book was not for me, it was for the glory of God.

I humbled myself and realized that I had spoken to over a dozen people about Jesus during that time and, by any measure, that is a good day.

Much like Moses, and I am not trying to compare myself, I then will look at how people I have spoken to and preached to are living, and I see that most have returned to living as they were before I had met them.

This is not unique to preaching, however, as I see the same thing happen at work when I teach classes to sales agents and then listen to their calls and realize that they applied nothing of what I taught.

We Must Work Together

The problem is that none of us can do this alone.

Moses should have been able to count of Aaron not caving in.

Aaron should have had the support of the Levites standing against the crowds.

The people should have taken some personal ownership and remained steadfast for the Lord who had been leading them.

Instead, we place people into leadership roles and then expect them to make us follow. A leader can only lead. It is our responsibility to put our feet into motion and go after them.

God knew people were not getting it. So, He came down to earth as Jesus to give us an example we could follow on how to withstand temptation. But we still must pursue the path Jesus has laid out for us.

Most of us stand there doing nothing. Waiting for God to make something happen.

Long before forty days pass and we do not see significant evidence that something has changed, we look around for something else to do because we all have limited attention spans.

The mountain, still covered and surrounded by lightning and thunder, was there for the people at its base to see. They should have said to themselves, that is where God is working, that is where I will be.Instead, they sought other gods.

Today, we need to all look around. Where is God at work? How are you going to join in that effort?

Tomorrow, we will read Exodus 33-35.

Day 27: Exodus 33-35: Friendship with God

You are in control of whatever kind of week you want it to be. Starting in God's word will lead you to have a fantastic one, I pray.

Today, we start by reading Exodus 33-35.

Going Alone

I can only empathize with Moses in 33:3, when God tells him, I will not go with you.

There have been seasons of my life, as a Christian, that I have not spent time in God's word. The only prayers I offered were the obligatory thanks for the meals I was eating. I would fall asleep at night, and toss and turn, without even praying, and never felt "right".

When I went to work the next day, everything would just be harder. Nothing seemed to fall into place. My wife would push back on me, the boss would be unhappy with me, even my cat would give me the stink eye.

I was just out of sorts.

So, I would double down and try harder. This left me more exhausted and not willing to wake up early to read my Bible. Cutting time, I would grab my lunch and gobble it down without a word of thanks. When my head hit the pillow, I would collapse, only to wake up an hour later and fight with the problems I was trying to solve the rest of the night. Watching the hours on the clock creep toward morning with no relief.

Moses had been through a lot. He may have had doubts at the beginning, when He was resisting God at the burning bush, but not anymore. He cherished and relied upon the intimate relationship he had developed with God.

Knowing the challenges of leading the nation of Israel, he was now hearing he would have to do so without God being with him.

Draw Near to God

Knowing my roller coaster of faith, I could only imagine that all people have this struggle. This would include world leaders, perhaps even President Trump.

I have no reason to believe the president reads my blog, but I still pray that when things get more challenging for him, and they will, that he realizes this as a call to draw nearer to the Lord.

Moses spoke face to face with God.

Verse 35:11 says, "the Lord would speak to Moses face to face, as one speaks to a friend." (NIV)

We often get too casual in our relationship with God. He is not the big guy, the man upstairs, or any other trivial title we place upon Him. He is God. We should always have complete reverence for His authority in our lives. He supremely deserves worship and obedience.

A Genuine Relationship

We should have a healthy fear for His awesome power, but here we read he will talk to Moses as a friend.

Like the old song says, "We've got a friend in Jesus." Proverbs 17:17 tells us "A friend loves at all times".

Romance comes and goes.

Some people stick with us out of necessity.

Friends are there for you because they love you.

God has no needs. Anything He may desire, He can have.

He spoke the entire universe into existence.

He desires friendship with us.

It would not be a genuine relationship if He did not give us a choice in the matter. So, He gives us free will.

That is His desire. That we have a close personal relationship with Him.

In Exodus 33:13, Moses asks God to teach him His ways so that he may know Him.

God responds to this request by staying close to Moses as he goes to the promised land. This gives Moses rest.

When I come to my senses and realize I am struggling because I am not walking with God the way I should be, and I submit myself to His will and make time with Him a priority. Life does not instantly improve, but somehow things get easier, and I realize that somewhere along the way, they improved.

Don't Leave Home Without Him

America, and everyone in the world, must have that same attitude Moses does, asking in 33:15 that if God is not going with them, don't send them.

God assures him He will be with them, but this does not make things easy. In 34:1, Moses is told to chisel out new tablets of stone. This is hard, tedious work.

He then must carve the Ten Commandments into the stone. God had written on the tablets that Moses threw down and broke. This time in 34:28 it states he wrote on the tablets. The word he is lowercase, so this is not God writing, but Moses.

Let His Glory Shine

My third point this morning is that God's presence shone on Moses' face after he had spent time with God. He was radiant.

We should all shine for Jesus. We are to be lights on a hill, not hiding under a bushel. People should not wonder what is different about us, or for that matter, not see anything different about us. They should recognize that we have been with Jesus. (Mat 5:15-16) When they do, we must not be like Peter and deny Him. (Mat 26:69-75).

This message applies to more than just leaders, like Moses. Exodus 35:29 shows that we should all willingly give the Lord whatever skills and talents He's blessed us with.

As the body of Christ, we must not allow ourselves to be like the limb that falls asleep and is numb. We must get on our feet and serve Him and commune with Him daily.

Tomorrow, we will read Exodus 36-38.

Day 28: Exodus 36-38: Every Gift Matters

Good morning, I hope you are enjoying the year so far.

Today, we read Exodus 36-38.

Everyone has a Purpose

Opening these chapters, we read how the Lord has given skill and ability to a great number of people whom He wants to build the sanctuary. Not all of them have the same skills or ability, but all are called to use those talents for God.

They are called, but in verse two it specifies "and who was willing to do the work" (Ex 36:2, NIV).

To me, this implies that there were some who were not willing. Perhaps they didn't think they could contribute. Maybe they thought enough people were helping, and they weren't needed.

It is possible they didn't want to serve the Lord. Maybe their personal experience of coming out of Egypt wasn't as stellar as others.

Or maybe they just felt that their own projects were more important.

Don't get Ahead of God

They may have even had a problem with Moses and his leadership, or had an idea that they could build something better and gain the Lord's favor.

There have been several times in my life, while working for someone else, that I thought I had a winning idea and went out on my own. I started an ad agency, a magazine and a restaurant, to name a few.

The enemy will tempt us with delusions of grandeur.

Perhaps they were supervisors when they were slaves.

Now they think they should lead the project. Or they could have received another important assignment.

In verse 4, we read that all those who were doing the work had to leave what they were doing.

Help Carry the Load

One of the great struggles most churches have is getting enough members to volunteer. For all the same reasons discussed about the skilled workers of Israel, they will leave it to the few who will step up to carry the load.

It becomes exhausting and many people just burn out.

The most common excuse I hear when trying to get someone to help is they have other commitments.

The people here had other responsibilities that they left to join the work of the Lord.

More than Money

In modern times, many people think that when a church wants people to help, all they have to do is write a check.

Money helps, for sure. The church I belong to is beginning a building project and we are reaching out to many for additional funding. But money isn't enough.

We see in verse 5 that the giving was going well. They had more than they could use, so Moses had to ask them not to give more.

Today, if a church had such a surplus, they would give it to mission work or helping another church in need.

Everyone has Talents

Frequently, people doubt the significance of what they bring to the table.

Chapter 38 reveals that, while most ark coverings and lampposts were gold, many items were silver, and some even bronze. These lesser materials were equally necessary.

They didn't make the bases out of bronze because they ran out of gold. The use of the base dictated the material used. Each type of metal, every fabric used, has a specific attribute that determines when to deploy it.

Silver is softer than gold, bronze is much harder. The melting point is unique. If you were to be shoveling hot coals out of a fire with silver, it would melt. The conductive properties would cause the heat to reach your hand.

You may think your only ability is to play the kazoo, but if you offer that talent to your church, they may have a project they wanted to do with kazoos and were just waiting for someone to have that talent.

If you give the Lord that talent, He will see you were faithful in what He had given you and will give you more.

When I first attended my church, the music director somehow knew I was a guitar player. She asked me if I would play with the praise team. That led to teaching classes, which led to helping with the IT needs and then preaching.

All of this led to God giving me the Book I released earlier this month.

When you resist helping your church, you are only preventing yourself from gaining the blessing God will provide.

Therefore, I encourage each reader to just reach out, ask how can you use me?

Tomorrow, we will read Exodus 39-40.

Day 29: Exodus 39-40:
Taking the Church to the World

We are reaching the end of our second book. Today, we read Exodus 39-40.

When They Won't Come to You

I'm no fashion maven, so maybe that is why the detailed emphasis on Moses Tunic and the placement of each element on it just didn't capture my attention. Each piece, I'm certain, holds great significance. Someday, I will read the commentaries and my findings will amaze me.

That's why I do these devotionals—we should all think more carefully about why these things are in the Bible.

What caught my attention was the passage in 39:33, which says, "They brought the tabernacle to Moses" (NIV).

We all should be inviting people to our churches. According to Scott Knowlton's blog, "82% of unchurched people are likely to attend if someone invites them".[4]

You can invite people all you want. In an area like Tucson, AZ, or most other cities I have lived in, the people you invite may live a great distance from your church.

What do we do when we can't get people to come to us?

According to this verse, we must bring the church to them.

They did not summarize the message for him. Alternatively, he did not receive a group visitation. The people brought the tent and all its furnishings.

Yes, I know that most times, that is not possible today. But the application of it is! Besides, the church isn't the building, it's the people.

So, if you have an unchurched friend, care enough about their eternal soul to suggest getting together, maybe at their house, or at least on their side of town with some friends from church to do a weekly bible study.

If you can't get an audience in person with them, will they let you share an online Bible study, or even this blog?

Can you take them a Bible and ask them to read through it with you and maybe talk on the phone once a week about what they are reading?

Say, "if you have questions, please write them down and I will call you every Thursday and help you understand. If I don't know the answer, I will ask around and find one." Then follow through and do it.

Your own spiritual growth will amaze you, and you may even lead someone to Christ. There is no greater joy.

Don't Hide the Key

Too often, Christians keep their beliefs a secret. We don't want our friends to think we are one of "those people".

What we are keeping from them is the key to eternal life.

When you are entering the gates of heaven and your friends are nowhere to be found, it will be too late.

When you stand before the judgment seat of Christ and He asks you what you did with the gift He gave you, what are you going to say? "I put it in a drawer and locked it to keep it safe?" Don't be the man who hid his talent in Matthew 25.

Wait for God's Leading

Sometimes people cannot come to church.

It is not God's plan for them in their life. They would not receive all He has for them. So, we must help prepare them for that time.

"Moses could not enter the tent of the meeting because the cloud had settled on it." (Ex 40:35, NIV)

There was a time in my life when I had such a cloud of doubt and confusion that if I had gone to church, I would have been bored. Chances are I would have mocked the people there, even to the point of being a distraction. It is possible I would have been driven further away, just because it was not time for me to come.

But my wife's steady influence eventually planted a seed in me that grew until the time came. If we attempt to go to those who can't, or won't, come to us, then we have fulfilled the commandment God gives us. He will then bring them to Himself. That is not our role, it is His. Just as Moses inspected the work the Israelites did in verse 39:43, God will inspect the work each of us does.

Is it just as the Lord commanded?

We will all have to give an answer. Before we drag someone to church and let them think the people there are hypocrites, which I assure you, to some extent, we all are. Let's not be hypocrites and take the church to them, so that they can see we don't just talk about faith but live it.

Tomorrow, we will read Leviticus1-4.

Conclusion of Exodus:

Now that you have read the second book of the Bible, take a moment to reflect. How have the events in Exodus mirrored lessons in your own life? Do you feel yourself growing in knowledge? Are you also growing in faith?

For fun, here are five questions I want you to answer (I will post some brief answers at the back of the book).

1. What major event led to the Israelites' freedom from slavery in Egypt?

2. What miraculous event allowed the Israelites to escape Pharaoh's army at the Red Sea?

3. What set of laws did God give to Moses on Mount Sinai?

4. What was the significance of the Passover?

5. What kind of journey did the Israelites undertake after leaving Egypt?

Chapter 2: Footnotes

1. Thom Linders, *Moving Ahead: How to Make America Godly Again* (Tucson, AZ: Book Writing Pioneer, 2025).

2. You compare Israel's rise leading to Egyptian fear with other nations overtaken in coups:

    - **China (1911):** The Qing Dynasty fell in the Xinhai Revolution, led by revolutionaries aiming to end imperial rule and establish the Republic of China. See: Jonathan D. Spence, *The Search for Modern China* (New York: W. W. Norton & Company, 1990), 276–282.

    - **Germany (1933):** Adolf Hitler's Nazi Party used the Reichstag Fire and Enabling Act to consolidate power and dismantle the Weimar Republic, marking a coup-like authoritarian takeover. See: Richard J. Evans, *The Coming of the Third Reich* (New York: Penguin Press, 2003), 329–345.

    - **Guatemala (1954):** Elected president Jacobo Árbenz was overthrown in a CIA-backed coup during Operation PBSUCCESS. See: U.S. Department of State, *Office of the Historian*, "The United States and the Overthrow of Guatemala's Democratically Elected Government," https://history.state.gov/milestones/1953-1960/guatemala.

3. 💎 **The High Priest's Breastplate: Urim & Thummim**
    - Exodus 28:29–30 describes how the Urim ("lights") and Thummim ("perfections") were placed in the breastplate worn over the high priest's heart "for the judgment of the children of Israel." Many scholars interpret these elements as sacred lots or divine instruments of revelation, possibly used to discern God's will in binary yes/no decisions.

- See: Jacob Milgrom, *Leviticus 1–16*, Anchor Yale Bible Commentary (New Haven: Yale University Press, 1991), 1041–1046; Cornelis Van Dam, *The Urim and Thummim: A Means of Revelation in Ancient Israel* (Winona Lake: Eisenbrauns, 1997)
- This directly supports your theological reflection regarding divine light and truth covering the high priest's (and by extension believers') heart.

4. Scott Knowlton, "8 Mind-Blowing Stats About Church Invites," *Scott knowlton*, blog, accessed June 30, 2025, https://scottknowlton.com/8-mind-blowing-stats-about-church-invites/.

Chapter 3:
LEVITICUS

Day 30: Leviticus 1-4: The Call and the Cost

Good morning and congratulations, you are now in the third book of the Bible. Today, we read the first four chapters of Leviticus.

Before I get into that, I would just like to ask that we all pray for the families of the victims of last night's horrific plane crash in Washington, CD.

Being Called

Leviticus starts out by saying that the Lord called to Moses.

There has long been a debate between the Calvinists and the Armenians over predestination. I will not jump in the middle of that, foremost because I don't believe it makes a difference in getting saved.

I will say this; however, I agree with a Calvinist point of contention that dead men don't make choices. Dead men do nothing; they are dead. My prayer is that those who were lost last night all knew Jesus as their Lord and Savior, though statistically, I think that is unlikely.

I was dead in my transgressions (Eph 2:1), and while in that state, the last choice I would have ever made would have been to follow Jesus.

Just like He called His disciples and told them to follow, He called me when I was still His enemy.

Here, we see He is the one who calls Moses, just as He was when he was in the burning bush.

Following Instructions

Moses would not understand how to gain atonement, but the Lord tells him the exact processes.

He instructs him on where to place his hands before slaughtering the offering, how to prepare the offering, and what to do with it after preparation.

At my day job, I train sales agents on the products we offer, but more specifically, on the processes to follow when having conversations with their clients. I then go back and test how often they comply with those processes, and it is not unusual to learn they do not.

None of us are that great at following directions. When I think of someone being lost, that term makes sense because you often end up lost when you don't follow instructions.

Spice It Up

Chapter 2 says they are to add salt to the offerings. (Lev 2:13, NIV).

In my youth, I felt that following the rules was boring. To add spice to life, I had to at least bend a few regulations and try not to get caught.

Living like this keeps you looking over your shoulder. Watching to see if you are about to get in trouble.

It was only after giving my life to Jesus that I found the greatest "fun" was the freedom I have in Him. I am free to serve and pursue what He has in store for me, because I can focus on what is ahead of me.

We see God wants us to have flavor in our life, some spice to it. John 10:10 says He wants us to "have life abundantly." The Christian life isn't about what we sacrifice; it is about accepting His sacrifice.

At the end of chapter 3, we read that "All the fat is the Lord's" (Lev 3:16, NIV).

The fat is the prized portion. Our very best is what the Lord expects us to give to Him. He gave us His very best. He wants nothing less in return.

We Fall Short

I believe most of us, at least when we first get saved, try to give our best to the Lord, but we fall short.

So, in chapter 4, we hear about times when we sin unintentionally. This happens to all of us, and often. I will realize I didn't give someone their pen back.

No big deal; it's just a pen, right? Wrong! Stealing is a sin, regardless of the value of what you stole or whether it was intentional.

I look at inappropriate things, have improper thoughts, and provide incorrect information. Does the fact I just didn't know I was wrong matter? No, it is still a lie.

Therefore, Romans 3:23 says, "All have sinned." Except for Jesus, who was without sin, we are all stained. It is why I would admit that even now, trying as hard as I might, I still sin many times every day.

We'd face certain destruction. Romans 6:23 tells us, "the wages of sin is death." That is what we all deserve.

God told Moses about all the sacrifices needed to atone for those sins. There would not be enough animals in the world to sacrifice if we still followed these rituals.

It would not be justice if God told that generation, sacrifice for your sins, but the rest of us don't have to. There was a price to pay.

Power in the Blood

Jesus paid that price and because He was the Lamb without blemish, His sacrifice would be great enough to cover everyone.

Instead of needing to sprinkle blood on the sides of the altar, Jesus's blood covers us.

I would imagine the altars would stink, and there would be flies, perhaps even maggots. The blood of Jesus cleanses us from all our sins so that these offerings are no longer necessary.

God still requires the offering, but it must be in Christ.

We must have ourselves fused into Christ Jesus by faith, so that when He died, we died with Him and the life He gave includes our lives.

Dying to ourselves, so that we can live in Him.

Tomorrow, we will read Leviticus 5-7.

Day 31: Leviticus 5-7:
The Weight of Sin, the Gift of Forgiveness

Good morning. As we bring our first month to a close, we will look at Leviticus 5-7. I have grown in the Lord this month. I hope you have as well.

Unintentional Sin

Some people live in denial of their sinfulness. When they do, 1 John 1:10 tells us they are accusing Jesus of being a liar. They claim that He did not need to die for their transgressions because they refuse to accept they have made any.

Here in Leviticus chapter 5, we read of the many unintentional sins we all commit. Many without our knowledge. Getting through life is messy. Unaware that we are enabling sin, our help implicates us in it.

Fearing accusations like those against Daniel Penny, we avert our gaze from certain things. We avoid helping when given the chance.

Sin is wrong, whether we intended to commit it. God is holy. He is light, not shadow. He will not tolerate some sin and prosecute others; that would be contrary to His holy nature.

Therefore, we all can trust the Bible when it claims we all sin and need a Savior. Even an unintentional sin requires a sacrifice.

Realized Sin

It also is important that we realize these sins.

We must go to the Lord, who is omniscient, and ask Him to show us areas where we have sin in our lives. He is faithful and will bring them to our minds. Allowing us to confess them.

Verse 5:17 establishes that our awareness doesn't change our culpability; we are guilty all the same. So, atonement would be necessary.

One time, when I was in financial distress. While returning an item to CompUSA when that store was still in existence, I needed the money back so that I could keep our utilities on. Even getting food to feed my family was in question. As I waited at the customer service counter, with no one around me, I looked at the ground, and there was a fifty-dollar bill.

When the clerk came up to the counter, I held it up and said I just found it on the ground, holding the currency up. He looked around and said, "Congratulations, I guess it's yours!" I put it in my pocket and went home to share the good news with my wife.

Leviticus 6:3 states that those who conceal lost property or commit perjury are culpable. Now, I had not lied about it, but I accepted the lie the clerk had said. To be holy, and we are to be holy (see 1 Pet 1:15), I should have said, "it is not mine."

Genuine faith would mean that God would have blessed me and provided more than what I gained by keeping the cash.

I don't make this point to cause anyone to feel guilty.

Let's not pretend we're all innocent.

Forgiven Sin

When we ask Jesus to forgive our sins, He forgives all our sins. Sins we had committed, sins we will commit. Sins we intended and the unintentional. Big sins, minor sins.

When I began my walk with God, I desired to be that detail-oriented. I knew that every word of the Bible was true and tried to keep each one.

That is why, over twenty-five years later, I remember that moment in CompUSA.

Over time, we become numb. The feeling of forgiven sins becomes commonplace, so we commit them without concern.

We know unintentional sins are happening, but as long as we don't think about them, we can sleep easier.

In Leviticus 6:13, we are told to not let the flame go out.

We are to read the Bible daily so that these details are fresh in our hearts and minds. So that we do not become complacent about sin.

When we do this, we live with the correct lens on what a mighty sacrifice it was that Jesus made. He died for us, knowing how sinful we all are (see Rom 5:8).

Having the correct perspective on this enables us to give him the thanksgiving offering we are called to give.

While praying about my sins, as God brings them to my knowledge, I can sometimes hear the hammer striking the nails that were driven through my Savior's hands and feet. I can sense the pain He endured for me, and each sin added to the guilt He took on for me.

God wants us to be aware of all of this, not because He still holds it against us. It is all forgiven, forever. But, so that we have that passion to tell others about our Lord.

Tomorrow, we will read Leviticus 8-10.

Day 32: Leviticus 8-10:
The Seriousness of Service

We begin our second month together by reading Leviticus chapters 8-10.

This is all about the ceremonial process of ordaining Aaron and his sons into the priesthood. Each had to be consecrated to the Lord.

Laboring for the Lord

Doing the business of God is an awesome responsibility that no one should take lightly. James 3:1 warns, "Not many of you should become teachers, my fellow believers, because you know that we who teach will be judged more strictly." (NIV).

I often hear preachers who seem oblivious to these commands. They believe that if they can draw a large enough crowd and collect enough money, they have done their duty. I do not see the commandment to grow your church anywhere in scripture. God grows the church (see 1 Cor 3:5-7).

In Leviticus 8:23, we see Moses taking the blood of the peace offering and putting some on their earlobe. This is so they will have an ear tuned to listening to God's word. Hearing Him as they serve the people.

They have blood on their right hand to signify the work which they must do. They are to let all their actions glorify God. (see 1 Cor 10:31)

They place the blood on their right toe because they are not supposed to sit and wait for the people to come to them. They should go wherever God leads them. God knows what people need and will provide the leaders to them.

God Is Listening, Are We?

I believe He has heard America's prayers. Not our wishes, but the righteous prayers of His children who have sought His guidance for our nation.

Though we did not deserve it, He has provided us a path. It is our responsibility to go down that path, always listening for His voice and performing the labor required.

8:36 says that Aaron and his sons did all that God commanded. We must be as faithful. God has provided all we require and we will see His glory upon our land, if we do.

When Moses and his sons went into the tent of meeting and did all the Lord had commanded, the glory of the Lord appeared for all to see.

Disobedience Has a Price

Then, in chapter 10, we see that two of his sons, Nadab and Abihu, acted on their own. Not waiting on the Lord's commands, they offered unauthorized fire before the Lord. For this, the fire came out and consumed them.

While Aaron, seeing his sons destroyed, may have wished to react, verse 3 shows God reminding them of His holiness and the honor due Him. Aaron remained silent. Moses then appoints others, because the work must continue.

The question is, will you wait upon the Lord and do according to His commands, or will someone else gain that opportunity?

You may think, I don't want the responsibility of being a priest or preacher. Then, by all means, you should not be in such a role.

This does not ease you from the duty to serve the Lord with the gifts He has given you. We are all called to serve in different ways. The body of Christ, aka the church, requires all its members to join to carry the load. It is too heavy for only a few.

Tomorrow, we will read Leviticus 11-13.

Day 33: Leviticus 11-13: Modern Defilement

Today, we read Leviticus 11-13.

Clean Living

How many of you start the year off with dietary goals or resolutions? I try to avoid doing that to myself because, by February, I have already failed to keep them.

These chapters detail the dietary rules God imposed on the Hebrew people. This was important in those times because there was no way to refrigerate and treat the meat to avoid salmonella and other more dangerous food-based toxins.

Jesus declared all food clean in Mark 7:19. It is not what goes into us that defiles us, but what comes out of us.

As I read the rules for being clean or unclean, my focus was on what is defiling us today.

For some, it is what we look at.

Fifty-eight percent of people watch pornography online.

When I was growing up, we had a clubhouse where we would hang out. There were a few old Playboy or Penthouse magazines that we hid under the mattress so that no one other than the club members would see them.

We didn't want our parents to know we were looking at that sort of thing.

My stepdad had stacks of much more disgusting magazines piled up on the back of the toilet in my parents' bathroom. The sixties were all about sexual freedom.

When I watch old sitcoms, they joke about watching porn.

Back in those days, you might spend a small amount of time partaking in such unwholesome activity. Today, the average person spends over six and a half hours online every day.

The mainstream television shows have gotten much worse over the years. When I was young, they would have restricted what we now watch as family entertainment.

I think all of that sexual content ruins the real thing when you fall in love, get married, and discover what God had meant for good. Sadly, people have twisted it into something evil.

My bigger concern is with the amount of hatred and violence we consume. When we saw gunfights and war scenes, we knew the people were getting hurt. We didn't need to see blood splatter across our screens.

Multisensory Participation

Visual input is one way we defile ourselves.

Another way is what we listen to. Music used to be love songs and maybe some protest songs. Now, it is as violent as the shows we watch.

That is all static. Now, we have ways to step into the action.

We play games that let our minds contemplate perpetuating harm to someone else. They may be images on a monitor, but can our minds separate those things? Can our hearts?

There are many ways we allow unclean thoughts and images to enter our minds. But the Bible says what comes out of a man defiles him. (Mat 15:11).

During the seventies and eighties, I enjoyed Richard Pryor and Eddie Murphy's comedic shock value. Since I worked in garages, the language wasn't new to me, but the delivery and use made it funny.

For three years, I attempted to be a stand-up comedian. The stories I told would be funny, but when they weren't getting a laugh, I knew that if I threw in some vulgarity. It would get the crowds going.

Coarse jokes and foul language show what is inside a person. You let those filthy words fly when you can't think of a more intelligent way to get your point across.

It Starts Deeper

What comes out of a person indicates what is in a person. What defiles us is our thoughts.

When we lust after someone, especially when we don't even attempt to stop ourselves, that defiles us. To covet what belongs to others while ignoring God's bounty is to defile ourselves.

When we hate others, hold on to grudges, and refuse to forgive. Evil forms, and from there, it flows out through our language and actions.

Today, I try to avoid what I allow into my mind. When I see images, I turn away. I'm repulsed that half the inquiries I get on social media are from people wanting to show me these inappropriate things. I delete, block, mute, etc., but I can't unsee what I have already seen.

I know to refocus my thoughts when my mind fixates on someone or something that I know violates God's will for me. It takes discipline, but if each of us tries to redirect our attention, I believe we will take our society to a better place.

Perhaps others will see this difference in us and want to know how to have that themselves, and we will explain how Jesus can give you that control.

Tomorrow, we will read Leviticus 14-15.

Day 34: Leviticus 14-15: Spiritual Cleansing

We only have two chapters today, but one is pretty long. Leviticus 14-15 focuses again on the topic of cleanliness.

Cleaning Up

Yesterday, we looked at what makes us unclean. These two chapters contain an extensive discussion of bodily emissions.

While there is plenty to discuss in that area, what kept coming to my mind was the length and depth of what the Israelites had to do to become clean.

Most of us today give little thought to this area.

Because of Covid, some people have become germophobic. I believe that a slightly less sterile environment is beneficial. God designed your body to have a healthy immune system.

We never have antibacterial soaps and hand sanitizers. Many studies recommend their use, but I have found others who claim they lower our immunity. I'm not a scientist or medical professional. But common sense tells me if you don't use something, it atrophies. It applies to everything else in the human body. Why not the immune system?

Even the Food and Drug Administration recommends skipping the antibacterial soap and using plain soap and water.[5]

I am fastidious about washing my hands throughout the day. I type on a keyboard all day and would not want to have an accumulation of filth. But, I wash with soap and water, and not the antibacterial kind.

Once a year, I might catch a cold, but I work around small children at church, so the risk is always there. My wife, who is always around children, has only gotten sick about two times in the last thirty-two years. She can sleep next to me when I am ill, and remain healthy.

Spiritual Cleanliness

Those are things people do to stay physically clean. But what do you do to stay clean spiritually?

Yesterday, we discussed not letting impure images, words, or thoughts into our hearts and minds.

Looking at the verses today about becoming ceremonial clean, I had to contemplate what we do to cleanse ourselves once the filth is already in.

I get a lot of disgusting spam on social media. Social media is used to promote my book and this website. When I get a response, I open it to see if it is someone reaching out with a prayer request or inquiry about joining us.

I see things I have no interest in seeing before I can stop the images from appearing.

What then? I can't unsee it, so how do I remove it? My sites have a delete button, but what about my mind?

Clean Thoughts

The only remedy I have found is Philippians 4:8. My focus is on all the good things the Lord has done for me. Then I think about the love I have and the love I am shown by my brothers and sisters in Christ. By focusing on what God is doing right now in America and the world, I can avoid those other thoughts.

Changing my focus to Jesus and everything about Him means those other things have no soil to plant themselves in.

Idle hands are a devil's playground, so I find activities like writing a sermon, helping in a ministry, or reading my Bible. I can't find time to indulge in those distractions, so they soon fade away.

You need to build spiritual muscle to counter the forces which will try to weaken you.

I would love to hear from my readers. What steps do you take to cleanse yourself when spiritually defiled?

Tomorrow, we will read Leviticus 16-19.

Day 35: Leviticus 16-19: The Scapegoat and Our Sins

Today, we have a lot to read. I tried to break up all the days into as close to 85 verses as possible without reading partial chapters or reading from more than one book on any day. Because of this, there are a few days like this where we will read a little more. Let's look at Leviticus 16-19.

Transparency

We read in verse 16:1 that there is to be a high level of respect for the sanctuary. While today, our churches are public and open, not everything is available to all people. Those who have the higher responsibility must be privy to the information needed to make decisions. They are to rely on good counsel, and at our church, we put many large decisions to a vote by the whole church.

This does not mean the whole church should have open access to all information.

The Scapegoat

Then Moses introduced us to the idea of a scapegoat. I remember that growing up, as the youngest in the family, I would often be the scapegoat. In that situation, it meant the one who would take the blame.

So, thinking of the scapegoat as the goat they would let free has a different meaning. When we think of the first goat being sacrificed, we see how Jesus, by taking our punishment and being the sacrifice for us, enables us all to be scapegoats.

Foreigners Must Respect The Law

We read that we must not mistreat a foreigner, but we should require them to keep the same decrees and practices the Lord expects from us.

We must hold them to that same standard.

When they break those commandments, they are guilty and deserve the same punishment as us. We should also offer them the same salvation we received.

Popular Is Not Right

Much of Chapter 18 deals with sexual immorality. So much of our society has turned a deaf ear to God's commands on these matters. God does not change. His rules have not either. Just because something is trendy does not make it right.

When a nation allows sin of this nature to go unchecked, the Bible says the land will spit us out. This means we will lose what God has provided.

From the time sin came into the world, the land has worked against us. We must labor to derive food from it, and toil to survive.

We only can persist because of God's grace and mercy toward us. When we are not willing to follow God's laws, He will withdraw that protection, and we will lose our land.

Even with the recent changes in our administration, our country is still on the brink of this disaster. We cannot take our foot off the gas. We must not tolerate sin.

People can throw a fit and cry on camera to gain our sympathy, and we must be careful not to harm the innocent, but we must never back away from seeking righteousness.

We also see that we are not to make offerings to other gods or any idol. Modern man has made an art of creating new things to worship. Do not let technology, profitability, power, or fame seduce you. These are all just a modern twist on offering sacrifices to foreign gods.

We must be holy, because God is holy.

Tomorrow, we will read Leviticus 20-22.

Day 36: Leviticus 20-22:
The Holiness of God, the Sinfulness of Man

Thank you for joining me. Today, we read Leviticus chapters 20-22.

Jesus Gives Repentance

Whenever I read through the books of the law, I become so grateful to Jesus, who fulfilled all these for me. There are so many transgressions and regulations that I would not have survived to the point I am in my life.

In those times, the punishment wasn't shame; it was death!

Because of Jesus, we now can repent and seek forgiveness. He not only took the punishment for those sins, He removes any desire for them.

When someone claims I am homophobic, they are missing the point. I am not afraid of them; I am afraid for them.

Because I love the person who practices these sins, I want them to repent. I know their flesh is weak, and they can't do it alone.

For them to make such a radical shift would require them to give control to Jesus. He can, and will, remove that from them.

We will get back to that in a moment.

Idolatry

First, I want to talk about Molek. This was the idol who looked like a bull with outstretched arms. Many compare it to the Minotaur. The name itself means sacrifice, and this wasn't limited to child sacrifice. It included passing a child through a fire, and if not killing the child, it would leave them scarred and disfigured.

There are many ordinances against disfigured and disabled individuals serving as priests because of this. It was a sign that the people were practicing the Canaanite rituals and serving their gods.

Knowing of these offenses and failing to report them brands you as guilty and deserving of death.

There are many sins for which a person would deserve death because, to God, the wages of any sin is death. He demands complete obedience.

I would say this is impossible for man, except one man proved it was not. Jesus had no sin and was a man.

Only God's Help

But, as with Jesus, with the help of God through the Holy Spirit, it is possible for man to live without sin. Only God can remove the curse of sin.

God will set His face against anyone who tries to intervene and provide a way that is not through Jesus. God condemned mediums and spiritists for this reason.

They are calling God a liar when someone says there is another way to be forgiven.

For this, they have cast their own fate.

Therefore, God says in Lev 20:8, "I am the Lord, who makes you holy."

We cannot make ourselves holy. Works will not be enough. Only God can make us holy.

For this reason, He tells them not to live by the customs of the people He was going to drive out.

This is a warning for us as well. Yes, I know the part of the country I live in was once part of Mexico. But they were driven out.

Before them, it was the Incas, Mayans, or Aztecs, depending on where you look. Those were driven out. When God allows this to happen in history, it is for His reasons.

He was creating for us a land based on Christian values.

When we allow major cultural influences to move in, we are shifting away from that ideal that God has for us.

In verse 20:23, we read God abhorred them.

We are to strive to be what God intended for us to be. He will not force it, but He is clear that it is a sin to be anything else.

Can faith in Jesus forgive someone with these sins? Absolutely. If they place their faith in Jesus, they will repent. This is a gift of the Spirit. If they refuse and deny Jesus to bring about repentance, they are not trusting in Him.

In love, we must help them see that remaining in their sins has eternal consequences.

Tomorrow, we will read Leviticus 23-25.

Day 37: Leviticus 23-25: Honoring God, Giving Our Best

I've said it before, but I will repeat myself. Thursdays are one of my favorite days. I love Sunday, just focusing on the Lord all day. Mondays have so much potential. Even with a challenging week, Thursday brings the opportunity for improvement, and your accomplishments fill you with gratitude.

Today, we read the greatest number of verses we will read in one day all year, except for October 9. Sorry, it just works out that way because I keep us to full chapters and try not to jump books. I say try not, because in December we will read two very short books in one day.

But, let's get into what Leviticus 23-25 were saying to me today.

The Festivals

Here, God is telling Moses how he and the people of Israel were to honor Him through festivals.

In Amos 5:21-24, we will get some clarification. God does not want the festivals; He wants an obedient and contrite heart. But, at this point in our history of communicating with the Lord, He is setting up the festivals.

These were to be sacred assemblies. This included the Sabbath.

Most Christian denominations worship on Sunday. God gave direct days for His festivals. The point was not the day; it was the Lord.

Sadly, what I see in churches today is a complete lack of reverence for the importance of that event.

People wear shorts, t-shirts with inappropriate messages on them, dirty clothes, and pajamas. I accept clothes are clothes and fashion changes. If that is what you are showing on the outside, what does the inside look like?

That is the real question. Are you in church because it's Sunday, and that is what you are supposed to do? Or is going to join your family in Christ to worship your Savior the pinnacle event of your week?

Is it a chore or duty you need to perform, or a passion you have?

Notice in 23:3 that this is an ordinance the Lord gives to people wherever they live.

Giving

Then we hear about giving. This is a topic a lot of pastors will avoid. They're uncomfortable making anything about money.

So, let's not make it about money. It is in everything you have; we are to give to the Lord.

The way I have always looked at it, and we will see in today's reading proof of this: everything I have belongs to God. Because of His love and mercy, He has allowed me to enjoy more of it than I deserve. If you don't feel that describes you, I would question if you understood what you actually deserve. None of us even deserves the days we have. We don't understand our sinfulness.

God gives us this incredible offer: Instead of justice, He gives us mercy, and along with that, He blesses us. If we are faithful in returning the first fruits, the best of what He gave us, back to Him, He will bless us more. (See Luke 6:38)

I am not talking about a prosperity gospel. God has a plan for each of us, and I learned a long time ago that financial wealth was not a part of His plan for me. Therefore, I don't focus on money. Jesus taught you can't love God and money. (see Matt 6:24).

What I am saying is we need to come to the Lord with our best labor, our best presentation of ourselves, and the best attitude in our hearts.

When we give irreverently, showing up Sunday half asleep because someone else "made" us be there. That is not what God is asking for.

Verse 23:24 cautions that those who do not deny themselves on that day will face being cut off (NIV).

Keep It Going

Sunday should be about honoring God in all we do.

If we approach Sunday in this way, we soon discover that Monday is Sunday, part 2, Tuesday is part 3, etc. God will bless your soul in ways beyond money, and you will yearn to serve Him more.

24:2 tells us to keep the lamps burning. While I am taking this out of context, it is still a valid point.

When we develop a relationship of mutual loving reciprocity with God, realizing He gave us His best, we give Him our best, and our best gets better, so we give even more. We soon realize how selfish we have been. How much we had been holding back.

I learned there were sins I was not giving to Him. Not out of shame of the sin but out of a selfish desire to keep the thing that was causing me to sin.

Then, we are taught that we must take all these commandments from the Lord seriously. Our reading declared a death penalty for those who blaspheme the Lord. They were to be taken outside the city walls and have the entire assembly stone them to death.

Because we have Jesus's forgiveness, that punishment no longer hangs over us, but it is important to realize that it was serious enough for God to allow His One and Only Son to be killed for us.

Share The Love

Then, in 25:17, we are told not to take advantage of each other. This is something I see too often. If someone gives of themselves, everyone else backs away and thinks to themselves, "Whew, I escaped that one?"

They feel relief. Instead, they should say, "Thank you for taking care of that this time. Let me help you with the next one."

Why do I feel that everything I have is God's? We read in 25:23 that even the land we live on, when we buy it, is still the Lord's. Everything that comes from that land, which in those days would have been the food, the materials to earn a living, etc. God owns everything, and we must return it to Him.

Today, we try to wrap our arms around as much as we can grab hold of and, like a stubborn toddler, declare, "Mine!".

Tomorrow, we will talk about the reward for obedience, but today, I challenge you to examine what you look like on the inside. How could you let what is in you shine brighter on the outside?

Tomorrow, we will read Leviticus 26-27.

Day 38: Leviticus 26-27: Blessings and Curses

Good morning. For those who wonder why I always start with good morning, it is because, as I write this, it is 6:35 a.m. That is when I normally have eaten breakfast, read my Bible verses, and booted up my computer.

Today, the verses we read were the last two chapters of Leviticus, 26-27.

There were two lessons from these chapters. I will take them in reverse.

God's Abundance

We see God's warning of the wrath He will pour out on people who do not keep His commandments. It is right for Him to do so.

God owns everything, and everyone. He blesses us to have all that we have, and especially in modern-day America, we have so much more than ninety-nine percent of the people who ever lived had.

Even the poorest among us are relatively blessed.

Think of the harsh conditions people in most eras had to endure. I know homeless people who have chosen that lifestyle. They don't want the responsibility of going to work and maintaining a home. For them, their freedom is more important.

With those of my acquaintance who choose this lifestyle, drugs, and alcohol have contributed to their choice, it is still their choice. Even taking those substances was their choice.

Help is available. They prefer what they have.

But God wants to give us life and not just life, but abundant life (see John 10:10).

Notice in Leviticus 26-46 that God repeatedly gives the people a chance to repent. He is a merciful God who does not wish that any should perish (see 2 Pet 3:9). He tells Moses that if they don't repent, He will punish them more. If that doesn't cause them to repent, He will add to it. This pattern repeats several times.

My life had gone sideways. But I didn't heed the warning. I had to close my restaurant; still, I didn't change my ways. My wife left me, and I moved on, unfazed. Even when I had a car wreck and broke my neck and back, I remained an atheist.

God never gave up trying to bring me back to Him, and I praise Him for His patience with me. I did not deserve to survive long enough to be saved.

Yet He kept me alive until I was born again, and then He blessed me.

A Season for Rain

Which leads to the opening 25 verses of chapter 26. I wanted to leave this to last, to end today on a positive note.

God has everything and controls everything. He can provide not only what we need but every wholesome desire we could have.

I say wholesome desire because He will not contribute to our sinfulness.

If we, as individuals and as a nation, return to the Lord and keep His commandments, He will make us prosperous by sending rain in its season and causing the ground to yield its crops. Since most of us are not in the agricultural industry, this also means blessing us with success.

For nineteen years, I was one of the top-producing sales agents at the company I still work for. People would ask me what my "secret" was, and all I could do was point to the Lord. I did nothing different from what they were doing, but He blessed me with success.

Peace In Our Time

He told the people of Israel they would live in safety.

Would we not want to know this in our own land? He grants peace, and we live in a world that is desperate for this.

We hear of the terror that will persist without the Lord, and He promises to remove it, but just like the people of Israel, we need to return to Him.

He will walk among us and be our God, and we will be His people, if we will humble ourselves and keep His commandments.

In verse 16, He warns that if we don't, He will bring on sudden terror and wasting diseases and fever that will sap our strength. Have we not seen this recently?

When will we turn our ears and start listening to the Lord?

He is still offering us a chance, but one day, He will remove that opportunity.

Please don't wait until it is too late. Call on the Lord Jesus Christ today. He is waiting.

Tomorrow, we will read Numbers 1-2.

Conclusion of Leviticus:

Now that you have read the third book of the Bible, take a moment to reflect. How have the events in Leviticus mirrored lessons in your own life? Do you feel yourself growing in knowledge? Are you also growing in faith?

For fun, here are five questions I want you to answer (I will post some brief answers at the back of the book).

1. What is the main topic of Leviticus?

2. What were the different types of sacrifices described in Leviticus?

3. What was the significance of the Day of Atonement (Yom Kippur)?

4. How did the laws in Leviticus relate to the Israelites' daily lives?

5. What is the overall message or theme of Leviticus?

Chapter 3: Footnotes

1. **Mangual, Rafael A.** "Unjust From the Start: The Case Against Daniel Penny Should Never Have Been Brought." *City Journal*, December 9, 2024.
https://www.city-journal.org/article/unjust-from-the-start..

2. **Cox, Daniel, Beatrice Lee, and Dana Popky.** "How Prevalent Is Pornography?" *Institute for Family Studies*, May 3, 2022.
https://ifstudies.org/blog/how-prevalent-is-pornography.

3. U.S. Food and Drug Administration, "Antibacterial Soap? You Can Skip It, Use Plain Soap and Water," last modified December 1, 2021,
https://www.fda.gov/consumers/consumer-updates/antibacterial-soap-you-canskip-it-use-plain-soap-and-water.

Chapter 4:
NUMBERS

Day 39: Numbers 1-2: Counting Our Blessings

Good morning. For the next two weeks, we will read the fourth book of the Bible, Numbers. Today, we focused on the first two chapters.

Know the Requirements

There were three thoughts that stood out to me as I read the details of the census that God told Moses to conduct.

It is important to God, who dwells within your community. By having them count their males, it is possible to determine the needs of a community.

It is impossible to calculate how many public resources will be required when a country does not have sovereign borders.

City planners have formulas to help them predict traffic flow. The calculations are based on the current population but factor in a reasonable amount of organic and inorganic growth.

They must speculate on how many jobs a new company will create when they come to an area.

This will also require supporting jobs to provide services to those people. It will affect how they forecast the need to widen roads or create new flow patterns.

With that much growth, will the electric grid hold up? What about water? I live in a desert and knowing if the water we can access will be adequate is crucial.

Controlled Growth

To know they will have enough tax revenue, they want a sustainable amount of growth.

Getting companies that offer higher-income jobs will enhance that tax base and enhance the local economy.

This will mean new stores, restaurants, service providers, etc.

While these are positive influences, they still need to be planned for and controlled.

Flip that and calculate an influx of lower-paid, even unemployed workers.

Impacts on Community

Just as with the growth we mentioned, they will have an impact. Their children will need schools, doctors, and public services.

Will there be an increase in crime? More need for fire and ambulance services?

How will the government provide these expensive services if those migrating in are not as proficient at adding tax revenue?

These genuine problems require planning and constant change.

Therefore, it becomes important to know how many people you must care for, and how many can serve.

Controlled Reduction

You need the same calculus when removing people from a community. Those people required food; they used resources; they provided tax revenue.

It is very possible that removing them will decrease the tax burden and allow the resources to be spread over a smaller group. There will still be fewer people eating in restaurants, less money spent on groceries, less collected in sales tax, etc.

Which businesses will prosper, and which businesses will suffer? How will you adjust, and is there a way for those affected to adapt?

God Knows Each of Us

Then I noticed God knew the actual names and told Moses who to assign to count.

I am sure The Lord had equipped these men from each tribe to do this task. God had given them talents and skills.

They had integrity. God was familiar with their identities and recognized their capabilities.

God knows each of the stars by name (see Isa 40:26).

We may think we can get away with things. No one is around. We are in the privacy of our own homes, in the middle of nowhere.

God is omnipresent and omniscient. He knows our actions. Every thought we have and our full potential, whether good or bad.

There were two to three million people in the tribe of Israel, and God calls out this small group by name.

We should all live our lives knowing He knows us.

Judah First

My last observation was in verse 2:3. God knows Jesus will come from the line of Judah. He knows that the sun rises in the east.

Therefore, He sets Judah to the east.

They will be the first to see the sun rise.

When Jesus returns, others will comprehend that something is happening. They will search and look around. Trying to figure out what is going on.

Those who belong to the Lord will already know.

He will gather us to Himself in the air. (1 Thes 4:17)

From then on, we will be with Him forever.

Those who are not in that number will go through such horrific tribulations that God will not require His children to be part of.

I encourage you to live with this thought.

Dealing with Tragedy

Last week, two airplanes crashed. The crashes claimed nearly one hundred lives.

A friend at church spoke of how people were at the airport waiting to pick up a loved one who would never arrive.

I posed the question: how many Christians who knew those people had "planned" to tell them about Jesus? Perhaps they had moved forward in doing so.

Maybe they invited them to lunch and were about to share their testimony, but the phone rang.

Or their friend told them about a personal crisis.

Figuring the time was just not right, they waited for the next opportunity.

That opportunity never came. It never will.

We must all seize the moments we have because one day, whether through rapture or the inevitable end of each of our lives, we will no longer have those chances.

Tomorrow, we will read Numbers 3-4.

Day 40: Numbers 3-4: Sharing the Load

8580. Think about that number as we read chapters 3-4 today. We will get back to that in a moment.

Firstborn

What stood out to me was how God had set all the firstborns apart for Himself. He had done this since the night of the original Passover.

Think about how often young ladies who get pregnant choose to abort their child. Later in life, they may have other children. We had a speaker from New Life Clinics come to share her testimony, and she had aborted her firstborn. She still languishes with that pain today.

When we take that life, we deprive ourselves of all the joy and love that every person brings. We eliminate heartbreak and sorrows, but every person I have ever heard talk about having gone through that process suffered from it. They didn't eliminate the heartache; they expedited it.

Instead of feeling the sting of rejection from a teenage son who decides he wants to do things his way. They forsake all that and suffer the loss immediately.

Getting past ourselves, however, we need to realize we are stealing from God. That was a child He had created.

If you subtract the impact all those individuals would have had on society, it is easy to understand why we are such a mess today.

These were to be the leaders, spiritual leaders in our communities. And now, they are not.

Before that, in Numbers 3:7, we see that these people, set apart by God, are to "perform duties for the whole community."

When we lose leadership, we see the ruin of the community they would have led.

The Sanctuary

Then, we focus on the sanctuary. This is the place where God would meet with the leaders He had appointed.

Don't confuse this with the church. The church is not the building. People are the church, but here he is talking about the sanctuary.

This was such a key area. We hear about the meticulous care that went into constructing it, breaking it down, and moving it.

That is where 8580 comes into play. The number is how many people it took to move and care for the sanctuary.

Today, most congregations have about 20 percent of the people doing the work. It takes a large team to accomplish all that needs to be done.

Look at how organized and precise each role was. They left the bread on plates as they covered them with the blue fabric and then the leather. After this, they place the poles in. These were not the people who would move it, just prepare it to move.

The Kohathites, Gershonites, and Merarites came in and carried the things assigned to them. They could not even look at the other things.

I have heard people burn out and complain that they always must do this or that, while other people only need help in an easier area.

God did not want the Merarites who were carrying the frames and posts, to look at the Gershonites and scoff that all they had to carry was the curtains. People can be petty.

We should all realize it is a blessing to serve God in whatever area He assigns us to.

The church is a body. We can't all be feet. Feet get to go places, but some of us must be shoulders.

Everyone loves to look deep into eyes, but we can't all be eyes. Some must be noses and deal with the smells.

For The Love Of God, Not Money Not all are paid, either.

We see Moses gave Aaron the redemption money for his sons. Not all Levites had the same duties or the same rewards.

Someone sold us this idea of communism. That everyone deserves to work the same amount and have the same rewards. This is nonsense.

We all have specific duties to perform, and whether we do, God chooses who and how He wants to bless us.

Moses and Aaron did not have to carry poles or even utensils, but they had the responsibility of determining if a family member needed to be terminated if they did not perform their given assignment.

I would rather labor under a heavy piece of lumber than condemn a relative to death for looking around the room to see what others were doing.

My takeaway from these two chapters is that we all have roles to play, and when we all carry our weight, the Lord can accomplish amazing things through us.

When I talk to people about their hopes for our country, their church, or individual families, they all have big dreams, but are they all willing to take on the burden?

Tomorrow, we will read Numbers 5-6.

Day 41: Numbers 5-6: Faithfulness and Purity

Good morning. Today, we have one of our shorter reading assignments. Chapters 5 & 6 only contain fifty-seven verses. The next chapter is exceptionally long, so I didn't include it in today's schedule.

Remaining Pure

The theme today is purity, or as it may be, impurity and faithfulness.

God is always faithful. It is a characteristic of holiness. We are to be holy as He is holy; therefore, we are to be faithful. Faithful to Him, faithful to each other.

He cannot be around sin. He created heaven for us to dwell with Him. Then, He had a problem. We are all filthy and defiled by sin.

This is like being around a smoker or someone who owns cats. You don't need to see them smoke; you can smell it on them.

The person with cats always has fur on them, and there is that ammonia smell that just permeates everything in their home.

The Price of Purity

God had a way to resolve this. He sent His One and Only Son, Jesus, to pay the price for our sin. This cost Him everything. But it removes from the believer all traces of sin. We can then dwell with Him in His paradise.

For the people with Moses, He set the precedent. Any defilement required their removal from the camp until they were clean again.

They applied this to anyone who sinned against God if the sin did not require death. It also applied to those who sinned against each other.

When we wrong each other, we are unfaithful to the Lord. He demands we love each other and respect each other.

Affirmation of Marriage

This applies to marriage. A woman must remain faithful to her husband. Faithfulness doesn't just imply the lack of adultery but the consistency of how she conducts herself. She should love her husband in such a way that he would have no reason for jealousy.

When we withhold our affection toward one another, we give our spouses reasons for doubt. Doubts about themselves as well as the relationship. Therefore, Ephesians 5:22-33 gives explicit details on the relationship between husbands and wives.

We must respect and cherish each other. We are to love the Lord first, then our spouse, then our children, and everyone else after that.

The modern family places a higher value on loving our children, and even ourselves, above our spouses and often even more than God. This is not scriptural.

Our spouses become jealous when we don't affirm that love. This puts a burden upon us by drinking bitter water. In the Bible, it is only the wife who goes through this test. The lesson applies to both partners.

By not being faithful in loving our spouse as God intended, making them confident in our feelings toward them, we bring upon ourselves unhappiness.

The Bread

Though there is much to contemplate about the Nazirite, the next thing that captured my attention was the idea of thick unleavened bread.

I picture flatbread or Matzah crackers when I think of unleavened bread. There are, however, dense loaves of thick bread made without yeast or sodium bicarbonate that form thick heavy loaves.

Dipped in olive oil, I am sure they are delicious.

The problem in America is it is hard to get undefiled flour. Our government requires enriching all flour. This means they have added Folic Acid, which is why Americans have so many complications of obesity and dietary diseases.

In Europe, people eat more grain than we do. It is in their pasta, their bread, and even their beverages. But they don't enrich their grains.

Without Folic Acid, their bodies digest them, and they don't gain weight.

Therefore, if you are to make unleavened bread, thick or thin, be sure to get non-enriched whole-grain flour.

Be sure to let your spouse know you love them more than anyone other than God as we draw into this week of Valentine's Day. Let them know it isn't flowers or chocolates that make Valentine's Day special, but the person you spend it with.

The final thought from today's verses: join Aaron as he blesses Israel by praying, "The Lord turn his face toward you and give you peace." (Numbers 6:26, NIV) Tomorrow, we will read Numbers 7-8.

Day 42: Numbers 7-8: Giving and Serving

Good morning, and happy Tuesday. Today, we read Numbers 7-8. While only two chapters, the first is extraordinarily long but repetitive. We will talk about that in a moment.

Equal Giving

There are two areas in America that have strayed from the path set by the Lord. These are the areas I believe have led us to this dysfunctional system we have. Correcting it will require a change in basic assumptions.

In chapter 7, we hear that all twelve tribes of Israel gave the exact same offering.

It would be foolish to believe that all the tribes were blessed and prosperous.

They were farmers, hunters, or warriors.

Nowhere do we see that when warriors returned with plunder, they had to split it among all the clans. We know there were markets, and people bartered and traded. However, society categorized several types of citizens, such as the shepherds, as lower class.

Two Lost Principles

Still, they were not to give based on their ability. They all gave according to the demand of the Lord.

The nation of Israel was a Theocracy. The rulers in the synagogue were the rulers of the government. Moses and Aaron were not just spiritual leaders; they were the rulers and the judges.

Later, God would appoint judges and anoint kings, but the church was the government.

I am not advocating for a Theocracy for America. We can see from history that governments and churches, for that matter, become corrupt.

We have lost the principle that God chooses and leads the people's leaders.

After ratifying the Constitution, each state insisted on Christian principles, if not Christian men, guiding their representatives.

These are the two guiding principles we have lost.

Instead of a nation led by God, through men consecrated to Him, we have a land led by a government that has placed itself in the seat of being God.

Therefore, the government wishes to be the provider and provisioner of everything within our society. The farther we get from God's leadership, the more corrupt we become.

They established the Levites as the government to minister to the people and relay the Lord's commands. They would meet with God and then relay the messages and administer the directives.

American people, persuaded by the media, choose our representatives, not God. They don't answer to God; they answer to the people who provide them funding.

We need to get back to a place where people of God, chosen by God, intervene for the citizens according to the will of God. Then, the people need to realize that it is God who provides and that all must give. If God blesses people with more, this doesn't mean they need to give more. They need to give more to God, that is separate. But, to the government, the precedent set here in Numbers is that all gave the same amount. Because of their faithfulness, God blessed them according to His will.

All According to God's Design

He is in control. If He were to make all shepherds wealthy, there would be no one to tend the sheep, and their food supply would be at risk.

He would take a shepherd and make Him into a king. That is God's prerogative.

We have twisted this to put ourselves in control, instead of God. Therefore, we believe all people deserve to have the same blessing and that those with more should share it with the rest.

We see in these chapters that is not God's design at all.

The next time you, or someone else you know, think they deserve more or should have to provide less, ask yourself: is this God's will, as shown in scripture? Or is this man's plan that leads to destruction?

Term Limits

The last point I would make today deals with Numbers 8:24-25. The Levites were all to serve from age twenty-five, but after age fifty, they could assist, but not do, the work.

We have people in our government who have been in office for over thirty years. This should never happen. Term limits are necessary.

There could be an avenue for them to contribute as advisors or in some other fashion, but the work needs to be done by people who have been part of the population they represent.

Someone who has been living in Washington, D.C., for over thirty years should not be representing the people of California, or Wisconsin, or anywhere else.

Tomorrow, we will read Numbers 9-11.

Day 43: Numbers 9-11: Following the Cloud

Good morning, today we read Numbers 9-11. There were some remarkably interesting things discussed in these chapters.

Share our Faith

It began with the Lord commanding Moses to celebrate the Passover. Why did He need to reiterate this commandment?

They received the Passover as an ordinance to keep in the land the Lord would give them. Now, they had been wandering in the desert due to their disobedience at Mt. Sinai. They had not reached the promised land.

According to Jamieson-Fausset-Brown Bible Commentary, this was the only time during the forty years in the desert they celebrated this festival.[1]

Here, God gives instruction that everyone was to take part, even the foreigners among them. As with our own faith, God never intended for us to keep these things to ourselves, but to share them with everyone we encounter.

There were to be no exceptions. Even those who were unclean needed to keep the Passover, but not until the fourteenth day of the second month.

If anyone chose not to partake, they would be cut off and "bear the consequences of their own sin." (Number 9:13, NIV) Keep in mind, "The wages of sin is death" (see Romans 6:23).

The Lord Guides Them

I found myself consumed by a bitter jealousy of their miraculous guidance. When the cloud remained over the tent, they knew to stay, and when it lifted, they moved.

There are times in my life when I wish I had clearer guidance from the Lord. I felt His presence and believed He wanted me to do something, but I still had doubts about the timing. I didn't want to get ahead of Him.

Should I build my house now? Or wait until I have saved more money? What about the job opening at work? Is that a promotion worth having? Or does God have a better plan for me if I stay still? When is the right time to retire?

Oh, how I wish for a pillar that could guide me, a celestial map to my life's journey! Instead, I have a cloud of doubt.

We all need to pray for each other to have more faith.

Sound the Alarm

Not everyone was watching the clouds. Therefore, the Lord had Moses make trumpets to sound the alarm and get their attention.

Do we need to increase our focus or change where we're looking to increase our faith?

It is intriguing that in 10:35 it was Moses telling the Lord to rise when they set out. This shows that we must move when we believe that is God's will, but only after praying and asking God to go before us.

Especially for a group, like a church or a nation. There are always those who are not watching the Lord or walking with Him. In 10:36, Moses asks the Lord, when they rested, to return to the masses.

Still Lacking Faith

It has always baffled me, knowing they were following a cloud by day and fire by night for all these years. God has brought them out of Egypt, led them through the Red Sea, and provided Manna for them. Yet, they would still find reason to complain.

The Lord has blessed me for years. Still, I find reasons to doubt and complain.

We always want more than we have.

In our house, we avoid carbohydrates. Unlike the Israelites, who were eating these loaves of Manna day after day and asking for meat, I have the opposite. I eat meat day after day, as they would for a month, and I crave a loaf of bread. Or a slice of real pizza. We always want what we don't have.

Moses grows so weary of their complaining that he would see it as a blessing if God took his life.

There are times, with all that God provides for me, that I long, more than anything, for Him to bring me home.

Life can be hard. Then, the Lord gives me a new assignment and renews my purpose.

I know what He is asking me to do, and I know it is impossible.

Just like Moses, I forget nothing is impossible with God. I need Him to remind me that His arm is not too short.

I pray we all have enough faith to move when we see the Lord moving, and when we don't, we will have friends who will alert us. It is time to go.

Tomorrow, we will read Numbers 12-14.

Day 44: Numbers 12-14:
The Humility of Moses, the Doubt of Israel

May God bless you for joining us as we read Numbers 12-14.

Humility

This passage speaks about the humility of Moses. Remaining modest is an arduous task today.

People will not take you seriously if you are. Society rewards boasting and arrogance in most areas.

In the presence of greatness, humility is effortless. Moses was collaborating directly with the Creator of heaven and earth.

Because of his humbleness, we read people were challenging Moses.

His wife was a Midianite, and the rest of the Jews did not think he was worthy to lead them any longer.

I'm certain this bothered him, but he pushed those feelings aside.

God was not so willing to turn a deaf ear. It is always great when the Boss has your back, and this was the case here.

Even though Miriam was in the wrong, for which God had stricken her with leprosy, Moses prayed for her.

When we pray for our enemies, we show God's character.

Because of Moses' prayer, God rewarded him, and Miriam's affliction lasted only a week.

Following the Lord's Command

God then tells Moses to send the Israelites into Canaan to spy out the land. It was just as God had promised a land flowing with milk and honey.

Just like us, they were greedy and wanted something better than what they had.

A land flowing with milk has great and healthy herds. This means there were lush pastures for them to graze on.

The presence of honey meant bees. Bees pollinate the crops and vineyards. Both are signs of abundance.

But they didn't want to have to work for it. When they found the people were enormous, they refused to fight them.

Only Caleb and Joshua trusted the Lord was with them.

Doubts Linger

How the rest, being aware of what God had already done for them against the Egyptians, could have such doubt is a mystery.

It is one we all struggle with.

I had to shut down a magazine I was publishing, and we were on the brink of bankruptcy, but God delivered us.

I remember the day I applied to my last employer. It was twenty-four years ago. I could not even finish the computer test.

I had been using Macintosh computers for so long that the Windows commands were foreign to me.

That night, I was at a baseball game with members of our church, and a friend asked if I had found a job yet.

"I know one place I won't be working," I told him.

The words got stuck in my mouth. "Let me rephrase that," I said. "Unless it is God's will, I know where I won't be working."

The next day, the company called while I was out applying for other jobs.

When I arrived home, my wife told me they had called. I asked if they were laughing.

"No," she replies, "I think they want to interview you!"

She was right, and I knew it was God's will for me to work for them. I have remained there for over two decades.

Still, I see other opportunities in life, and I struggle with doubts. Is it too much to ask for God to deliver me again?

Verse 14:9 tells us not to rebel against the Lord.

They were told not to fear the people in the land because God would be with them.

God asks Moses how long the people would treat Him with contempt. (Num 14:11).

We must ask ourselves when we fail to move because of doubts about our abilities. Are we treating the Lord with contempt?

If we are doing what God wants us to do, will He not go with us and assure us of success?

Tomorrow, we will read Numbers 15-16.

Day 45: Numbers 15-16: Defiance and Consequences

Let's begin our day by discussing chapters 15 & 16.

Beware of the Heart

We should not trust our hearts; they are deceitful and desperately wicked. (see Jer 17:9).

Today, we read that while everyone has unintentional sin in their lives, we also have sins of defiance. These are sins where we believe God's way is not acceptable to our lifestyle choices.

As a hormone-crazed teenager and even young adult, knowing that sex outside of marriage was a sin didn't matter.

Even if I were not an atheist, I would not have let this description of those actions inhibit me.

We rationalize God would not make us the way we are if He did not intend for us to enjoy it.

It's that self-centered, narcissistic perspective that justifies abortion. My body, my choice.

The LGBTQ community also demonstrates this mindset.

We all determine on our own that our god would not have a problem with this behavior.

Dr. David Jeremiah says in a sermon I watched – "this is true, because your god does not exist."

This is another form of idolatry. Making our own god that we can worship instead of respecting the God that created us.

Numbers 15:30 calls this blasphemy against the Lord. We must shun those who commit it.

Actions Have Consequences

Is it a cultural difference? This verse says we must drive out the foreigners for these actions.

Our society's emphasis on universal acceptance directly contradicts this.

While God loves everyone, He never tolerates intentional defiance.

If we choose to rebel against the Lord, there will be consequences.

We see a man gathering wood on the Sabbath. It doesn't say he was chopping wood or cutting a tree down. He was merely gathering it.

For this action, because they had been told to do no work on the Sabbath, God tells Moses that the man must die. The whole assembly took him outside the camp and stoned him to death.

People might say it was different back then, and in one way, this is true. Today, we have grace.

Jesus says, "For truly I tell you, until heaven and earth disappear, not the smallest letter, not the least stroke of a pen, will by any means disappear from the Law until everything is accomplished." (Matt 5:18, NIV).

Jesus accomplished something. He died for you to forgive your sins.

This requires surrendering the lordship of your life to Jesus. If you are making a different god for yourself, one which allows for immoral conduct. You have not given Jesus that control. Therefore, you are still under the Law.

Keep it Top of Mind

Numbers 15:39 tells us that God gave the Israelites tassels to remind them of his commands.

We have the Cross of Jesus to look at. This reminds us not only that He paid the price for us, but how seriously God will judge sinfulness.

If we do not submit ourselves to Jesus, this is the fate we are accepting for ourselves.

We should look upon it, as they did the tassels, so that we would not chase "after the lusts of your own hearts and eyes." (Num 15:39, NIV)

The Rebellion

Just as now, there were those who remained bent on defiance. This included Korah, Dathan, and Abiram, along with two-hundred-fifty other men.

God swiftly dealt with this bold resistance by opening the ground and swallowing these men in chapter 16.

It is poetic justice that when they defy God and choose to be of the world, they are consumed by the world. The earth swallowed these sinners, along with their families.

The third mystery is after seeing all this happen, the people still resisted Moses and Aaron.

For this, God sends upon them a plague. Even though Moses prayed God would remove the plague, another 14,700 people died.

Today, we have a society dedicated to defying the Lord. Believing they can flaunt their sinfulness. They see plagues pouring out and remain defiant.

We must help these lost souls come to know the Lord.

They believe they can endure what lies ahead of them, but no one can. It is not loving them to allow them to make these choices without trying to show them the light.

As we celebrate God's love, let us all love enough to share the Gospel with those who need to hear it.

Tomorrow, we will read chapters 17-20.

Day 46: Numbers 17-20: Grumbling and Guidance

Today, we will read Numbers, chapters 17-20. That might seem like a lot after so many days, with only two chapters, but the first chapter is noticeably short.

Repeating Mistakes

The most hilarious thing about the people in the Bible is they repeat the same mistakes.

My first response is to mock them. Then I realized I do the same things.

Therefore, it is no surprise that the people I train at work, or the children I teach in Awana do the same thing.

Even the adults I have shared researched and thought-out sermons with, those who came up to me after the message and thanked me for sharing such a deep truth. We all share the same burden of guilt.

This opening chapter again depicts the people grumbling about leadership. They are sure they should replace Moses and Aaron. So, God does this test with the staff with all their leaders' names written on it.

Nothing happens to any of the other men's staff. The Lord is tired of the pattern, so He goes beyond. Aaron's staff sprouts, buds, blossoms, and produced almonds.

After their latest defeat, they lament their lost state. They are sure they will die.

Newsflash: we are all lost, and all will die. Those who trust in Jesus, though they die, yet will live. (See John 11:25)

Responsibility is a Gift

The Lord clarifies that each man has a responsibility.

Our communities require effort and commitment from all of us. When we don't carry our load, it places a burden on everyone else.

The recent call to preach humbled me. Upon seeing the wording in 18:7, the Lord says, "I am giving you the service of the priesthood as a gift." (NIV).

It is a gift to feel the power of God working through you. To know He is guiding my very thoughts and controlling my mouth as I speak.

I am not a priest, but I am a preacher. This is also a gift.

We are all called to share the Gospel. When we do, especially when the Lord allows us to lead someone to Salvation, we realize what a gift it is.

With power comes responsibility. God declares He will put to death anyone else who approaches the sanctuary.

God Always Exceeds

Just as God did not stop with having Aaron's staff sprout, He doesn't stop at giving the gift of the priesthood. He adds that Levites get all the tithes and meat from the offerings.

I do not serve the Lord because of what He will give me. He has already given me more than I could ever deserve or ask for.

The privilege of serving Him is far beyond what I deserve.

But I would have to admit, He has never stopped blessing me beyond all of that.

While always grateful for all He provides, I know it comes with responsibility.

Even Aaron and Moses suffered for failing to follow the command of the Lord.

When God tells them to tell the rock to give water, they decide in anger at the people to strike the rock with their staff. God still provides the water, but because of this inability to follow His commands, Aaron will soon die. Spoiler alert: Moses will never enter the promised land.

It would be easy enough to blame the people who were grumbling, but as I stated, we all do the same thing. We forget all that God has done for us. It becomes what have you done for me lately.

God is holy. We all must honor Him. I know I fail to do that daily. Let us all show God the gratitude He deserves.

Tomorrow, we will read Numbers 21-23.

Day 47: Numbers 21-23: Speaking God's Word

Good morning. Today, we will discuss one of my favorite stories in the Bible as we read chapters 21-23 of Numbers.

Intruders

I'm speaking of the story of Balaam and his talking donkey.

You may think it is the idea of a talking donkey who can see an angel blocking the path. While that is interesting, that is not what caught my attention.

I was drawn to the Moabite and Midianite elders' willingness to pay for divination.

Balak did not know what to do with this horde of people crossing his plains.

He could have been hospitable and agreed to let them pass. What if they didn't? He knew his own forces could not stand against them.

We have watched as millions and millions of migrants from all over the world pass through Mexico on their way here to the United States. Mexico allowed them to pass through since they had no choice.

Moses tells Balak they would pay for any water they drank or damage they did. He could have accepted this offer.

You need a plan of how to get them to leave when you allow such enormous masses of people to come into your country. His plan was to have people who dealt in the dark arts curse these people.

Everyone Has a Price

Balak offers this job to Balaam, who accepts the role.

Then God intervenes and tells Balaam not to curse His people. Balaam decides to listen, but Balak ups his offer.

With sagacious insight, Balaam rejected the offer. He knows he is no match for the Maker of the Universe.

They wear Balaam down and he sets out with the Midianite officials.

God becomes angry and sends an angel to oppose him.

Even a donkey can see to stop when an angel of the Lord stands in his way.

We choose not to notice when God is putting things in our path. Instead, we double down, believing it is just a challenge to overcome.

A donkey doesn't have its own agenda. Selfish desires do not blind it. It sees the angel and turns. Then it lies down. When it is beaten by Balaam, it decides to speak up.

We often see people we love walking, contrary to God's will. We say nothing. Not that any of us have a problem speaking, but in those situations, we don't.

Because we make these choices, life beats us down. We don't understand why, but the more we resist God's demands, the more obstacles we face.

Get on Board

Listen to that voice in our hearts. God is asking why we are beating ourselves down. Where does our strife come from? It comes from our hard heart, which is refusing to listen to God.

I lived in that denial for years. Knowing God wanted me to serve in bolder ways.

When I accepted more responsibility in the ministry, the enemy would attack me. Troubles would multiply.

Therefore, I hid behind excuses. Not enough time. Too many obligations. Not enough qualifications.

Like a complete donkey, I realized I had to listen to the Lord. But, I refused.

We all must speak what the Lord puts in our mouths. Just like a donkey, we can trust the words are His, not ours.

If those around us continue to get us to consider other perspectives, to keep us away from serving the Lord. We need to turn aside or stop and speak up.

Tomorrow, we will read Numbers 24-26.

Day 48: Numbers 24-26: The War on Truth

Today, we read Numbers 24-26

More Than Money

Chapter 24 opens with Balaam repeating his message. Balak gets upset that he won't curse the Israelites.

Balaam told him there was no amount of compensation that would get him to speak anything other than the words the Lord gives him.

We see people who sell out for a price.

In the news, we hear of trillions of dollars our government wastes on programs that only benefit a tiny group of people.

The question of why a politician would spend millions to obtain an office, paying around $250,000 annually, has always puzzled me. In the Washington, D.C., area, this amount would equate to modest living.

Then we see bartenders who turn into congresspeople and become millionaires. It is easy to speculate some of that money is coming back into their campaigns and pockets from the projects they fund.

Hopefully, there will be an investigation into these phenomena. One day, we may have an accurate explanation.

Integrity

This also happens in churches and in private businesses. Integrity has become a fluid concept.

The company I worked for had always had a guiding value called Integrity Without Compromise. I have always thought that it was redundant. If you compromise, you lose integrity.

This is the new war on truth. People think the truth is only true if it applies to their beliefs.

God provides us with a different definition. Truth is truth. Jesus is the truth. God is the truth. The Bible is the truth. (John 14:6, 17:17).

In John 16:13, Jesus tells us the Holy Spirit is the Spirit of Truth.

Postmodern thinking would have us believe truth is a personal concept. That your truth may differ from mine. This is far from any biblical truth.

Temptation

We encounter a truth in chapter 25. Men, when the opportunity presents itself, will choose to sin.

The men of Israel began practicing sexual immorality with the Moabite woman. For this, the Lord told Moses to take them all out and kill their leaders in broad daylight.

The execution of the death sentence against the Midianite Kozbi and the Israelite Zimri. They had caught both in the act. Executing them ended the plague that killed 24,000.

Allowing the sin to continue to infect the entire society.

Therefore, I applaud our current attempt to end these wasteful programs and their promotion of immorality.

Peace

When we are moving in the right direction, walking with the Lord, we can see a covenant of peace is possible.

I enjoy sex as much as anyone but cannot imagine any sexual activity that would merit the scriptural denouncement these two executed individuals have endured for millennia.

In chapter 26, we see that the largest clan was Judah. Reading this, I think of how small the nation of Israel is. In this spacious region, surrounding forces have hemmed these people in for generations.

Verse 26:54 says that a larger group should have a larger inheritance. Therefore, I do not believe it is God's will for Israel to be so confined.

In 26:62, we read the Levites did not receive an inheritance. Those who God calls to serve, should not be doing it for material gain. Their inheritance is the Lord.

We should provide for them. They deserve the offerings and much more.

Those who will not follow the Lord will not gain that inheritance.

Only Joshua and Caleb may go into the promised land. The descendants of Israel may enter with them. All those who sinned in Sinai wandered in the wilderness and died there.

Therefore, it is important to avoid sin, not support funding sin, and make a choice to follow the Lord.

We live under grace but still need to honor God with the way we live our lives.

Tomorrow, we will read Numbers 27-29.

Day 49: Numbers 27-29: Women's Rights and God's Will

Welcome. I hope you are enjoying learning more about God through this book.

Today, we read Numbers 27-29.

Women in Scripture

People have claimed the Bible is misogynistic. While there was a heavy emphasis upon men throughout scripture, it was based on a nation's ability to defend itself. When they did a census, they counted the men. This told them how large an army they could draw on if needed.

In Numbers 27, we see God intends for women to have rights as well.

Our society needed to go through rough years of oppression before the suffragette movement allowed women the right to vote.

Biblical kings and leaders centered their decisions on battles.

There were also decisions within the family. Men are to be the spiritual head of our households Eph 5:22-23)

The direction within the church is clear: men should not allow a woman to lead them. (1 Tim 2:12).

Jesus included women in His ministry.

In Numbers 27, we read God affirms if there were no sons, then daughters deserved the full inheritance.

Consequences of Sin

Everyone likes to take what God provides but will go too far until it becomes sin.

Moses sinned when he struck the rock for water in the Desert of Zin. Sin has consequences even for the one chosen by God. Moses may not enter the land he is taking them to.

It would be up to Joshua to finish taking them into that promised land.

How would you respond if God told you, "After years of serving me, I want you to come up to a mountain to see the land that you will not enter because on the mountain you will die?"

Would you walk to the mountain top slowly? Kicking the stones as you prodded along. Or would you sprint to the top, knowing that the end would be entering the kingdom of heaven?

Guided by The Light

Verse 27:21 tells us Joshua will need to stand before the priest who will inquire of the Urim. The meaning of the word Urim is light.

Today, for the believer, we can go boldly to the Light. Jesus is the Light of the world. (John 8:12)

At the command of the Urim, Joshua would lead the people of Israel into and out of the land.

Jesus will lead us when we submit ourselves to Him.

When we are not seeking the Light, we walk in darkness.

Chapters 28-29 get very repetitious about the offerings and festivals they were to keep. That can cause us to overlook these verses.

We should overlook no part of scripture. Instead, we must ask why God is making this point repeatedly.

The answer is, because it is important to God that we have reverence for Him and follow instructions.

He never intended for us to figure out whatever works for us. He gave us precise instructions on how to live in His presence.

Valuing work

The last sentence of verse 29:7 caught me. "You must deny yourselves and do no work." (NIV)

When we approach a holiday, our reaction is – we don't have to work as if it is a reward not to have to labor.

We should correct this modern mindset. It is evidence of a declining work ethic.

Work is a reward. God gives us all jobs to do. He could have just given us all the houses and tables overflowing with food and drink. Instead, He gives us labor to do and demands we sacrifice food and drink to Him.

We have become so self-centered we miss the point.

The work God entrusts us to do is a blessing. Rejoice in the work. I feel blessed by God's generosity in giving us such abilities.

Tomorrow, we will read Numbers 30-32.

Day 50: Numbers 30-32: The Weight of Vows

Good morning, today we read Numbers 30-32.

Marriage Vows

In our culture, we celebrate Valentine's Day. Known as one of the most romantic days of the year, it is an extremely popular day for marriage proposals.

I'm a complete sucker for romance. But asking someone to marry you because it is a romantic holiday is foolish.

Marriage is a sacred commitment ordained by God. It is a lifelong vow to love each other all the days of your life.

I have been engaged five times and married four. My current marriage has lasted thirty-two years, and I recommend marriage. But you need to enter marriage for the right reasons, not because of a commercialized holiday.

Why bring up Valentine's Day today? Chapter 30 is all about how God views vows.

I failed to keep my vows the first three times I was married.

The only reason my current marriage has survived is because I have learned to love God and keep His commands. He commands me to love my wife.

There were no qualifiers. Not love her if... It is love her like Jesus loves the church.

The church is a group of people who fail the Lord daily, yet He loves us so much; He died for us.

According to Numbers Chapter 30, a woman's vows are not as binding. They only count if her father, or her husband, knows about the vows and does not object to them.

God's Commands Are Difficult

I have read this chapter twice today, and I am not sure why God commands this. Nevertheless, that's what the text states.

We don't have to comprehend God's ways. Trust that He has reasons and accept and follow His commands. His character tells me His reasons are just.

God commanded Moses to take vengeance on the Midianites in chapter 31. Moses had to accept God's reasons.

The Israelites killed all the men but took the women and children captive.

Moses reminds them it was the women who caused them to sin by following Balaam's advice in Peor. Therefore, he sends them to kill all the women and boys, leaving only the virgin daughters to capture.

Because women can lead men to sin. I understand why God puts restrictions on their vows and obligations.

Share the Blessing

Earlier this year, I had noted that not all tribes were prosperous because we had not read that the warriors had to share their plunder. Chapter 31 describes a shift, mandating equal sharing with everyone but the Levites. They were all required to support the Levites in their sacrifices and tithes.

Then, in chapter 32, even though they had seen how their ancestors had wandered in the desert and died there, because they would not cross the Jordan and take the land God was giving them, that the Gadites and Reubenites were once again trying to stay on the wrong side of the river.

They agreed to send their warriors to help the rest of Israel, so it was not because of fear. Therefore, Moses permits them to remain.

Accept Responsibility

They received a warning: if they failed to keep their agreement, their sins would find them out.

Which brings us back to those vows we make before the Lord when we get married. Keeping this vow is important. There is no wiggle room.

We trust God can work out any issues within our marriages when we trust him. I believe this weighs more heavily on the men because of what we read in chapter 30.

If we don't, our sins will find us, and we will not find the promised land. We will wander endlessly.

Fortunately, my first three divorces were while I was an atheist. My salvation created a new person. (2 Cor. 5:17) There are limitations on me because of those choices. However, He has blessed me with my present wife. For this, I praise Him.

Tomorrow, we will read Numbers 33-34.

Day 51: Numbers 33-34: Remembering Our Past, Embracing Our Future

We have shared in reading the Bible now for fifty days. Today, we read chapters 33 and 34.

Our Heritage

It is appropriate that chapter 33 is all about looking back at where the Israelites had been.

Reflecting on past hurts allows for healing and future growth. It shapes our identity.

Remembering strengthens our resolve.

God's actions, though harsh, serve a greater purpose. We gain when we reminisce on His justice and how we have watched His plan unfold.

The Israelites' journey has similarities to settling the Americas.

The conquest of Canaan, though described as dealing with "savages," requires further examination of the complexities involved. God drove out people who worshipped idols.

Their immorality and displacement need careful consideration.

God delivered them into the hands of the Israelites. He did not want His people to assimilate their practices.

This is true of the Indigenous tribes in North America. They had their idols and rituals. God gave them over to Europeans, who would bring with them Christianity.

We need to remember this. When we don't, we end up adapting their images, like the Kokopelli. Soon, we forget that it was God who brought us to this land.

When we forget what He has done, we push Him out of our lives.

Break the Cycle

This cyclical pattern of forgetting origins leads to spiritual erosion and societal instability. Ignoring our past invites repeating its mistakes.

The Israelites' experience serves as a cautionary tale, mirroring modern societal struggles. We must learn from their errors to avoid a similar fate.

America's current challenges highlight the urgent need to remember our heritage and God's role in our nation's founding. This remembrance fosters strength and unity, preventing future conflicts.

God's chosen people faced internal strife, mirroring contemporary societal divisions. Their reliance on divine intervention without personal responsibility proved insufficient.

The Value of Character

Our current emphasis is on instant gratification. Ignoring the tedious processes that brought us all we have leads us to expect rapid rewards.

This focuses on the energy of youth as opposed to the wisdom of the older generations.

Aaron was eighty-three years old when he led the people out of Egypt.

Because of their sins at Mt. Sinai, they wandered in the desert for an additional forty years.

Anything worth having requires patience and persistence.

In Numbers 34, God appoints their leaders. Regardless of our outward appearance and actions, He knows our character.

Ignoring God's warnings led to repeated cycles of disobedience and divine judgment. Strong leadership is crucial for societal stability. However, leaders must ground themselves in faith and obedience to avoid repeating past mistakes.

The Israelites' story underscores the importance of both individual and collective responsibility.

The belief in divine intervention fueled a fervent movement, urging a return to faith. This conviction, however, sparked controversy and division.

We are witnessing God moving in our nation today. I believe President Trump's return signified God's favor. This demands national repentance.

Others question such interpretations, highlighting societal complexities. Holding to their love of sin, they view the speed he is moving as oppressive.

A spiritual awakening presents a challenge: can faith and political action coexist, or will divisions persist?

Can we embrace a return to godly living?

Tomorrow, we will read Numbers 35-36.

Day 52: Numbers 35-36: Refuge and Redemption

Today, we finish the fourth book of the Bible. Most people stop reading while still in the Book of Genesis.

The main reasons include lack of relevance, boredom, and not understanding what they are reading. I hope sharing my thoughts with you, even if you may not agree with my perspective, will help you stay engaged.

Our Actions Impact Others

In chapter 35, we read that there are to be six cities of refuge. These are places where someone can flee when being pursued for killing someone unintentionally. We call that manslaughter. It is tragic, but it happens.

When I was recovering from my car wreck, I shared a room with a local celebrity. While feeling depressed, he walked in front of a vehicle.

I felt great contempt for anyone who would put the driver of that car through the guilt and trauma they suffered.

He was oblivious to the impact his actions had on anyone other than himself.

Imagine if he would have perished. Lack of sufficient evidence may have resulted in a criminal conviction. Fortunately, there were no charges, and he survived.

The Bible clearly states that any intentional killing constitutes murder. The avenger of blood shall put any murderer to death.

This is not a job I would relish. I agree with the death penalty, but the weight of taking life after life would have to be heavy.

Keeping the Law

There were only six refuge cities, three on each side of the Jordan. Was it that people would flee across the river for protection, or was there more killing on the west side?

Only two and a half tribes chose not to cross. Was their unwillingness to follow God's earlier command reflected in continued lawlessness?

This bothers me about immigrants to the U.S.

I have family members whose families were immigrant farmers. When they came here, they did everything necessary to become citizens and have all become significant members of their communities.

I appreciate anyone seeking an opportunity for a better life. America's founders established it as the land of opportunity.

When an individual has already established a lack of respect for the law, why do we believe they will become law-abiding after getting here?

It would be like a carnivore saying if we give him one cow, he will become a vegetarian. This lacks logic.

Grace is the Answer

Verse 35:31 tells us to not accept a ransom for the life of a murder. Only Jesus can pay a ransom for such a sinner. Aside from that, we must execute them.

There are states with prisons filled with murderers who have been there for decades and will be for more. This is not pursuing God's will but the will of man.

Verse 33 says we should not pollute our lands with bloodshed.

The text says that tolerating such activity prevents atonement for these places. This is another example of how men like to usurp God.

These were Old Testament teachings. God has not changed.

He provided Jesus as a fulfillment of the Law.

All people can receive forgiveness because of grace.

While this means that we no longer must marry within our clan, like Zelophehad's daughters, we take more liberty with this than we should.

Only Jesus can pay the ransom for the murderers, and there are many serving life sentences who want nothing to do with Jesus.

They have not received eternal forgiveness, nor should they in this life.

We must try to introduce them to Jesus, but when they reject Him, that is their choice. The consequences are their own.

Tomorrow, we will read Deuteronomy 1-2.

Conclusion of Numbers

Now that you have read the fourth book of the Bible, take a moment to reflect. How have the events in Numbers mirrored lessons in your own life? Do you feel yourself growing in knowledge? Are you also growing in faith?

For fun, here are five questions I want you to answer (I will post some brief answers at the back of the book).

1. What was the main purpose of the census taken in the Book of Numbers?

2. Describe the journey of the Israelites in the wilderness, as detailed in Numbers.

3. What were some of the key laws and regulations given to the Israelites in Numbers?

4. What is the significance of the bronze serpent in Numbers?

5. How did the Israelites' rebellion and disobedience affect their journey in the wilderness?

Chapter 4: Footnotes

1. Jamieson, Robert, A. R. Fausset, and David Brown, *Commentary Critical and Explanatory on the Whole Bible* (Hartford, CT: S.S. Scranton Company, 1871).

Chapter 5:
DEUTERONOMY

Day 53: Deuteronomy 1-2: Strength and Courage

Welcome to our fifth book, Deuteronomy. Whenever I hear that word, my mind flashes to a TV show called Psych and Shawn Spencer calling it "do the right thing". Sounds like good advice to me. Today, we read the first two chapters.

Age is Irrelevant

Moses is one-hundred-twenty years old. It is easy to feel like our best years are behind us. We like to rest on our laurels and leave the earth shaking for the next generation.

Soon, we will read about the death of this outstanding leader, but in verse 4 of our opening chapter, we read he had just defeated Sihon, king of the Amorites, and Og, king of Bashan. Old does not mean decrepit.

We see this today with President Trump.

I can only hope to age so well.

Moses' time is ending. God tells him to appoint wise, understanding, and respected men from each tribe. God will anoint them as judges. These are three important qualities that mattered then and still do today.

To be wise

Wisdom is not just possessing intelligence. There are smart people who have academic acumen. This does not always equate to wisdom.

They can string together enough words to convince people of their ability, and this can make them dangerous.

Google defines wisdom in a few ways. I like this one best: the soundness of an action or decision regarding applying experience, knowledge, and good judgment.

It is that combination of experience, knowledge, and good judgment in action.

Some people have experience. I have lived an incredible life and have experience in many things. That does not make me an expert or qualify me to lead in all those areas.

I love learning and reading a lot.

This provides me with knowledge. Knowledge can help me discern when something doesn't seem right.

Even in those situations, I have proceeded only to learn I should have listened to my inner voice.

Leadership Requires Action

I lacked good judgment. It's crucial to have all three.

There are academic people who may possess all three attributes, and yet they remain on the sidelines as spectators. Connoisseurs of experience. Never acting themselves.

A person with all three who will step up is a worthy leader.

There are leaders who inspire and leaders who disappoint. A good leader must also have Christ so that they act with love and compassion.

Verse 26 reminds us that ten of the twelve spies who went into the promised land refused to step up. This was a rebellion against the Lord, and they would never enter.

This is hard to comprehend since the cloud had led them by day and fire at night. They had everything provided for them along the journey.

Still, their fear of the people with their walled cities was greater than their fear of the Lord. Because of their fear, God became angry. He would only let Moses see the land, not enter it. We don't hear Moses whining about this or arguing with that decision.

He takes ownership of his failure as a leader. He had not instilled in them the proper regard for the Lord.

Don't Get Ahead of God

They went without God and were defeated. Another valuable lesson.

We get impatient and try to force things into our time frame. We need to move when God says move and wait when He tells us to.

There were some tribes that God gave over to them. He warned them not to go up against others. We must fight the battles which the Lord gives to us. To push our own agenda can end in disaster.

Then, in chapter 2:21, we hear there were other people as large as the Anakites who had already suffered defeat. We must not impose our fears on others but maintain a healthy fear of God alone.

We read that when they moved with God, they destroyed all the towns they encountered, leaving no survivors.

The adage is there is nothing to fear but fear itself. I would say there is nothing to fear but God. A God who loves you when you keep his commands.

Tomorrow, we will read Deuteronomy 3-5.

Day 54: Deuteronomy 3-5: Choosing Our Battles

There is so much we could talk about in Deuteronomy, chapters 3-5, but I will try to stay focused.

God Provides the Victory

Recall from yesterday that Moses was 120 years old when he was leading an army against all these kings. For this reason, he knows the Lord is the one giving them victory.

We may not be involved in conquests of cities or battles with kings. But each of us fight our own battles daily.

All of us have loved ones who we worry about. They are having health issues or financial struggles. There are children who have moved away, and we fight the emotions of missing them.

Attempting to fight these battles with our own strength, we forget the greatest weapon in our arsenal. God is with us.

We need to give everything to Him in prayer and trust His will and timing. Asking Him to comfort us and provide for us the assurance that everything we are experiencing is for a good that we may not perceive yet.

We take solace in knowing that one day, He will show us the reason, and we will rejoice.

Seek God's Will

Does this ease the burden now? Yes, if we accept it is His will and that there is no other place we would want to be.

When we do this, we learn to acknowledge that all the valleys we pass through are for His will. All the mountains we climb are for His glory. This means all the victories we win are His, too.

In Christ, we have victory over sin and death. We shortchange ourselves when we limit the victory to these areas.

It is a little confusing to hear Moses state God gives them the victories but then verse 3:8 claims he gives Gilead to Makir. Moses claims he was giving other lands to various tribes. It is God who does the giving.

He could give nothing to anyone unless God had provided it and moved him to give it. Everything we have is His, and He is the sole provider.

We Make God Angry

Moses knows this because he pleads with the Lord. He tells the people to not fear because God himself will fight for them.

His doubt comes in as he accepts the Lord will not listen to him because He is angry with him. God does not want to hear about the people any longer because of their sins.

Therefore, God gives them a clear roadmap of what He expects from all of us.

In Christ We Have Grace

Scripture says not to subtract from or add to His commands. Jesus explains that grace does not remove anything from the Law. (see Matt 5:18)

In 4:4, it says that those who held fast to the Lord are still alive today.

This is the message of grace. Not that we are not responsible for our sins, we are. But Jesus has paid for them.

They would not need to be atoned for if they were not still sins. He would not have had to die.

Verse 4:6 tells us to observe personally and then share that wisdom and understanding with others. When we see someone who is worshipping an idol, we need to help them realize that there is only One God.

We need to be aware of how our actions reflect our faith. If we don't act on what we say, people won't pay attention.

He tells us this in verse 9 and ends it with the admonition to instruct our children and grandchildren. They are the ones who are seeing our actions the closest. Only if those actions match our words will they want to emulate them.

Reject Idolatry

He turns his focus again to idolatry. This is our ongoing battle. We love to make idols for ourselves, and even of ourselves.

Because of their idolatry, the Lord's wrath burned against Moses, barring his passage across the Jordan.

Verses 4:25-26 warn us that corruption is inevitable and that practicing idolatry leads to destruction.

Verse 29 assures us that even then if we seek the Lord with all our hearts and souls, we will find Him.

Few of us seek Him in this way. We feel that reading a few passages and attending a couple of hours of church should keep our ledger clean.

This is not what God commands. Therefore, He lets us sink into those patterns until we have distress and then we will seek Him again.

We must remember there is only One God. Only He deserves our highest praise.

When we repeat these mistakes, we need to drop to our knees and reconnect with the Lord.

Then, we move into Chapter 5 and the Ten Commandments. There is enough in these verses to camp for a week, but I will just leave you with a question: Which commandment do you struggle with the most? What steps could you take, knowing this is your weakness?

Ask God to help you with that struggle and have faith that He will.

Tomorrow, we will read Deuteronomy 6-9.

Day 55: Deuteronomy 6-9: Loving God with All Our Heart

Hello, and welcome to the last week of February. Today, we read Deuteronomy 6-9.

The Greatest Commandment

This section starts with the commandment to love the Lord your God with all your heart and all your soul and all your strength. This was identified as the greatest by Jesus in Matthew 22:37.

What I find amazing about this commandment is that anyone would struggle to keep it. But we do. Like a dog chasing a squirrel, we scatter and easily divert our focus.

We go through our days without giving thought to our Savior. Conducting our lives as if He can't see what we're doing. Believing like Adam that we can hide from God. Gen 3:8-10)

God's goodness shines upon us constantly. He has provided all we have and sustains our breath. Without Him, not only do we have nothing, but we also are nothing.

Show and Tell

But you would struggle to see that in the way most Christians live their lives.

Love is an action, not just an emotion. We may feel like we love God, but if our actions don't match, it leaves questions.

We are to keep it in front and center and share it with the world. Putting Him on our foreheads. This means we should outwardly display our blessings and salvation. Drawing others to want to know Him.

Instead, many Christians look beat down. We get this way because we are trying to face the world with our own strength.

We forget we have God on our team and keep looking for a receiver who is open to catch the ball. Meanwhile, Jesus is in the end-zone corner waving his arms so that we will see Him and toss it to Him.

We don't want to lean upon the Lord, so we hesitate and suffer sack after sack. Losing yards and becoming more desperate than ever for a big play.

What We Show

Verse 6:9 says we are to write them on the doorframes of our houses and on our gates.

In my neighborhood, some houses still have Trump-Vance flags waving. Other neighbors still display Biden-Harris flags.

The encouraging thing is that we can still be neighbors and get along even with varied political preferences. But when I read this verse, I must ask, do I know which neighbors are Christians?

I should know because, as a good neighbor, I should have invited them to church and shared my testimony with them. Since I haven't done that, how would they know I am a Christian?

Driving by my house, you will notice a large metal dragon in my yard. But you won't see anything that shows my allegiance to Jesus.

Can you say differently?

This passage tells us we need to do these things so that we don't forget all that God has done for us. We have already admitted that we live our lives without thinking about all God has done.

The Fire Starter

We give Him the credit, but we just stop thinking about it. We are dealing with the new fire we have to put out.

That is Satan's greatest trick. He keeps us engaged in our troubles, so we forget to think about God. It is like when Peter takes his eyes off Jesus and sinks when he was walking on the water. (Matt 14:25-33).

When our focus comes off God, we seek to make idols that will solve our problems. We earn more money so we can solve our problems. Now, money is our idol.

We believe team effort can influence changes that will solve our problems. Now, a candidate or group becomes the center of our activity. That is our new idol.

In chapter 7, they are told when they defeat an enemy, they must destroy it completely.

Freedom in Discipline

This is true today. An alcoholic can't drink casually. An addict can't "use" lightly. If we call upon the Lord, He will deliver us. Then, we must destroy that enemy.

When we are faithful to do this, verse 7:15 says the Lord will keep us free from every disease.

Our current news cycle aims to keep people in constant fear of everything. They sensationalize every story to make it seem like the sky is falling. They try to blame it on someone if they will make that connection, often when it does not exist.

However, with all that God has done for us, we read in chapter 8 that God will discipline us when we are not following Him. We see the father-son paradigm: a good father will use what discipline is necessary to help their son develop proper character. So will our heavenly Father.

Trials remind us that when God feeds, clothes, and houses us, we often forget Him. We have no problems, so our success becomes our idol.

It is often when we have problems, we seek the Lord, but when we don't, we neglect that relationship. Chapter 9 warns us against this practice. We need to show our gratefulness by keeping Him the priority in our lives.

No person knows the days they have left, and we should remember to share our faith with everyone daily.

Tomorrow, we will read Deuteronomy 10-13.

Day 56: Deuteronomy 10-13:
Blessings and Curses, Idolatry and Truth

You should all be proud of yourselves for having the discipline to make it this far. Today, we read Deuteronomy Chapters 10-13.

This is one of the longer reading days we have this year. More than the quantity of pages, there is an abundance of content to consider.

If what stood out to you was different from me, that is fine. The challenge is to spend time in God's Word and listen to what it is saying to you.

But create that discipline to read daily and try not to read to mark off that you did it. Read with curiosity.

Peaks and Valleys

In chapter 11, God tells His people, through Moses, that He is setting before them a blessing and a curse. In life, we must take the good with the bad. Our jobs are a blessing, but some mornings, we just aren't feeling up to doing them.

Our children are a blessing. But there are pains they will put us through as well.

Having a personal relationship with God gives us eternal life. We can approach life knowing everything we are going through is a small fragment of time compared to the eternal glory we will know. The losses of loved ones aren't any easier, nor the anxiety of dealing with disease and heartbreak.

It should comfort us knowing we will see those loved ones again. The time away from them will one day seem so brief it is not significant. Ahead of that reunion, we will have eternity with them.

In verse 11:29, it tells them to go to different mountains to proclaim their blessings and their curses. There is a 700-foot-deep valley between the two peaks. This is not about distance. Instead, it shows that we need to separate those peaks and valleys mentally and physically in our lives.

Enjoy the triumphs and be in the moment. God intended you to have that joy.

When you do go through trials, realize it is just a different peak. We should rejoice always (see 1 Thes 5:16) while also being in the moment. Accept that it is a different place. God gave us both places for His glory.

There are other mountains we will climb in our lives. Some will have more significance to the people who were there before us.

We can respect their feelings toward these places, but Deuteronomy chapter 12 tells us to destroy the altars. We should embrace the people. God loves everyone. But we must never accept their idolatry.

Dwell in Him

Verse 12:5 foreshadows that God will choose among the Israelites a place to put His Name for them to dwell there. Seeing the word Name capitalized signifies this is the Name of God, a.k.a. Jesus. In Him, we should all dwell.

Later, we are told not to do as they do, and everyone does as they see fit. This is a stark warning against this age of apostasy we live in.

A path to salvation

God loves all people, even though all of us are sinners. God hates all sins, even though there is no one who does not commit them. It was because of this dichotomy that God provided Jesus to atone for everyone's sins if they repent and put their faith in Him.

We should be sure to love everyone enough to let them know that our sins, like their own, will never be an acceptable way to live.

This life is a training ground for us to learn to live in His presence. We cannot practice living as if He did not exist and expect to be welcomed into His house. We cannot make our own places to offer sacrifices.

He has set before us a table of abundance, which we may eat. Even while we are unclean.

If anything I say here offends you, please realize I love you. I do not say this to offend you but to help you see that we all have a pathway to salvation.

What God provides

Moving into the last part of today's reading, God gave us animals to eat. He said we may eat as much meat as we want.

I have struggled throughout my life with weight problems. I was a chubby kid, and if I am not working out, I will put on weight today.

We had a pyramid that encouraged us to consume more grain than meat, which has influenced our American diet. The human body wasn't designed this way. We are omnivores but with teeth designed to tear meat.

To lose weight and control my blood health, I have found a carnivore-heavy diet is most beneficial. Our diet is not carnivore. I have gone weeks, months, with nothing other than meat and eggs, but it gets monotonous.

To maintain a healthy weight and high energy levels, we eat very few carbs, even fewer grains. We eat a lot of meat and animal products.

I am not a dietitian or a doctor, so I will just say this has worked for us.

People take dieting to the point of being a religion for them. Chapter 13 cautions us not to give anything so much importance.

We should worship only God. One must avoid anything that seeks to displace that affection.

Tomorrow, we will read Deuteronomy 14-17.

Day 57: Deuteronomy 14-17: Children of God, Called to Obedience

Good morning. I hope today finds you in good health. Today, we will read Deuteronomy 14-17.

There is much to discuss within these four chapters, beginning with the opening verse.

Children of God

Moses tells the Israelites they are God's children. Matthew Henry claims this is a sign of election.[1] We cannot choose to be born or even adopted. It is the choice of the Father to adopt us as His children. Without this choice, we are orphans with nothing to offer.

Benson emphasizes God adopts into His family those who were pious and followed Him.²

John 1:12-13 would agree with both, "12 Yet to all who did receive him, to those who believed in his name, he gave the right to become children of God 13 children born not of natural descent, nor of human decision or a husband's will, but born of God." (NIV).

When we place our faith in Jesus, He gives us the right to become His children. But it is not our decision, but that of God's.

It was not I who was seeking God when He found me.

Being dead in my sins, I was comfortable as an atheist. I had to humble myself and admit I was wrong and a sinner, which was difficult to do. This was not my nature. He found me when I was hiding from Him.

For this, I worship Him.

Do Not Harm Ourselves

In the same verse, we are told not to cut ourselves or shave the front of our heads.

The idolaters at that time would do this during the ceremonies for their dead. They would cut themselves or scratch deep gouges in their faces, through their eyebrows, as a sign of hopelessness during the burial ceremonies of their loved ones.

God wants us to have assurance and hope. In Him, we have eternal life. Death is not the end but only the beginning. The moment we leave this body; we are in His presence for eternity. (see 2 Cor 5:6-8) John Piper covers this well in Desiring God.³

First Fruits

We could talk about the dietary laws given in Deuteronomy. We must compare those with Acts 10:9-16 and realize that God has permitted us to enjoy eating all the animals. It is not what goes into the stomach that defiles us, but what is inside our hearts.

If there was something wrong with consuming these other animals, and even roadkill and animals found dead. He would have permitted no one to eat them, but 14:21 says they can give or even sell that meat to foreigners.

The Bible reminds us to tithe the Lord with the first fruits of all He gives us. I believe this should include our labor as well.

Seek God first, then everything else afterward (Matt 6:33).

Not all people can serve in the same way, however, so in 14:25, we see that exchanging our tithe for currency and giving the money is acceptable.

Financial Responsibility

In chapter 15, we read about canceling debt and not being debtors. It is all right to lend, but we should not borrow. When we lend, it should not be for the gain of interest. We should benefit those whose needs we can help meet.

It is God's will there should be no poor people in the land. He has blessed us with plenty, and when we share those blessings, they will be more than sufficient. We choose not to do this, and so there are poor people. God chooses not to bless us. All suffer because of this greed.

When we lend it to someone and then forgive that debt, we are told to give them more. To supply them from our flocks, and threshing floors. (v 15:14).

I owed money on the GMC Jimmy that rolled and broke my neck and back. Because of my disability, I contacted GMC, and they forgave my debt.

All of this seemed great until I tried to borrow money years later and discovered their action had destroyed my credit. This doesn't match what these passages say.

Chapter 16 reminds them they were once slaves. None of us deserves the blessings we have received from God. We have earned His wrath. Our wages should be death (Rom 6:23), but He took that punishment for us and gave us eternal life.

Proper Guidance

Then Moses describes the appointing of judges and kings. These stages of Jewish tradition will come later as we read the history books.

Until now, it had been Levites and priests who provided the governance.

Although Moses had given them divorce because of their hard hearts (Matt 19:7-12), Chapter 17 says that we are not to take many wives. Those women will bring with them new idols and traditions which the husband will follow.

Men will do what pleases their wives, and that will lead them away from seeking God.

I was fortunate in that while I was an atheist, God gave me a Christian woman who led me to her Lord. Jesus Christ saved my life. I am now a child of God.

Though this worked well for me, the Bible directs us to marry within the faith (2 Cor. 6:14). Therefore, if you are not married, seek a believer.

Tomorrow, we will read Deuteronomy 18-21.

Day 58: Deuteronomy 18-21: Avoiding Evil, Defending the Innocent

We're approaching the end of our second month together as well as completing the Pentateuch, the five books written by Moses. Today, we read Deuteronomy 18-21.

There are many things I could write about every day. I try to focus on three or four.

Today, I will examine the ideas of avoiding evil, enjoying what God has given us, defending the innocent, and the rights of the firstborn.

Avoid the Occult

Most tribes throughout the world were hedonistic. These polytheistic pagans believed in an unknown deity that controlled each element in their world. There was a god of fertility, of water, of grain, etc.

The people had abundance when those gods were pleased. If they had lost favor, there was scarcity.

These practices of worshipping the creation instead of the Creator are detestable to God. For this reason, He chose a people, Israel, from among all those nations.

They were to conquer all these other tribes and introduce them to Himself.

Sadly, the men, after conquering these people, would adopt their practices. The Israelites would become corrupt. Therefore, God demanded that they annihilate these nations along the way.

It was their idolatry that condemned them to destruction.

When we allow this into our own lives, we are seeking God's wrath. Witches and goblins may seem harmless and entertaining, but they are not.

I know many who enjoy the Harry Potter stories and are still devout Christians. We invite corruption when we embrace the occult. Therefore, chapter 18 warns against these practices.

Discernment is Necessary

We then read about following false prophets, and there have been many throughout history.

I pray every time I write, asking God for a message from Himself. If you ever read anything from me or anyone else, please take the time to investigate. Does it align with scripture? If it does not, please reject it.

In chapter 20, we see God wants us to enjoy the things He has provided.

If anyone has built a new house, planted a new vineyard, or started a family, they are to stay behind to enjoy those things. God does not want them to perish. Nor should we leave them for someone else to enjoy.

This also includes not forcing someone who is fainthearted to join them in battle. Let each of us fully devote ourselves to the Lord.

If you have someone who enjoys being around you but is not a believer, they are there for you to evangelize.

You should not, however, assign them responsibilities to serve. They will not become saved through service. Instead, they will profess a watered-down faith, leading to uncommitted converts.

The End of Innocence

We read throughout today's chapters about the refuge cities. They were to make a place for the innocent to flee. What spoke to me was the need to protect innocent blood.

When I think of innocent blood being shed, I can't help but picture all those babies who end up in abortion. This happens simply because someone believes they have a right to end these lives.

We never have a right to take a life with malice or forethought. If you have "decided" to get an abortion and reasoned why you would proceed with that decision, you have had forethought. Your guilt is a heavy burden; only faith in Jesus can lift it.

He will forgive all our sins. Even those atrocious ones. But once we seek His salvation, we agree that we have sinned and repented. Turn from those practices and seek His righteousness. He is faithful and just.

Don't Play Favorites

Then, in 21:16-17, there is a discussion of firstborn rights.

We are not to give those rights to a son we may love more because he was born to a wife we loved more. Instead, this right must go to the actual firstborn.

Jacob violated this birthright when he tricked Esau into selling it for a bowl of stew.

Again, when Jacob gave his blessing to Joseph's sons instead of Reubens.

While it is disturbing to see these violations, it is a reminder that none of us are without sin.

We all, Jew, and Gentile, need a Savior.

Standing on our own merit, we all fall short of the glory of God. (Rom 3:23) We all need redemption.

Jesus offers salvation to everyone who calls on Him and repents. Each person must make this decision for themselves. You must choose this while you have time.

Tomorrow, we will read Deuteronomy 22-25.

Day 59: Deuteronomy 22-25: Decency, Faithfulness, and Fairness

I use a phone app, Bible Gateway, when I do my daily Bible reading and highlight the verses that stand out to me. Then, I think about the topics for a while. As I am writing, I look at each highlight and make a comment. I must do some research along the way.

If I had done that today, while we read Deuteronomy chapters 22-25, this post would have been too long to read. There was just so much to contemplate in these final chapters.

Be Decent

There are three major themes: Be a decent person; don't cheat on your spouse because divorce is not an option; treat each other fairly.

It starts with being a decent human being. In 22:1-4, we see how to look out for our neighbor. If someone messes with his property or injures an animal, we should help.

We lived in a 1970s-era mobile home for twenty-seven years. Because of my disability and the effects of age, we knew someday we would need to build a wheelchair-accessible home.

After saving up enough to build our new home, we moved into a rental property and had our old house torn down. Repairing it to the point where it could pass inspection would have cost more than we would have recuperated.

As the new home was under construction, we received a text from one of our neighbors who noticed someone was taking wood from the site. It was the contractor removing debris, but we appreciated our neighbor was watching out for us.

This was a fitting example of what this verse was saying.

Later, we read to not hold their cloak for collateral overnight. We would not want them to be cold. We need to be good to each other, even when someone owes us.

Respect Marriage

Beyond being a decent person, we are to not commit adultery with another man's wife.

First, adultery is a sin.

Second, we are not even to covet our neighbors' wives. These are just two ways this would be wrong.

What is interesting is how emphatically God tells them to purge the evil from among them.

When people are violating these laws, the Lord says to execute them.

Today, we read about a love triangle that ends in murder. Murder mortifies us, but adultery doesn't even shock us. We have become so comfortable with certain sins they have become mundane.

Yes, we live in a time of grace. But Jesus never intended to pay for our sins so that we would have license to sin more. As Paul often said, heaven forbids (Rom 6:1-2).

Our salvation should help us break away from sin, not become tolerant of it.

Work Past Divorce

It all starts with becoming complacent about divorce. Here I am, pointing three fingers at myself. My first three marriages ended mostly out of boredom with each other and in a matter of months.

Fortunately, my wife and I celebrated our thirty-second anniversary this year. She had never married before and told me she would not allow a divorce.

We had to work through disagreements and complacency.

Divorce is a word we won't even use in our home.

Jesus said it was because of men's hard hearts that Moses allowed them to get divorced, but it was never God's intention for marriage (Matt 19:8-9).

Be Honest and Generous

Chapter 23 reminds us that the Ammonites and Moabites refused to welcome Israel as it passed through their land. They even called on Balaam to curse them.

God turns those curses others wish to place on His people against them. He brings good out of situations for those who love Him and obey His commands (Rom 8:28).

Next, we get to Miscellaneous laws, such as protecting a slave who is taking refuge. This brought to my mind Philemon and the slave Onesimus. Paul was right in befriending him. It was for God's glory that he returned to his master.

Circling back to being decent people, and I use the word decent, not good. No one other than God is good. We read they are to leave gleanings in the fields and vineyards and to allow the poor to have them.

They are to use equal weights and measures and not oppress the poor.

Then, we revisit adultery and more rules around divorce, including not remarrying the person you divorced.

And not to forget, we make another trip through purging evil from the land. This time for kidnapping.

Motivate Others

One last thought in 25:4, which tells us not to muzzle an ox while it is treading out the grain. People place a muzzle over an animal's mouth to prevent it from biting. When wearing a muzzle, an ox cannot eat the grain and will lose interest in pulling the plow. This was just a heavy board that would separate the grain from the husks.

They would also grow weak without being able to replenish their strength by eating as they went.

The intention of this verse, however, is that we should have a reward for our labor. Being compensated but also enjoying the work we do.

Thank you for allowing me the pleasure of sharing these insights with you for these last two months. I look forward to what next month has in store for us.

Tomorrow, we will read Deuteronomy 26-28.

Day 60: Deuteronomy 26-28: Choose Life

Time marches on, and now we enter our third month together. Thank you for taking this journey with me.

Today, we read Deuteronomy chapters 26-28.

Joy Not Sorrow

The opening section of chapter 26 is interesting. Verse 14 reads, "I have eaten none of the sacred portion while I was in mourning, nor have I removed any of it while I was unclean, nor have I offered any of it to the dead." (NIV)

I had to look this one up in the commentaries, and Benson says that the Israelites could not eat anything consecrated to God while in mourning. This stems from the custom the Egyptians had of offering a portion of their first fruits to the idol Isis.[4]

He says it may have just meant they were not sorrowful about having to give up so much of their prized possession. The first fruits were the best they had. To give them up to the poor may not have sat well with them.

Instead, these verses say they did as the Lord commanded and ate them cheerfully.

The Lord wants us to have His best, His One and Only Son, Jesus. He wants us to enjoy with gratitude but also with joy. We must recognize that no one killed Jesus against his will. He died for us, so that we could live for Him.

Do Not Defile Yourself

There were other idolaters who would take a portion of the first fruits to offer it to idols.

Jesus is God's first fruit. (1 Cor. 15:20) The firstborn of creation. It is imperative that we are worthy recipients of His sacrifice. If we eat unworthily, we bring upon ourselves condemnation. (1 Cor 11:27-29).

Moses commands them to avoid this to remain clean.

Then he says they must not offer this food to the dead. This was another thing the Gentiles of that time did. They offered part of the first fruits to the dead idols.

It may have also just been alluding to the Jews, who would send food, like a wake, to the relatives of the dead at the funeral.

In times of distress, when someone suffers the loss of a loved one, it is still customary to bring them food. Not for the dead, but to help keep the living going while they struggle through grief.

Separate the Good from the Bad

We need to separate our blessings from our curses. God instructed the Israelites to create an altar of stones, with the Ten Commandments written upon them, on Mt. Ebal. This was where they would sacrifice fellowship offerings.

It is also where they would offer their sacrifices. They were to eat these sacrifices together, in fellowship, with joy.

Just as a parent wants to see their children happy, God wants us to rejoice in Him (1 Thes 5:16, Phil 4:4).

The Levites were to curse the people from Mt. Ebal.

Others were to go up to Mt. Gerizim and bless the people there.

We see a complete list of curses and blessings. They all boil down to one thing: when we follow the Lord's commandments, we will receive blessings.

God has blessed me for the twenty-seven years I have been a believer. Not every day was great, but overall, God has gotten me through every trial and provided for every need I have.

Before, when I was an atheist running from God, in tragedy, I could find no comfort. My wants found no hope. Sin was my refuge because I didn't know what else there was (Rom 6:20-22)

These chapters go through an extensive list of curses, and the people say, Amen.

Curse of Sin

Then they hear from the other mountain all the blessings of obedience. What is strange is that they are silent during the blessings. I think there would be more celebration of these.

Knowing the conditions of our hearts, it is hard to rejoice. We know how often we fail God. We all deserve the wrath we hear mentioned in chapter 27.

So much so that they continue to mention more curses at the end of chapter 28.

Life is hard because we don't obey God the way He asks. If we did, life could be so much greater.

I'm not talking about a prosperity gospel. Any true gospel must account for our sinfulness.

When we move from sin to obedience, we will still have troubles. But when you face any challenge with God, He assures you of victory.

I challenge you to read those last two chapters again and think of all the ways we are being cursed today. Realizing those curses reflect our ongoing love for all the idols we have made for ourselves.

My prayer is not that God will bless me with more blessings. Not that He will remove more curses. He is all I need and the only reward worthy of having.

Therefore, my prayer is that I would be more obedient. That He would bless me with obedience to Him.

Tomorrow, we will read Deuteronomy 29-31.

Day 61: Deuteronomy 29-31: A Change of Heart

Good morning. Today, we have a light reading assignment: Chapters 29-31 of Deuteronomy. This is only seventy-nine verses. We need to enjoy the lighter days when we have them.

Blessings

It always amazes me that the Israelites continued to doubt God. As Moses states in 29:3, they have seen all the wonderful things He had done for them with their own eyes.

We must walk by faith, but they walked following the cloud, etc. John 20:29 tells us that believing without seeing is a blessing.

This is a blessing given to us by God. The people of Israel, though they had seen, still lacked one thing: God had not given them eyes to see, ears to hear, or a mind to understand.

God was there with them and wanted them to know it was He who was providing for them.

Since we don't have the fire hovering over us at night, telling us when to move and when to stay; He gave us this greater insight, the Holy Spirit, so that we could still have faith.

Our clothes and shoes wear out, but we can trust God has provided a way to replace them.

Curses

God warns us against idolatry. This includes idolatry of the self. We think we can claim God will bless us even when we sin. This is blaspheming Him. Scripture says we will be cursed. To believe the contrary would be foolish.

There will be calamities and diseases plaguing the lands. Stop me if this sounds familiar.

We don't enjoy thinking of an angry God. He is a faithful God. His word is true and whether we like the message, we must love the messenger.

These verses tell us our land will be desolate. His wrath and zeal will burn against us. The worst part is that the Lord will blot out our name from under heaven.

I can endure anything in this life. Despite my paralysis and the loss of loved ones, I still find hope in the promise of heaven.

To have one's name blotted out would be the end of hope.

The reason the Lord would do this is not because He is a mean God. He showed His love toward us while we were still sinners, by dying for us (Rom 5:8).

In verse 29:26, He gives us the answer for our misery. We have gone off and worshipped other gods and bowed down to them. Our land, this entire world, is overflowing with idols that He had not given us.

Hope

But, before we lose all hope, chapter 30 assures us, if we return to Him, He will restore our fortunes and have compassion on us.

When we place our faith in Him, He will circumcise our hearts so that we can give them to Him. His Word will be in our hearts, so we will have the power to obey Him.

He will make us more prosperous than before. Not when we seek prosperity. That is one idol we struggle with. But when we seek Him, He will delight in us.

Verse 30:19 says today, we have a choice before us: life and death, blessings and curses. He tells us to choose life so that we and our children, will live. He will give us that heart to love Him and hear His voice.

Our own faith is weak. Like the people following Moses, we had hearts of stone. When we

are born again, He gives us a new heart of flesh (Eze. 36:26)

This new heart has given us more courage.

They were too scared to approach the immense walls and gigantic people posing an insurmountable threat. God gave them this new heart. They had the courage to follow Joshua.

Hearts Can Break

We see in 31:17 that He knew there would be a day when our hearts would turn away from Him.

Sin is always there to tempt us. Satan is prowling like a lion, seeking to destroy us (1 Pet 5:8).

God sees eternity laid out before Him. He knew this would happen and warns that He would become angry and forsake us.

When He turns His face away, we lose the protection we need. We embrace sin and debauchery, and disaster comes on us.

This is not a surprise. The scriptures foretold it.

Tomorrow, we will learn a song He gave Moses. The song is not the important thing. The important thing is that we remember Him in all we do. We recall all He has done and is doing for us.

When we do this, He is always willing to allow us prodigals to return. He loves us and wants us to be with Him always.

Tomorrow, we will read Deuteronomy 32-34.

Day 62: Deuteronomy 32-34: The Eagle and the Rock

As we begin this week, we end these five books we call the Books of the Law. Tradition credits Moses as their author. Today, we read chapters 32-34.

Sing It

We begin with the Song of Moses.

I have been a songwriter for as long as I can remember. When I was four or five years old, I remember playing a little plastic guitar and making up lyrics.

In my teens, writing songs was my refuge. When someone would break my heart, I would grab my dog, Java, and drive to a place overlooking the city. There, I would sit on my car's hood with my Yamaha guitar and notepad and draft songs.

In my twenties, I struggled against facing life with a disability. Playing music in nightclubs made it easier to talk to women. I was always shy, and dancing was not a viable option. So, I sang and played. Then, all I had to do was respond when they came to tell me they liked my songs.

Because I have a unique voice and never sounded like anyone else, I would play songs I wrote. The advantage was I couldn't play them wrong. No one had ever heard them before.

God's Protection

I wish I could have written a verse as beautiful as 32:11, "like an eagle that stirs up its nest and hovers over its young, that spreads its wings to catch them and carries them aloft."

In my mind, I can visualize this majestic sight. They say animals don't love, but seeing this, it is hard to accept.

The mother eagle is teaching her young and still protecting them. Allowing them to face danger but refusing to let them suffer harm.

This is a picture of how God allows us to experience hurts and fears.

The baby eagles with their undeveloped minds, wondering why their mother would forsake them and let them fall. Learning when she rescues them, they can always trust her.

God uses trials in our lives to teach us these same principles.

They Fly Away

At a certain point in their development, the eagles will leave the nest.

As a father who rarely sees his son or grandkids, I know the pain this mother eagle would experience. Still, you have let them go. It is the natural process.

God provided everything the people needed, and as they reached the promised land, they grew fat and abandoned Him. He understands our pain. They rejected the Rock, their Savior. (32:15).

They deserted Him and forgot the God who bore them. So, the Lord hid his face from them. He calls them "a perverse generation, children who are unfaithful." (32:20)

God Allows Suffering

People will question why a loving God allows famine and disease. When we lose loved ones, it is painful.

We watch the news and see violence everywhere and contemplate how God doesn't step in.

Verse 32:24-25 answers this question.

We read how God was ready to destroy these people, but Moses intervened. He reminded Him that the enemies would claim He couldn't deliver them. So, He tolerated their actions.

Knowing they lacked sense and had no discernment, He provided an answer.

He would come down from heaven, like an eagle from above. He would live as one of us and die for sins He did not commit.

If we refuse to acknowledge Him as Lord, we read that disaster will come to us and we will look to our idols.

Our wealth will not save us.

Armies and technology will not protect us.

Government will be powerless against what will come if we refuse to repent and turn to God.

He is God, and only He can put to death or bring to life.

We can trust Him to heal our land if we repent of our idolatry.

We can be certain that we will leave these short, wonderful, sometimes miserable lives. He will gather us to our people. Those who went on before us and are waiting beyond for us.

Tomorrow, we will read Joshua 1-5.

Conclusion of Deuteronomy

Now that you have read the fifth book of the Bible, take a moment to reflect. How have the events in Deuteronomy mirrored lessons in your own life? Do you feel yourself growing in knowledge? Are you also growing in faith?

For fun, here are five questions I want you to answer (I will post some brief answers at the back of the book).

1. What is the main purpose of the Book of Deuteronomy?

2. What are the Ten Commandments, and why are they important in Deuteronomy?

3. What are the blessings promised in Deuteronomy for following God's laws?

4. What are the curses mentioned for not following God's laws?

5. What instructions does Deuteronomy give about having a king in Israel?

Chapter 5: Footnotes

1. **Sun Tzu** Tzu, Sun. *The Art of War*. Chichester, England: Capstone Publishing, 2010.

2. **Dale Carnegie** Carnegie, Dale. *How to Win Friends and Influence People*. New York: Simon & Schuster, 2009. Part 1, chapter 1.

3. Matthew Henry, *Matthew Henry's Concise Commentary on the Bible*, s.v. "Deuteronomy 14," accessed via Bible Hub.

4. Joseph Benson, *Benson Commentary on the Old and New Testaments*, s.v. "Deuteronomy 14," accessed via Bible Hub.

5. John Piper, *Desiring God: Meditations of a Christian Hedonist* (Sisters, OR: Multnomah Publishers, 1986).

Chapter 6:
JOSHUA

Day 63: Joshua 1-5: Leadership and Obedience

Good morning. We are just over two months into our reading, and today, we begin the Book of Joshua by reading chapters 1-5.

Strength and Courage

First, the theme of strength and courage is so prevalent. God tells Joshua this three times in the first chapter. He has just lost his leader, Moses. Now, He is telling him that he will be the one to lead the people into the promised land.

The Lord reminds them that He will be with them just as He was with Moses. He tells them to be strong and courageous.

Second, God tells them to be careful to obey all the laws. Not to turn from it to the right or the left.

The book of the law is not to depart from their lips. They were to meditate on it day and night.

For us, that would be the whole Bible. God's Word should be at the forefront of all our thoughts and actions. If we do this, the Bible promises we will be prosperous and successful.

Third, Joshua tells them to get their supplies ready because, in three days, they will cross the Jordan and take possession of the land.

He had no reason to doubt. No need to hesitate. God had spoken. Joshua, empowered by faith, acted.

Leadership

We see how the people were divided, and two and a half of the tribes remained on the other side of the river. He reminds them of their commitment to send their warriors ahead of them into battle. They agree.

This shows that good leadership is vital to any group's success. He knew these men would keep their word, and they did.

He then sends in two spies. When they return, they report the people of Jericho are melting in fear of them.

Their fear comes from knowing all the Lord had already done for them. This report encourages the people and gives them the strength and courage needed for the upcoming battle.

The Battle Plan

God then gives them the strangest battle plan I have ever heard of. But Joshua does not question. He obeys.

We need to learn to obey God without questioning. When He has a plan, our job is to listen and follow.

The people followed Joshua just as he had followed God.

I once worked for a manager who gave me an assignment. I did as he asked, but then, he was not there to see me through it. I had to continue without his guidance and was sure that I would be in trouble.

At the time, I didn't know the Lord. I did not realize then that it was He who had guided me. He was trying to show me that I could do more than I imagined. He was preparing me for greater things. He was showing me I could lead.

I have spent many years reading Sun Tzu's book, The Art of War.[1] There are a lot of good lessons there. I also have an entire bookshelf of books on leadership. The best is Dale Carnegie, in his book How to Win Friends and Influence People, who says, "If You Want to Gather Honey, Don't Kick Over the Beehive."[2]

I thought I could go on to do great things, but it would always involve me making other people do them for me.

The last thing I want to mention today is that the people had to consecrate themselves. They were to be holy, just as God is holy. We too, must come to God in that same way.

Tomorrow, we will read Joshua 6-8.

Day 64: Joshua 6-8: Obedience, Sin, and Victory

This morning, we read chapters 6-8 of Joshua.

Unusual Commands

There is so much in these verses that we could discuss for days. First, we see God's plan of attack is unusual. March around the city once a day for six days. On the seventh day, march around it seven times. Then, shout, and the Lord will give them the victory.

This is a testament to the power of God.

The Price of Disobedience

Then, we see Achan sinning against God. He took some of the devoted things for himself, and for this, God allowed the men of Ai to defeat them.

Sin always has a price. Because we are a body of Christ, one person's sin can affect the whole.

We are to purge sin from among us. When we don't, there are consequences.

Joshua was mortified. He and the leaders tore their clothes and fell facedown before the Lord.

How many times do we see our country, our church, our families, or even ourselves fall, and our first response is to blame God?

Taking Responsibility

It is a great lesson to learn that we all must accept responsibility for our sins. We must repent. Ask the Lord to show us what we have done wrong.

It is only then that God will allow us to see what His plan is for us.

He had given them the city of Ai, but because they had sinned, He could not deliver it. When they repented and purged the sin from among them, they found victory.

God is a great military strategist. This time, instead of marching and shouting, He gives them a different plan of attack. He sets up an ambush, and Ai is defeated.

After this, they build an altar and write on it a copy of the Law of Moses. All the people stand, half in front of Mt. Gerizim and half in front of Mt. Ebal. Just as they were commanded in Deuteronomy.

The priests read all the words of the law, the blessings, and the curses.

We cannot just hear God's word and then not act upon it.

We cannot listen to the parts we like and then ignore the parts we don't.

We must accept it is all God's Word and that He knows what He is doing.

When we obey, He will bless us. When we don't, we will suffer curses. There is no middle ground. There are no other options.

Which path will you choose today?

Tomorrow, we will read Joshua 9-11.

Day 65: Joshua 9-11: Deception and God's Sovereignty

Today, we read Joshua, chapters 9-11. As we have seen so many times before, these people make a lot of mistakes.

Deception

First, the Gibeonites deceive them. They tell them they are from a distant land. So, Joshua makes a treaty with them.

Verse 14 says that the Israelites sampled their provisions but did not inquire of the Lord.

How many times do we get so sure of something we don't even take the time to pray about it?

When they discover the deception, Joshua makes them woodcutters and water carriers.

God's Intervention

Then, five kings of the Amorites go to war against them. Joshua is afraid and inquires of the Lord.

Verse 10:8 says, "The Lord said to Joshua, 'Do not be afraid of them; I have given them into your hand. Not one of them will be able to withstand you.'" (NIV) God is faithful and gives them victory.

He even makes the sun stand still so they can finish the job. There has never been a day like it, before or since.

I had always thought it was so Joshua could see, but that wasn't the case. Verse 13 says it was so they could avenge themselves on their enemies.

I had to look at some commentaries on this one. I found that they believed it was not because God wanted them all to die, but that He was showing them His power.

They were to completely destroy their enemies because their culture and practices were so detestable to the Lord. He did not want these people to be a snare to the Israelites.

When God is with us, who can be against us? No one.

We need to remember this as we face our own battles. We can have victory if we trust in the Lord and follow His commands.

The Lord will fight for us.

Tomorrow, we will read Joshua 12-15.

Day 66: Joshua 12-15:
Inheritance and Incomplete Victories

Good morning. We read chapters 12-15 of Joshua today.

Listing the Victories

The first few chapters are just a listing of all the kings they had defeated. It is good to remember our victories. They give us the courage to face the next battle.

Unfinished Business

Then, in chapter 13, the Lord tells Joshua that he is old and there is still a lot of land to be taken.

God had given them the land, but they still had to go in and possess it. They had to fight for it.

The Lord tells Joshua to divide the land among the nine and a half tribes. The Levites did not get an inheritance. The Lord was their inheritance.

Caleb then reminds Joshua of the promise Moses had made to him. He was eighty-five years old and still as strong as he was when he was forty. He asks for the hill country, and Joshua gives it to him.

This is a great story of faith. Caleb knew God was with him and that he could defeat the Anakites who lived there.

Then, we see in chapter 15 that Judah could not dislodge the Jebusites. They live there among them to this day.

This is a cautionary tale for us. When we don't completely destroy our enemies, they will always be a snare to us.

We can't just cut back on our sinning; we must completely destroy it. If we don't, it will always be there to tempt us and lead us astray.

I pray we all have the strength and courage of Caleb to fight our battles and claim the inheritance God has for us.

Tomorrow, we will read Joshua 16-19.

Day 67: Joshua 16-19: Allotments and Responsibility

Today, we read four more chapters that are mostly just a listing of the allotments of land for each tribe.

Details Matter

It is easy to get bogged down in the details and miss the bigger picture. I have done this many times in my life. I get so focused on the task at hand that I lose sight of the overall goal.

The details are important. They show us that God is a God of order. He has a plan for everything. He is not a God of chaos.

He gives each tribe their own inheritance. He knows their needs and provides for them.

Our Role

But they still had to go in and possess the land. They had to fight for it.

God had given them the victory, but they still had to do the work.

We can't just sit back and wait for God to do everything for us. We must be active participants in His plan.

We see in chapter 17 that the daughters of Zelophehad come to Eleazar and Joshua and ask for their inheritance. They knew the law and that they were entitled to it.

We must know God's Word so that we can claim the promises He has for us.

Then, in chapter 18, Joshua scolds the people for not taking possession of the land. They were being lazy and not doing what God had commanded.

He sends out men to survey the land and divide it into seven portions. Then, he casts lots to see which tribe gets which portion.

We must be diligent in seeking God's will for our lives and then act on it.

God has a plan for each of us. He has given us all an inheritance. But we must be willing to fight for it. We must be willing to do the work.

I pray that we will all be like the daughters of Zelophehad and know God's Word so we can claim His promises. And that we will be like Joshua and be diligent in seeking and acting on God's will.

Tomorrow, we will read Joshua 20-22.

Day 68: Joshua 20-22:
Refuge and Misunderstanding

Good morning. We are working our way through the Book of Joshua. Today, we read chapters 20-22.

Cities of Refuge

First, we see the establishment of the cities of refuge. These were places where someone who had unintentionally killed someone could flee and be safe from the avenger of blood.

This shows us that God is a God of mercy. He does not want the innocent to suffer.

God's Provision

Then, we see that the Lord gave them the land He had promised. He gave them rest from their enemies. Not one of their enemies withstood them.

God is faithful. He always keeps His promises.

He also provided for the Levites. He gave them towns to live in and pasturelands for their cattle.

God always provides for His people.

A Misunderstanding

Then, we have this story of the altar built by the Reubenites, Gadites, and the half-tribe of Manasseh.

The other tribes see this altar and think they are turning away from the Lord. They are ready to go to war against them.

But they send Phinehas to inquire of them. He was a man of God, and he handled the situation with wisdom.

He reminds them of the sin of Peor and the punishment that came with it. He was concerned that their actions would bring God's wrath on the whole community.

But they explain that they built the altar as a witness between them and the other tribes. They were afraid that in the future, their descendants would be excluded from the community.

This was a great misunderstanding that could have led to war. But because they communicated with each other, they were able to resolve it peacefully.

We need to be careful not to jump to conclusions. We need to communicate with each other and seek to understand each other.

When we do this, we can avoid a lot of conflict and live in peace.

I pray that we will all be like Phinehas and handle situations with wisdom and that we will communicate with each other to avoid misunderstandings.

Tomorrow, we will read Joshua 23-24.

Day 69: Joshua 23-24: Choose Whom You Will Serve

Today, we finish the Book of Joshua. We read the last two chapters, 23 and 24.

A Final Charge

Joshua is old and is giving his final charge to the people. He reminds them of all the Lord has done for them. He warns them not to turn away from the Lord and worship other gods.

He tells them, "Be very strong; be careful to obey all that is written in the Book of the Law of Moses, without turning aside to the right or to the left." (Joshua 23:6, NIV) He tells them that if they turn away from the Lord, they will be destroyed.

A Choice

Then, in chapter 24, he gathers all the tribes together and gives them a choice.

He says, "But if serving the Lord seems undesirable to you, then choose for yourselves this day whom you will serve, whether the gods your ancestors served beyond the Euphrates, or the gods of the Amorites, in whose land you are living. But as for me and my household, we will serve the Lord." (Joshua 24:15, NIV)

This is a choice we all must make. We can't serve two masters. We must choose whom we will serve.

The people respond, "Far be it from us to forsake the Lord to serve other gods! It was the Lord our God himself who brought us and our parents up out of Egypt, from that land of slavery, and performed those great signs before our eyes. He protected us on our entire journey and among all the nations through which we traveled." (Joshua 24:16-17, NIV) They make a covenant with the Lord to serve Him.

This is a covenant we all must make. We must choose to serve the Lord and Him only.

I pray that we will all make the same choice as Joshua and the people of Israel and say, "As for me and my household, we will serve the Lord."

Conclusion of Joshua

Now that you have read the sixth book of the Bible, take a moment to reflect. How have the events in Joshua mirrored lessons in your own life? Do you feel yourself growing in knowledge? Are you also growing in faith?

For fun, here are five questions I want you to answer (I will post some brief answers at the back of the book).

1. What primary task did Joshua receive after Moses's death?

2. Describe the Battle of Jericho and its significance.

3. What is the significance of the crossing of the Jordan River?

4. How was the land of Canaan divided among the Israelite tribes?

5. What was the overall message or theme of the Book of Joshua?

Chapter 6: Footnotes

1. Sun Tzu, *The Art of War*, trans. Lionel Giles (Boston: Shambhala, 2005).

2. Dale Carnegie, *How to Win Friends and Influence People* (New York: Simon and Schuster, 1936).

Chapter 7:
JUDGES

Day 70: Judges 1-2: The Importance of Obedience

Welcome to the seventh book of the Old Testament, Judges. Today, we will only read chapters 1 and 2.

This is the next step in the evolution of governance. We should always be leery when anyone adds a layer of rulership between us and God.

Jesus, through His resurrection, has made it possible for us to go boldly to God. We have been adopted as the King's children. Therefore, we need no other layers.

Pledging Allegiances

The third verse describes Judah's request that the Simeonites accompany them to Canaan.

Such alliances can be beneficial to all involved. We all need to band together to complete the will of God.

But, I feel their fear over the people and cities they had seen when they spied out Canaan. Instead of trusting, they had God; therefore, they needed nothing else, they were looking for earthly answers.

This is a theology based on works. All religions other than Christianity believe that man must do various things to earn salvation.

The Bible is clear that Jesus is all we need. He did it all for us.

What could we add that would bear any significance beyond what He did on the Cross?

But Judah and Simeon formed an alliance and attacked the Canaanites and Perizzites, who were victorious.

Not because of their combined strength. I believe the Bible would have been clear if that were the situation. It would have said, with their combined might, they slew ten thousand.

That is not what it says. Instead, it states God gave them into their hands.

God was and is their strength. Whenever we believe we need more resources than we have, we forget we have the only resource we will ever need.

Disabling the Resistance

In verse 6, they catch Adoni-Bezek, who was a brutal king and warrior.

He was known to cut off the thumbs and toes of the people he defeated. The reason he did this was to render the people unable to fight. Without thumbs, they could not hold a sword, and without the big toe, they would lack balance.

Because he had been doing this to his enemies, Judah returned the treatment to him.

Then, we see how the tribes did not destroy the people they were to drive out. Trusting only in God and following His commands, they would have eliminated those people from the land.

Coexistence is a Sin

Instead, they went for diplomacy and allowed them to coexist. God had warned against this. It would lead to them worshipping the foreign gods.

To think we have a better plan than God is a foolish mistake. Trust in God and follow His commandments. This is the only way to create peace and lasting prosperity.

God sends an angel to tell them to stop making covenants with the people of the land they are taking. They continue to disobey Him.

All disobedience to God is sin.

As generations pass, we get further and further from knowing the truth that God provides.

Today, we have schools that don't acknowledge the truth at all. They refuse to talk about the Bible except to refute it.

Their administrators grew up in the school system, which taught this. Now, each generation is more corrupt.

A similar dynamic was happening in chapter 2 as they began serving Baal and Ashtoreth.

The result was that God turned His back on them.

The Lord was against them when they went out to fight.

He will always keep His word, and He had warned them this would happen if they sought idols.

Judgment Needed

Because they lacked judgment, He gave them judges to guide them. God works through these judges to lead the people.

It is easy to scoff at these people.

If we are honest with ourselves, don't we try to make our own rules?

I know I often strike out on my own, relying on myself. If I am not enough, I call upon a friend for help. I count on my finances, and I trust in my credit rating.

This is how we make wealth into an idol and why Matthew 6:24 warns we can't worship God and money. We need to seek the Lord, and when we know we are doing His will, we must trust Him.

Tomorrow, we will read Judges 3-5.

Day 71: Judges 3-5: Strength in Trials

Good morning. I hope you are enjoying these daily devotionals as much as I enjoy writing them to you. Today, we will read Judges 3-5.

Immune to Trials

People often wonder why we must go through so many trials in our lives.

It is natural for parents to want their children's lives to be perfect and stress-free.

There is a line in the Pixar movie Nemo where Marlin, Nemo's overprotective father, states he wouldn't want his son to face any dangers. Dori, the absent-minded fish he was getting help from, states, "Then he would never do anything!"[1] She is right.

This is like allowing our children to get dirty and play in the mud. It is disgusting, but the exposure helps strengthen their immune systems.

Over-vaccinating ourselves has resulted in compromised immune systems. A study from the National Library of Medicine supports this.[2] As does a report by the Children's Hospital of Philadelphia.[3] Other reports refute that evidence, such as the Medical News Today report.[4]

My belief is that God designed our immune systems, and stress from germs strengthens them. There are limitations to this, but the evidence and natural processes back the theory.

Judgment of War

Likewise, war is a reality. There has always been warfare. Until we reach the last peace described in Revelation, we will continue to deal with this scourge.

Verse 3:2 implies that God gave wars to the people of Israel to equip them with the tools to triumph under challenging circumstances.

Verse 4 states it is also to assess if they will obey God and trust in Him. Or, will they try to create alliances for themselves?

We see a couple of verses later that they did the latter and took daughters into marriage and gave away their daughters.

This resulted, as forewarned, in them chasing after the foreign gods such as Baal and Asherah. This is evil in the eyes of God.

The Lord is faithful and allows these experiences to strengthen them. Then, He always rescues them.

We see a string of deliverers, including Ehud. The treachery of how he slew Eglon is graphic and vicious.

Avoid Easy Street

Life is hard. It is supposed to be.

An easy life breeds weak people. Easy faith creates weak faith.

Only when we embrace the Lord's commands, even when they seem brutal to us, do we prosper.

When we don't slaughter all the enemies, they infect us. This leads to idolatry and the cycle repeats.

When they kill all the Moabites, they have eighty years of peace.

This is how we must fight battles. Not to find a stalemate, a peace accord. But, to achieve a lasting victory.

Strong Women

The Bible is clear about not having women lead men.

I enjoy seeing strong women in these chapters. The prophetess Deborah gets credit for leading the victory because Barak was not willing to do so without her.

Jael proves women can be lethal. Her service to God is commendable to everyone other than Sisera and his mother.

My third point is from the Song of Deborah. The opening verse teaches that when leaders lead, people will follow.

So many initiatives base themselves on the populace making sacrifices, while the ruling class remains exempt. Instead of loyalty, contempt follows.

God's heart is with the leaders and with the willing volunteers. Requiring service, dictating giving or compliance, does not drive people to give of themselves.

Peace For Our Children

The song concludes that those who give to the Lord with a grateful heart will be like the sun. Peace will last forty years.

As a grandfather, I would love to see a world where my grandkids could grow up in peace. The thought of their safety eclipsed all other concerns, even the certainty of future loss.

The pathway to a peaceful future is obeying God.

It must start on an individual level.

What things in your life could you repent of to help show your allegiance to Jesus Christ?

Tomorrow, we will read Judges 6-8.

Day 72: Judges 6-8: Gideon's Faith

Thank you for sticking with me. Today, we read Judges 6-8. There are lessons we can learn from Gideon.

Nothing to Fear

Midian was oppressing Israel.

These were the people of God. He had delivered them from Egypt, parted seas and rivers, brought down walls, and helped them defeat giants. That wasn't enough, I guess, because here comes Midian and they run off and hide in caves.

Today, the news focuses on the pervasive fear affecting everyone. We are all waiting for the next pandemic.

Certain if our health doesn't disrupt us, the economy will.

Whatever political party we align ourselves with, we are sure the other one is trying to destroy everything we hold dear.

Fear sells more than sex these days. Advertising and storylines used to focus on raw sensuality. Now, it is all centered on fear.

George Orwell, in the books 1984 and Animal Farm, foretold this.[5] Although I do not believe in later-day prophets, he was spot-on in predicting the days we are living in.

We Lose Focus

The problem arises from Israel thinking too highly of themselves. This is a failing we also have.

When they think it is their own efforts. They worship the leaders God had placed over them instead of God.

This does not differ from worshipping the creation instead of the Creator. Idolatry in any form is a sin.

When God provides us with success, we turn to worshipping the success, instead of the Lord behind it.

We join a fitness program and start feeling better than ever. We start a new sport and soon are riding bicycles on Sunday mornings instead of attending church.

It is natural to make idols of things and activities.

God blesses us, and we soon want the blessings but stop wanting God.

Center on Jesus

Jesus must be our everything. That may sound like it is limiting, but it is liberating.

When we make Jesus, the goal of all we do, we eliminate the stress of maintaining our success.

God had warned Israel not to get involved with the gods of the Amorites, but they didn't listen. So, an angel appears to Gideon, who is the least likely person to be leading them, and tells him he needs to step up.

Like Moses questioning the burning bush, Gideon needs proof and challenges the Lord. All the tests prove he is speaking to an angel of the Lord, so he fears death. God assures him, "You are not going to die." (Jud 6:23, NIV)

Remove Idols

Before we can get back to serving God, we must tear down all the false altars.

This disrupts the status quo. His father had erected them. The rest of the people were comfortable with them.

So, they were hiding in caves, crying out to their gods for help. Baal and the Asherah pole were not delivering them. How could they?

We live in fear when we place our faith in the wrong things.

We fear disease when our faith is based on health. If our faith is in wealth, we fear inflation. When our faith is in power, we fear the opposing party.

Gideon had nothing to fear. Men made those lifeless idols.

We figure if we have enough of something, we won't need God. Our strength is not in the size of our army. Better technology or bigger weapons will not deliver us.

Build With Confidence

As I have mentioned, our church is undergoing a building project. The old mobile structures need more repairs than would make sense, so we are building a new sanctuary. This requires more financial resources than we have.

We would all like to have an excess of resources before beginning any project. Knowing we could cover the costs ourselves would make the decision easy.

In that scenario, thankfulness for our resources would overwhelm us, and we would place our complete faith in them.

Life can take away anything we possess.

Thinking our savings were sufficient, my wife and I decided it was time to build our house.

As soon as we started, the costs of lumber skyrocketed. Everything else did, too. Had we built a year earlier, we would have saved money.

But we waited until we thought we had enough.

When we are measuring anything other than God, there is never enough. Only God is enough. All other things, money, time, and labor will come up short. We must not put our faith in these things.

Not About the Numbers

Gideon figures if his troops outnumber the Midianites, he has a chance.

God doesn't want them to think it is their strength that delivers them. He wants them to remember He is their strength.

So, he cuts their number down to a few thousand, then cuts again. Now only three hundred, he divides into three small groups of only one hundred each.

When this works, all the people know, it is God.

Terror gripped the Midianites; it wasn't the hundred men that frightened them, but the Lord who stood behind them.

God's greatest working conditions are when things are impossible. When there is no other explanation, that is when He delivers.

Yet, we still try to create favorable conditions. Favorable to us. Even favorable to investors or banks.

Those conditions are not what God wants. God wants conditions that will glorify Him.

God will drive us to our knees so that we must look up to see Him. Those are His favorable conditions. Then, God will receive glory.

Tomorrow, we will read Judges 9-11.

Day 73: Judges 9-11: The Danger of Pride

Today, we continue to progress through the book of Judges, reading chapters 9-11.

Our Choice

The question in verse 9:2 intrigues me.

Is it better to have many rulers, or one?

Nobody wants a dictator, but can there be too many chefs in the kitchen?

Gideon's family had grown both in size and power, and his sons were in charge.

Abimelech wanted the power all to himself. Power has a way to corrupt. It is addictive and can lead people astray.

Abimelech must have been a persuasive speaker because the people chose him.

To pay him, they take money from the temple, which violates their covenant with God.

This is evil and leads to a greater atrocity; he hires reckless scoundrels and has all the other sons of Gideon murdered on a single stone. Killing so many in one location shows a slaughter.

They make Abimelech their king.

Jotham hears about this, climbs to the top of Mt. Gerizim, and shouts out a warning. We spoke about Mt. Gerizim being the mountain from which they shouted curses.

Learn from Trees

We hear this parable of trees. Ellicott claims these stories originate from Lokman, a slavephilosopher of the time who wrote fables.[6]

I favor what Matthew Henry states: "To rule involves a man in a great deal, both of toil and care. Those who are preferred to public trust and power must forego all private interests and advantages for the good of others. And those advanced to honour and dignity are in great danger of losing their fruitfulness."[7]

This is a warning all leaders must protect against.

Trees have no need for kings. A sense of deep appreciation for God's timely rain fills each tree. He protects them from fire and damage. Even when people chop down a tree for construction, it finds honor in being chosen.

Why would an olive tree want to rule over the other trees? That is not what God had intended for it.

Each tree refuses, but then they ask the worthless bush, which produces no fruit. The bush decides that being nothing but kindling for the fire is pointless. So, it accepts the call to lead.

Humility Required

God looks for humility.

Abimelech does not have this quality. Hell awaits him. His choice is to rule over others, taking a place that belongs only to God.

To avoid death at the hands of a woman or burning in the fires as he had done to others, Abimelech ordered a servant to kill him.

The people then sin against the Lord. We continue to do this today.

Giving Control

We might not appoint kings to rule over us, but we give the power to control our lives to lesser things.

Our jobs dictate how we spend our time.

Hobbies and activities we enjoy soon become our masters and demand money we shouldn't spend and time we could use more productively.

We prioritize entertainment and recreation over time spent worshipping God.

How long will God tolerate our behavior?

He tells them in verse 10:13, "You have forsaken me and served other gods, so I will no longer save you."

We must be like the Israelites and state that we have sinned against God, and we must repent. (10:15-16)

As Christians, we find assurance of our salvation (Heb 10:22).

But repenting means we stop seeking a tree and remain steadfast in seeking our true King.

Tomorrow, we will read Judges 12-15.

Day 74: Judges 12-15: The Downfall of Samson

Today, we read Judges chapters 12-16. This is the tragic tale of Samson, the leader of Israel, which also ends in his death.

What's in a Name?

Before we get to that, let's look at verse 12:6.

My first thought was, why would you kill forty-two thousand people because of how they pronounced a name? Was it something about the name they said?

Nope! It was simply a dialect issue.

The people in Ephraim could not pronounce the "sh" sound.

Think of parts of our population that say certain words incorrectly.

From my heritage, we have injected the word wash with an "r" sound. We mispronounce it "warsh," as in "we warsh our clothes."

I live in Tucson, and we have Spanish words in the names of streets and of businesses.

If you're talking to a winter visitor, they will often confuse you by asking for a location. The way they pronounce the name is so different you don't even recognize it.

This can make them feel stupid for the mispronunciation, but it would never be a valid reason for a massacre.

Tolerance

People will call me intolerant.

I will tell them, "Jesus is the way, the truth, and the life. No one comes to the Father except through Him," which is John 14:6. They will say that I'm racist for not being open to other religions.

I am not open. The Word of God says all other paths lead to destruction. I don't want anyone to face that result without knowing the truth.

You can disagree with it. Just as in the linguistic problem in our verse today, there will be a slaughter.

God Loves Babies

Later, in verse 13:5, we see babies come from God. Even before their conception, He knows them. Samson had a purpose and a destiny before his parents knew him.

This is true of all humans. God has reasons for each of us.

We may not be historic and grand like Samson. But He would not have made us if there was no need for us.

As with Moses and the burning bush, and Gilead, we see how Manoah had a tough time accepting the words the angel spoke. (see Ex 3:1-22, Gen 18:12) Manoah was much like Thomas needing a first-hand encounter (see John 20:25).

Prayer is a positive and beneficial practice for us. Why are we always so surprised when God responds?

Do we not understand that our Father loves us?

Manoah thinks they will die because they have seen the angel of the Lord (Jud 13:22).

Respect

Fear the Lord, and have complete respect and reverence for Him and His power.

I was chatting on social media with a person from New York who was lamenting the wildfires in California. This was a tragedy.

I claimed government mismanagement played a large part in the scope of the devastation.

She was more worried about global warming and not caring for the planet.

I told her we have more respect for the creation than we do for the Creator, and things like this will continue until we repent and correct this sinful condition.

The Sweetness of Sin

One of my favorite animals is the Lion. They are so majestic and powerful. It would be horrifying to see Samson tear one apart, as in verse 14:6.

But the Lord created the Lion, and it was the Spirit of the Lord that provided the means to destroy it. God had His reasons.

Samson, especially as a Nazarene, should not touch a dead body. He reaches in, eats the honey, and even shares it with his parents.

We can see he has lost his respect for the Laws of God.

He creates riddles about this atrocity instead of remorse for his sinfulness.

Today, people want to celebrate their sins.

Wrong Choices

His weakness for the wrong women backfires on him.

As sin does, this escalates to him striking down thirty men and robbing them of their clothing. Sin always takes us farther than we intended to go.

He then goes further and ties the tails of foxes together and burns down their crops. Adultery follows.

Adultery raged until Samson slew thousands of men with a donkey's jawbone. Sin is insatiable.

Lust results in another poor choice of a woman.

How often does a wife need to trick you?

Wouldn't you stop letting her tie you up?

Pride Goes Before the Fall

His pride causes Samson to make a game of this all.

He has more respect for his hair than the God who gave him strength.

Even after all this happens, God hears his prayer and restores his strength.

No matter how far we have allowed sin to take us, we can still repent.

You may think you are beyond saving, but Samson shows us no one is.

If you have never trusted God to forgive your sins, I urge you now to seek Jesus as your Savior.

He is ready to restore you, too.

Tomorrow, we will read Judges 16-19.

Day 75: Judges 16-19: Doing Your Own Thing

Today, let's move on to chapters 16-19.

The King

These chapters focus on the story of Micah, or so it would seem. He is the main character in the first two chapters.

The true focus of these chapters, however, is idolatry.

Starting in 17:6, we read that "Israel had no king, everyone did as they saw fit." This line really hit home.

Here in America, we have elected officials and are diligent to resist giving them too much power. We don't want a king. This is a good thing. No person should have control over us.

The problem is that few people allow Jesus to be their king.

He is our King (Mat 17:22-27) whether we submit to Him. All will one day bow to Him, and we will have to give an answer. (Phil 2:10-11).

Like the people of Dan, who did not want to give lordship to anyone, we all like to do our own thing.

We gather up sums of money, as Micah had done, and we make an ephod. Making an idol of wealth.

Then we find someone who supports the worship of this idol, and we make them our priests.

This is not a person God has anointed. They have no authority. But we allow them to lead us, even if they are heading in the wrong direction.

When someone else comes along to take them away, we rise to defend them.

Because God does not anoint them. They are just false idols which cannot save anyone. Therefore, these intruders steal this ephod.

Three Questions

At Micah's house, the men heard the Levite's voice. They ask three important questions:

"Who brought you here? What are you doing in this place? Why are you here?" (Jud 18:3, NIV)

I must ask myself these questions daily.

Who?

Who brought me here? As told in the preface of my book, I was not seeking God. He brought me to the place where I fell to my knees and put my faith in Him.

If your answer does not acknowledge God bringing you to where you are at, I would ask: Are you sure you are where you are supposed to be?

I have done every job I could imagine doing.

I had a solid plan in mind, but it didn't lead to where I thought it was going.

After realizing my misdirection, I pivoted and found a fresh course.

After surrendering control to Jesus, I am exactly where Jesus wants me to be.

Even when I do not know why I am there, or how I got there.

What?

When I recognize my location, I must ask the next question: What am I doing there?

God has a purpose and a plan for all of us.

We must pray and seek His guidance to figure out what we should do in the place He has brought us to.

There are days I feel lost. I look around and see a lot of activities that I don't understand.

When I submit to His will and pray for guidance, it clears up, and I realize my purpose.

Why?

Then, I must determine the answer to why I am there.

Do I have a special attribute the situation needs me to contribute?

What is that skill, and how can I apply it?

Or am I there to learn something I don't know?

Often, situations seem like I am there to lead, but then I realize I am there to follow. To gain something that will prepare me for something else later.

Henry Blackaby stresses the importance of finding where God is at work and participating in His work.[8]

When you get there, you may realize they lack leadership.

If that is one of your qualities, you may think, "Oh, they need me to lead!" It is right up your alley.

You then find yourself stuck there because that wasn't what they needed.

They needed you to develop a leader for them.

Sometimes, the best way a strong leader can lead is to allow someone else to lead but to provide guidance as you follow.

Determining why you are in a situation is important.

Do The Work

Once you understand where you are and what your role and purpose are, you must get to work.

Chapter 19 is all about procrastination.

We see this other Levite whose wife leaves him. He goes to her father's house and tries to get her to return with him. The father keeps delaying him.

Procrastination is a fantastic way to defeat momentum.

You may have a great plan. It may be God's plan.

The enemy will give you an extensive list of "better things" to do. He does it to prevent you from accomplishing the goal God has set for you.

I consider procrastination to be a demon, and I pray asking God to remove it from me.

When we don't, we end up in places we have no business in.

Tomorrow, we will read Judges chapters 20-21.

Day 76: Judges 20-21: The Consequences of Sin

Good morning. Are you all ready for another wonderful week of exploring God's word? I am. I refer to it as exploring, because there is always something new.

They say it is a living word, referencing that the Word, Jesus, is alive.

But I also know that God speaks to us from His Word, the Bible. He shows us every day what we need to know.

It may be answers to questions we have or maybe answers we will need to know soon.

Either way, God participates in the lives of His children.

That is why I encourage each of us to read through the Bible, listening for His voice.

Not just completing an assignment but trying to learn something new.

They Had No King

Today, we finish the Book of Judges. While we only have chapters 20 and 21 to read, we need to reference back to what happened yesterday in chapter 19.

The opening sentence in chapter 19 is, "In those days Israel had no king." This is also part of the last sentence today, "In those days Israel had no king: everyone did as they saw fit." (Jud 21:25, NIV)

I'm writing this after receiving an invitation to join in a "Pride" celebration. Pride itself is a sin, but in this case, it is celebrating a lifestyle that scripture defines as sin.

Like the Israelites in Judges 19-21, when we live with no king, everyone does as they see fit.

We all like to follow our hearts, but Jeremiah 17:9 tells us, "The heart is deceitful above all things and beyond cure. Who can understand it?" (NIV).

Our hearts lead us to sin, but the "wages of sin is death" (Rom 6:23, NIV).

I have acquaintances who revel in this "Pride" lifestyle. They may consider my viewpoint as hate speech. I assure you; I do not hate anyone.

In truth, I love all people. Because of this, I hate the sin, which God hates. He hates it because of its destructive and terminal consequences to those who practice it. This applies to all sins, even my own, and there are many.

The Concubine

This is what we see in today's reading.

Because of their sinful hearts, the people of Benjamin wish to sodomize this man. Instead, they rape and kill this poor concubine.

As stated, the wage of sin is death, hers.

Then, all of Israel rises and attacks Gibeah.

I have not added up the carnage, but we read of tens of thousands of soldiers dying from both sides.

The men attacking this concubine were only thinking of their own pleasure. Who is it harming, other than this concubine, for whom they had no respect?

That is the nature of sin.

We figure it is our choice, and it's not affecting anyone other than ourselves.

That is not the case. There are always lingering ripples of people who will be affected by our choices.

Even after this devastation, God shows mercy. He allows the remnant of Benjamin to receive wives.

The Israelites must conceive a way around their oath to not provide their daughters to Benjamin, which is my second point.

Instead of accepting our lot and the consequences of our choices, we try to find loopholes.

As Christians, we know that God forgives us.

If we sin without feeling remorse, I question the condition of our hearts. Have we trusted Jesus as our Lord?

We still enjoy dancing on that line, assuming salvation is ours. We get as close to sin as we can, getting none of it on ourselves.

The Stench

We step away from it, thinking we escaped. Those who love us can smell it on our clothing. It lingers like the aroma of a cigar.

When I was in high school, I had friends who smoked marijuana during lunch. I didn't enjoy the effect it had on me, so I didn't.

My fourth-hour class was Mr. Mattison's Physical Science class.

As they all came back to class, the room smelled like pot smoke.

I would go off campus for lunch and would smoke the biggest, smelliest cigars I could afford. The odor that was on me was stronger than what they had on themselves, so it would cover for them.

One day, as we were sitting in class learning about inertia, Mr. Mattison looked up and said, "Linder's, I know everyone else has been getting high. Please stop smoking those cigars!" No one believed the deception. We hadn't gotten away with anything.

The Price is High

This is the same with sin. The people of Benjamin thought, "It's just a concubine, who will miss her?"

God loves all His children.

He required atonement for this sinfulness. The price was exorbitant.

No price was higher than the one He paid by giving His One and Only Son, Jesus, to die for you and me.

We all have sin, and we all deserve the death these multitudes of soldiers received.

We can never go back and undo what we have done.

If the people of Gibeah had intervened, they could have saved lives.

The rapists didn't have enough control of their own urges, but others could have stepped up to defend her. They chose not to.

People will choose not to say anything today, because they don't want to offend anyone.

When we condone sin, we start a sequence of events that can be devastating.

We all must have enough love in our hearts to speak the truth.

Even when that opinion is not popular.

Tomorrow, we will read the Book of Ruth.

Conclusion of Judges

Now that you have read the seventh book of the Bible, take a moment to reflect. How have the events in Judges mirrored lessons in your own life? Do you feel yourself growing in knowledge? Are you also growing in faith?

For fun, here are five questions I want you to answer (I will post some brief answers at the back of the book).

1. What was the cycle of sin and deliverance that the Israelites experienced?

2. What was the role of Deborah, and what was significant about her story?

3. Describe Gideon's story and its significance.

4. What is significant about the story of Samson?

5. What is the overall message or theme of the Book of Judges?

Chapter 7: Footnotes

1. *Finding Nemo*, directed by Andrew Stanton and Lee Unkrich (Burbank, CA: Walt Disney Pictures, 2003).

2. Alberto Boretti, "mRNA Vaccine Boosters and Impaired Immune System Response in Immune Compromised Individuals: A Narrative Review," *Clinical and Experimental Medicine* 24 (2024): article 23, https://link.springer.com/article/10.1007/s10238-023-01264-1.

3. Children's Hospital of Philadelphia, "Immune System and Vaccines," accessed July 1, 2025, https://www.chop.edu.

4. "Does the COVID-19 Vaccine Weaken the Immune System? What to Know," *Medical News Today*, last modified April 2023, https://www.medicalnewstoday.com/articles/is-your-immune-system-weak-aftercovid-vaccine.

5. George Orwell, *Nineteen Eighty-Four* (London: Secker & Warburg, 1949); George Orwell, *Animal Farm* (London: Secker & Warburg, 1945).

6. Charles John Ellicott, *Ellicott's Commentary for English Readers*, s.v. "Judges 9," accessed via Bible Hub.

7. Matthew Henry, *Matthew Henry's Concise Commentary on the Bible*, s.v. "Judges 9," accessed via Bible Hub.

8. Henry T. Blackaby, Richard Blackaby, and Claude V. King, *Experiencing God:*

9. *Knowing and Doing the Will of God* (Nashville: B&H Publishing Group, 2008).

Chapter 8:
RUTH

Day 77: Ruth: Finding Hope Amidst Loss

Today, we will read the Book of Ruth.

Any section of scripture contains a hundred messages I could share. I will narrow it down to about three so that you all can get on with the rest of your lives.

Emptiness of Grief

We see in 1:5 that Naomi's sons and husband had all died.

Ruth lived around 1050 BC. During this time, the average life expectancy was much like ours today, 70-80 years.

From what we know, Ruth was between 45-50 years old. This would mean her sons were in their 20s or early 30s when they died.

For anyone to deal with this tragedy is significant. A parent should never have to bury their children, but it happens often.

I sense Naomi isn't going home to resume her life. She is going home to finish her life.

From her words, we hear that her life is over. She is too old to have more children and feels there is not much left to live for.

She is running out the clock.

Over Medicated

I know people in this situation.

My grandmother, who died when I was in my 20s, was dying every day I knew her.

She lived alone sometimes. At other times, she lived with my cousins.

There was a myriad of health problems stemming from being overweight and overmedicated.

Her hypochondria likely led to polypharmacy. A condition where the medications you are taking cause the need for more medications. This increases the likelihood of adverse drug reactions.

I remember staying with her, and she always had popsicles made from frozen Kool-Aid on toothpicks.

She had a dachshund hound dog and was always quirky.

Because I was young, I didn't understand. She was a lonely lady who felt she had little to live for.

She loved God and was waiting to go home to be with Him.

This is what I see in the earlier chapters of Ruth. Naomi believes her life is over and wants to conclude everything.

The Encouragement of a New Light

Ruth would have been in her 20s, maybe early 30s. I would imagine, based on Boaz's reaction, she was beautiful.

This beauty was not skin deep. She had a lovely spirit and dedication to her mother-in-law.

Her commitment to being buried with Naomi is admirable.

Her story is significant because she is an ancestor of Jesus.

A Moabite woman who marries Boaz and bears him children, even though he was older.

Dedication, steadfastness, reliability. I don't know if these traits are genetically determined, but this family clearly displays them.

She showed great humility, working tirelessly and always obeying her mother-in-law's wishes. Each of these qualities is commendable and respectable.

Redemption

Boaz is a lucky gentleman. He wakes up with this woman at his feet.

I can imagine being an older man, waking up with a beautiful young lady at my feet. I imagine it because I do it every day. Well, she's next to me, but you get the point.

He does not take advantage of this situation but offers her to the guardian-redeemer. This person, though not named, decides not to accept the proposition.

I am glad we no longer barter people, the way we trade land. In those days, this was a common practice.

All of this was a foreshadowing of God's redemption plan.

Before He spoke the universe into existence, He knew we would sin. He always had a plan to save us.

Where We Walk

I find it amusing how they would hand a sandal to someone as a sign of redemption and transfer of property in ancient Israel. Using a sandal signified walking on land. God gave the Israelites all the land they could walk on.

When the guardian-redeemer refused to take ownership, he removed his sandal. This meant he would not be walking onto the property.

Therefore, he transferred it to Boaz.

How We Witness

For something to be binding, others must witness it.

Boaz shared with those at the gate His intentions to marry Ruth and continue the family line for Mahlon, his relative.

The public nature of the ceremony allowed the elders at the gate to bless the marriage. God then rewarded the marriage with a child. Had this not happened, there would be no line to Jesus.

When we witness to others about our faith in Jesus, we are doing a similar action. We are allowing them to see how God is working in our lives and bless us. For this, God blesses us and creates for Himself other adopted children.

Have you recently shared your testimony with anyone?

Tomorrow, we will read 1 Samuel 1-3.

Conclusion of Ruth

Now that you have read the eighth book of the Bible, take a moment to reflect. How have the events in Ruth mirrored lessons in your own life? Do you feel yourself growing in knowledge? Are you also growing in faith?

For fun, here are five questions I want you to answer (I will post some brief answers at the back of the book).

1. What is the key setting of the Book of Ruth?
2. What is the significance of Ruth's gleaning in the barley fields?
3. What is the significance of the kinsman-redeemer custom in the Book of Ruth?
4. How is the lineage of King David connected to the Book of Ruth?
5. What is the overall theme or message of the Book of Ruth?

Chapter 9:
1 SAMUEL

Day 78: 1 Samuel 1-3: A Legacy of Faith

Good morning. I hope everything is going well so far. Today, we will begin the ninth book of the Bible, 1 Samuel, reading the first three chapters.

Family trees

I didn't get far before having my first epiphany.

In the first verse, the writer or writers tell us of Elkanah's family tree. The writer(s) introduces us to his father, grandfather, great-grandfather, and great-great-grandfather.

This genealogy was particularly important to the writers of the Bible.

It made me think of my lineage.

I could say I am Thomas, son of John, son of Kenny. Beyond that, I do not know.

There are services that would provide me with a longer, more detailed view of my family tree. The problem is that it is not a fruit tree; it is a nut tree.

One sinner, followed by another, and more beyond that. I was a nut that fell off that tree.

When I did, I became rooted in the Gospel and became Thom, son of Jesus, son of God. He adopted me into His family.

I trust you are my siblings.

Our heritage should not limit us.

God offers us the option of being heirs to the King of Kings.

Earthly Treasure

Then, we see how Elkanah gave Hannah a double portion because of his love for her.

When we love someone, we like to give them more.

However, when we have more of the world, we may have less of God.

It's better to suffer in this life and receive a reward from the Lord.

It is not a matter of one or the other. The Lord wants us, His children, to have an abundant life. (John 10:10)

He also loves us with an everlasting love that transcends the impossible, so He gives Hannah the child, Samuel.

She is faithful in her promise to dedicate him to the Lord.

When she does, He gives her other sons and daughters. We can never out-give God.

Anything we offer to Him, He will replenish in a way only God can.

Please don't mistake this with the prosperity gospel.

Giving without a pure heart will cause nothing.

It is only through heartfelt allegiance to the Lord that He will bless us.

This takes faith.

Perceptions

The world will watch us giving our resources, including that most limited one, our time. They will think we are delusional.

Like Eli watching Hannah pray, they will think we're drunk or perhaps even crazy.

It does not matter what the world thinks.

Relying upon them is a sad form of idolatry. The world cannot give us anything.

God, who made the heavens and earth, can give us everything He wants us to have. He will meet all our needs. (Phil 4:19).

We Must Ask

Still, in the first chapter, verse 20 says, "She named him Samuel, saying, 'Because I asked the Lord for him'." (NIV)

James 4:2 tells us, "You do not have because you do not ask God." (NIV) I know this is true. It's in the Bible.

Beyond that, I have seen it happen. God is faithful.

We are not. At least not always.

Here I Am

We mean to be, but we don't always follow through. It means sacrifice and making tough choices.

Because we would need to forfeit the world, we don't always answer, "Here I am." Saying those three words is scary.

When God first called me to preach, I was sure it was a mistake. How could a Holy God use a sinner like me? An enemy who had spent so many years fighting against Him.

He can, because "there is no one holy like the Lord…there is no Rock like our God." (1 Sam 2:2, NIV)

When I placed my faith in Him, He took my sin and gave me His righteousness (2 Cor 5:21).

Verse 2:4 proclaims that strength arms those who stumble.

I was not prepared or equipped. He didn't need me to be. All He needed was for me to be available.

Humility and Response

Humility was not even necessary, as He was the one who humbled me. (1 Sam 2:7)

I had no strength, but it was "not by strength that one prevails." (2:9)

Our own power is useless.

We are all sinners (Rom 3:23). There is nothing we can do to remove that stain.

But Jesus, through the cross, removed it for us.

Verse 2:25 tells us that "God may mediate for the offender." (NIV)

Eli's sons would not repent. They would lose their position. The Lord would hand that stature over to Samuel.

Even though he did not know the Lord, God called to him.

I will never understand why God has called me to write this devotional or the books I do.

We may not even know what is causing you to read these words I wrote.

When we do these things, all we can ask is, are we hearing the voice of the Lord? If we are, how are we going to answer?

I pray your answer, like mine, is, "Speak, for your servant is listening." (3:10)

When you hear God calling you, please respond, "Here I am."

Tomorrow, we will read 1 Samuel 4-7.

Day 79: 1 Samuel 4-7: The Weight of Disobedience

Good morning. We have reached another turning point in our study of 1 Samuel. Today, we will read chapters 4-7.

Discipline

I say the turning point because we read in these chapters that the Lord has turned against His people, Israel.

He never forsakes Israel and continues to preserve a remnant. His Word is true and faithful.

When we sin and refuse to repent, He will chastise us. This is a prime example.

It should serve as a warning to us about our own behavior.

We should also learn from it the importance of discipline in parenting our children.

God loves His people, but when they are walking on the path of perdition, He will cause them to stumble.

We had been reading of how Eli's sons had been taking the best for themselves and carrying on with the women. This was not pleasing to the Lord.

Therefore, He delivered thousands of them into the hands of the Philistines and allowed them to capture the Ark of the Covenant of God.

Their enemies had more fear of God than the people of Israel. When they heard the shout of joy in verse 4:5, they trembled.

God was still not ready to redeem His people. Another thirty thousand, including Eli's sons, perished in the battle.

In a tragic yet comical scene, Eli falls over backward, breaks his neck, and dies.

He was ninety-eight and very heavy, according to the Bible.

Weight

This was always my mental image of a man of God.

From Saturday morning cartoons and the story of Robin Hood. I pictured them all to be Friar Tuck. Round, drunk, and not involved in the action very much.

Later, I met a minister one summer. I was launching fishing boats in the Northern California village of Trinidad.

He was big and heavy and cussed like a sailor. This guy had a beautiful boat but was one of the meanest customers we had all summer.

When I learned of his profession, it cemented my image of the pastorate.

Now, I know how hard a pastor works. It is a tireless and unending job to care for even a medium-sized congregation.

A recent study on the health of pastors in Africa found 90% to be obese.[1] In America, I would trace this to always being on the go.

They need to eat at restaurants every day, either in meetings with members or while traveling to see others.

Restaurants like to provide more food than is healthy to eat. This leads to poor health conditions.[2]

Please pray for your pastor and encourage them to remain fit.

Repentance

The Glory had departed from Israel.

Even a false, handmade idol, like the half-man, half-fish Dagon, could not stand before the Ark of the Covenant of God. It fell. They stood it up. It fell again and broke.

We must realize God is sending trials into our lives and allowing them to humble us.

If we don't humble ourselves, trials will defeat us.

Verse 5:6 says God's hand fell heavily on the people.

Before God had broken me, I would not come to repentance. Like the Philistines, I resisted.

They sent the Ark to one city after another. Each time, disaster followed. Then, they offered sacrifices to the Lord and gave their worship to Him. But they did not use the correct form of sacrifice. He kept His weight on them for a couple of decades.

The people of Israel all repented in verse 7:2. They confessed their sins before the Lord in 7:6, and Samuel offered the proper sacrifice for them.

He is faithful to receive us when we do this. Our nation needs to continue a path back to God.

This involves each of us making a personal recommitment to the Lord.

Are you ready to humble yourself and pray?

Tomorrow, we will read 1 Samuel 8-11.

Day 80: 1 Samuel 8-11: The People's Choice

I hope you had a wonderful week. Today, we will read 1 Samuel chapters 8-11.

Parental Heartache

We know that Samuel's dedication to the Lord began from birth, as mentioned in 1:28. He devoted his life to leading Israel for God.

As a parent, I know we all try to set good examples for our children. Sometimes, that is not enough.

They still go the way they want. It's heartbreaking.

My mother always loved me. She had one thing she would ask: that I do not take illicit drugs.

Our sinful nature makes us crave rebellion, even against those we love the most.

Knowing drugs were the forbidden fruit, I fell into that temptation before entering high school.

As with any sin, I would then try to hide my activity with lies.

I remember coming home from school and telling my mom I didn't feel good so I could just go to my room and lie down. Preventing her from seeing my eyes.

Years later, after turning my life around, I confessed that to her. She assured me my rouse failed. She knew all along. Parents just do, especially mothers.

I can understand the heartbreak that Samuel would have felt to see his sons turning aside for dishonest gain. (v 8:3)

Rejecting God

Then, to have the elders of Israel call you out on this and ask for a king.

God tells him it isn't Samuel they are rejecting, but Himself. (v 8:7)

Fear gripped me when I first accepted the call to preach the Gospel.

Not for me. I doubted anyone would attack me for sharing the Word of God.

Nor was I worried they wouldn't like me. I never cared about being popular.

I worried that, somehow, I would mishandle the Word of God. That because of me, they would reject Him.

I would know for eternity that they were in hell because of my inadequate leadership.

My sermons, the ones that are excellent and others less so, have shown me the overwhelming power of God to conquer any failing of mine.

I understand the fear when you feel led in your heart to share the Gospel. Trust me, no, trust Him. You can't mess up the work of God.

You may quote a passage incorrectly or learn that you were wrong in your interpretation. That doesn't matter.

God will still work in their hearts, and when they come to faith in Jesus, you will know a joy that surpasses all else.

Accepting Failure

Getting back to Samuel, God tells him the people of Israel were rejecting Him.

The devastating truth of that would level me. It was his job to lead the people to God.

If they lost in a battle, it was God's job to provide the victory or not.

If they prospered in growing crops or breeding livestock, that was all in God's hands.

Samuel's duty was to lead them to the Lord. God is telling him, "You failed!".

When my boss tells me he is putting me into a different assignment, that hurts. No one likes to fail.

To fail at the most important assignment in life? Ouch!

Pain or Gain

In sales, we use pain and gain questions to create value in using our solutions.

Our marketing campaigns focus on the gain and what the product can do for you.

God had already shown for generations what He could do for Israel.

When a gain question doesn't create value, salespeople will go to pain questions.

What are you losing if we don't solve this issue for you?

God instructed Samuel to use this tactic.

They're going to have to live with the repercussions of their decision.

The In Crowd

They respond, "We want to be like everyone else."

I've never cared about popularity. Being like everyone else seems boring to me. If we were alike, no one would be special.

Why would we value a friend if we could replace them with a replica?

America is trying to be like Europe.

Europe has turned away from God and is suffering because of it. Why would we want to follow that example?

Our uniqueness makes us special. God created each of us to be who we are. We should never coalesce into homogeneity.

God Anoints Leaders

God made Saul stand out. He was taller than the crowd. He had a heart for God, even wondering what to bring to the man of God.

Then, He set up circumstances, the lost donkeys, to bring Saul and Samuel together so that He could anoint him as king.

Like Moses, Gideon, and others, Saul can't comprehend why God would choose him.

God doesn't choose us because we are special.

He does so because He is special. He is holy.

In verse 10:9, "as Saul turned to leave Samuel, God changed Saul's heart." (NIV)

When you take that deep breath and move past your fear to speak, God will change your heart.

He did mine. I realized, like Saul, I was trying to hide from the Lord.

He is omnipresent. Attempting to hide is futile.

Tomorrow, we will read 1 Samuel 12-14.

Day 81: 1 Samuel 12-14: The Perils of Power

Good morning. Today, we read 1 Samuel 12-14.

Leadership

Reading these verses, considering all that is happening in America these days, brings me concern.

I love President Trump and believe he is doing a fantastic job.

The Department of Government Efficiency (DOGE) is also completing its assigned tasks.

There is the potential for great days ahead for the United States and the world.

The Cycle

The similarities to the days of Samuel and Saul, however, are notable.

God had delivered the people of Israel, and then they rebelled.

He allowed the natural course of things to bring them to their knees.

Without His protection, they were no match for the surrounding tribes.

Israel cried out, repenting of their sins, and the Lord rescued them again.

This repeats so often it sounds like a broken record.

We Wear Out

They had the greatest King of any, God Himself. Yet, to be like the "cool countries", they ask for an earthly king.

God loves them, and even though it breaks his heart, he gives them over to their wickedness.

Samuel had served diligently. He had taken no bribes, acquired no benefit the Lord had not provided, and was innocent of any wrongdoing. Now, he was tired.

You can give your all to the people for the sake of God, and it is fulfilling.

Witnessing people's lives change and sensing their devotion to God encourages you.

Then you realize it is a show, and they are still walking with the world.

So, you try harder and call on the Lord to give you more wisdom and strength.

There comes a point where you have gone to the well too many times. The bucket comes up dry.

Shiny Outside

Saul was at this place in his life.

He had given his all, but the people kept cleaning themselves up outside. All the while allowing their hearts to rot.

Despite tearing down their altars to Baal and Ashtoreth, their hearts remained filled with wickedness and idolatry.

America has turned away from the sinful self-indulgence of the last few years.

We've suffered through pandemic and inflation.

The DOGE investigates the corruption and realizes they were robbing the taxpayer's blind.

We asked for a new leader, and God delivered.

The question remains: where is our heart?

Have we repented of our selfish entitlement and returned to the Lord? Or are we still worshipping the same sins we had before?

God Let Them Go

I can sense God saying, "You said to me, 'No, we want a king to rule over us' – even though the Lord your God was your king. Now here is the king you have chosen." (1 Sam 12:12-13)

We must realize President Trump can only do so much. He can seek God, and I pray he is, and lead.

But if the people's hearts remain corrupt. If we continue to worship the idols of self, wealth, health, and sinful self-indulgence, nothing will change.

We will see temporary improvements, but God knows our hearts.

He will see through the deception.

Prayers Needed

The people went to Samuel and asked him to pray to the Lord for them. (1 Sam 12:19) This is what America must do.

Samuel rebuked them and told them they had not repented. They needed to turn to the Lord and serve Him with all their hearts.

He warned in 1 Sam 12:25 that if they "persisted in doing evil, both you and your king will perish." (NIV)

Saul's Mistake

1 Sam 13 tells us that Saul was acting on his own.

He was getting things done, but it was making Israel obnoxious to the Philistines. (v 4) Because of this, Israel retreated and was running and hiding in caves.

You can defeat giants when you know God is with you.

Knowing you have lost His presence, all you can do is live in fear.

Saul makes a crucial mistake, which we read about in 1 Sam 13:11-14.

I pray President Trump does not repeat this.

He panics and is determined to offer the sacrifice himself. Samuel is the only one who should have done this.

He does not wait upon the Lord's timing. Instead, he takes matters into his own hands.

Samuel tells him he has done a foolish thing. (v 13)

God would have established his kingdom forever if he had waited. His actions have doomed his kingdom.

No Fair Trade

Because of their obnoxious actions, the Philistine blacksmiths were gouging them for the price of sharpening their weapons and even their plows for farming. Therefore, when they needed to go to battle, they were not prepared. (v 22) Only Saul and Jonathan possessed weapons.

The Lord is Our Strength

Jonathan still has faith, and in 1 Sam 14:6, he acknowledges that it is not by strength, but because of the Lord they can prevail.

This was true in those days and still is.

Saul makes the right correction in verse 18. He brings in the Ark of the Covenant of God.

All the weapons in the world will not help without God.

With God, having two armed men can be enough.

Opposition Imploding

Because God is with them, the Philistines (v 20) get confused and start attacking each other.

We are seeing the people who had caused the problems for America turning on their own.

They don't have to worry about the actions Elon Musk is recommending.

They are condemning themselves.

Jonathan's Mistake

Those following President Trump must take warning of what happens with Jonathon.

Because he had not heard Saul's edict, Jonathan felt entitled. Therefore, he ate some honey.

No big deal. It was just a snack, and it was there for the taking.

It was only an issue because the king issued the edict.

According to the rule of law, they should execute Jonathan for disobeying the king.

If their king was the Lord, as it should be, he would have been.

Because Saul is not God, the people override his decision and defend Jonathon. Further showing the weakness of an earthly king.

Escalation

Sin always leads to greater sin. The next thing we see is vs 32-33, the people are eating meat with the blood still in it. They have broken faith.

Saul then sins again. He builds an altar.

Then he calls on God, and there is no answer.

This happens when people take upon themselves the actions which God has not directed them to do.

There's Still Time

We are in the middle of this story.

Israel is about to get a new king, David.

He will bring the people back to God because he has a heart for the Lord.

America has a new leader. If we put him above the Lord, we will suffer the consequences.

If that leader does not seek the Lord in all he does, we will have trouble. No one will be there to rescue us.

We, as Christians, must be praying for our leaders and imploring them to seek God in all they do.

The opportunity is there, but we must wait on the Lord for His timing and His delivery.

Tomorrow, we will read 1 Samuel 15-17.

Day 82: 1 Samuel 15-17:
David's Faith, Saul's Downfall

Good morning. I hope you are all taking part in your local church.

I know online services are convenient, and we cast our service online, but you get so much more out of being with other believers.

Not only what you get, but you grow from what you bring. Just be there for them.

Today, in our Bible study, we will read 1 Samuel 15-17.

We are about to get into the most famous storyline in 1 Samuel, the battle between David and Goliath.

Long before I was a believer, I remember watching a Sunday morning cartoon, The Adventures of Davy and Goliath. Therefore, I knew this story.

I didn't understand its significance. But I knew that the youngest son slew the Giant with a stone.

We will get to that in chapter 17.

For now, let's back up and examine what led to this event.

God Remembers

Verse 15:2 recounts the Lord commissioning Saul with a mission. He is to punish the Amalekites for how they oppressed and abused the Israelites on their way out of Egypt.

God had not forgotten their transgression.

We all have sins in our past that we have forgotten.

When circumstances arise, we recall them and are ashamed, but we push them down and move on.

We hope everyone else, including God, has long since forgotten what happened. God never forgets.

When I was in my early twenties, I attempted to launch a business. We were selling soda to drivers caught in hot traffic.

I would see vendors selling newspapers from the medians, and thought, I don't need the newspaper; I need a cold drink!

Therefore, my first wife and I went out, filled an ice chest with soda and ice, and evaluated the idea.

We sold out in a couple of hours.

I calculated the profit margin. Then, I wrote a business plan and thought through the potential obstacles. One was visibility.

We didn't want our salespeople to be confused with the newspaper vendors.

We also wanted to ensure, for safety reasons, that our salespeople were clearly visible and distinguishable.

This had to be feasible and affordable.

A friend owned a tuxedo shop. She was able to make us a deal on some brown vests.

My wife had a background in the theater, and we assessed various ideas. The winning concept was a set of rabbit ears.

Brown shorts, a white or tan T-shirt, a brown vest, and a set of rabbit ears.

Drivers loved the idea.

We talked to the Humane Society about donating a percentage of sales. They allowed us to mention that on a sandwich sign.

The idea came to life with the name Dem Cwazy Wabbits. DCW, Inc. formed.

Underfunded, we hired a handful of high school kids. We put them on a couple of corners. Sales were surprisingly strong.

The problem was we were not covering the margins as I expected. We needed to grow fast enough to make it up on volume. It never came together.

Those industrious kids had received a couple of paychecks, but when we ran out of money their last check was short.

Despair overwhelmed me. I was anguishing over the debt. My family feared for my safety.

I never had contact information or even all their names.

Though the amounts were small, the problem is I have never had a way to make this right.

They may have forgotten. It was three weeks in their lives forty years ago.

I have never come to peace with it.

God has forgiven me of all my sins. This doesn't mean He forgot what happened.

It was one of the sins He died for, in my place.

Following Orders

God remembered the Amalekites and told Saul to punish them.

The punishment they deserved was total annihilation. God told Saul to kill everyone, even all their livestock. (v 15:2-3)

Saul's men wanted to keep the plunder. Saul was not following the Lord, so he feared his men. (v 15:24)

He let them keep the best of the livestock and killed the rest.

For Agag, watching his people perish would be worse than death. Therefore, Saul captures Agag.

He is continuing to make his own rules, which means denying the orders God has given.

Then, when Samuel questions him about this, Saul attempts to justify his reasons.

We all do this.

I would have paid those kids if I had the money. If I could have found them, I would have made it right. Since then, I have done other virtuous deeds to atone for that sin.

Sorry, Saul, those are all the wrong answers.

You also put up a monument to yourself.

In Verse 15:22, Samuel asks if it is better to offer sacrifices or to obey the Lord.

He compares rebellion to the sin of divination and arrogance to idolatry.

Saul confesses, but because of his actions, Samuel tells him the kingdom will not remain his. (v 15:24)

This was the last time Samuel ever saw Saul. (v 15:35)

Fearing Saul, Samuel was still obedient to go seek one of Jesse's sons.

He assumes, since Saul was tall, that the first son is the right one.

God tells him not to judge by outward appearance. (v 16:7)

Therefore, cleaning up our outside will not impress God. He knows our heart.

When we get to the youngest son, who is out tending to the sheep, we meet David. The Lord confirms this is the one. (v 16:12)

Soothing the Soul

Then, the spirit leaves Saul, and evil spirits torment him.

God puts this in place so that Saul will invite David to come into his presence and play the lyre for him. The music calms him and quiets the torment he is experiencing.

Music has always been my safety zone.

As a teen, I experienced all the emotional upheaval of developing relationships and understanding love. I would deal with the heartache by writing songs.

At night, I would play the FM radio stations on my Fisher Stereo system so loud it could wake the dead. It calmed me and helped me sleep like a baby.

Walking into a bar after my accident, with crutches or a cane, people would try to avoid making eye contact.

They would avoid the "elephant in the room" and not ask what happened to me. Instead, I felt invisible.

Then I got onstage and played my guitar and sang into the microphone. Through the songs I wrote, they would believe they knew me.

As I returned to my table, they would come over and strike up a conversation.

Music was my ticket back to normal. It made me human again.

Facing Giants

I understand why God would gift David with this talent and use it to get him into the company of Saul.

This leads up to chapter 17 when this young man brings provisions to his brothers as they battle the Philistines.

Among them was this obnoxious giant, Goliath, whom Barnes claimed to be nine feet nine inches tall.[3]

He has no fear of the Israelites but, worse, no fear of the Lord.

David has no faith in the army, but complete trust in God.

When we face enormous problems in our lives, we need to remember it's not about the size of the problem. It is always about the size of our God.

David knew this and trusted it.

The armor, he felt, would only weigh him down, so he didn't trust it.

Goliath, a mighty warrior, would have prevailed, so a sword wasn't necessary for him.

Choosing Our Weapon

He has faith in God. His choice of weapon, five smooth stones, epitomizes this.

Jesus is the Rock of our salvation. He is the foundation of our faith.

David places his faith, and the fate of Israel, in the Rock.

With no hesitation, he hurls the stone into Goliath's forehead. As the behemoth lies on the ground, he uses Goliath's own weapon against him.

We like to put our faith in things that not only will fail us but can harm us.

I have trusted in wealth; I have trust in alcohol. Love always seemed like the thing that I was missing, so I put my faith in women.

These things failed me.

God is the only one who will never let you down.

Have you placed your trust in Him?

Tomorrow, we will read I Samuel 18-20.

Day 83: 1 Samuel 18-20: Jealousy and Friendship

I'm sorry if I was long-winded yesterday. I will try to be briefer today.

There are so many things I always want to write about; it is hard to control myself.

Today is no exception. We are reading 1 Samuel 18-20.

Jealousy

We had watched David rise to prominence with God and with men yesterday.

Today, that 'green-eyed monster' we call jealousy raises its ugly head. Saul doesn't like how the people love David more than they do him.

I don't have to worry about that too much. Being the backup preacher, I know I won't overshadow my pastor.

His years of experience and polished delivery are far beyond my skills.

At my last job, I trained sales agents. They had direct managers they reported to.

I didn't have to administer any discipline; therefore, it was not unusual that they embraced me more than their leader. This caused resentment and animosity.

I worked through this by including the managers in all my planning.

We'd be a stronger team if we were all in agreement.

Avoid Abuse

Saul wasn't concerned with teamwork.

He was just annoyed by the song the townspeople were singing. It said David killed ten times as many as Saul. His ego couldn't take it.

An evil spirit came over him, that same monster we spoke of before, and he hurled a spear at David.

The young warrior's reflexes were true, and he dodged the murder attempts twice.

Before that, we see in verse 18:8 that Saul was overcontrolling.

People with these insecurities will try to separate people from their families.

This is true in abusive relationships.[4]

They will praise the person and lavish them with gifts but then try to possess them.

When that person forms additional friendships like David did with Jonathon, they will strike out with physical violence. Like we saw with Saul.

The Bible teaches everything we need for life and righteousness.

Here, it teaches how to avoid abusive relationships.

I would like to say that I am immune to this. But there have been women in my life who mistreated me. Even though they were abusive, I would continue to take them back.

None ever attempted to murder me, but David continues to give Saul opportunities.

Insecurity

It is impossible to say where Saul's insecurity may have come from. Knowing the Lord had left him could have been a driving factor.

When distance is forming between God and me, my first thought is to spend more time with God.

Sometimes, I just don't feel I am walking with Him the way I used to.

I must remember; He didn't move. My wandering caused our separation.

Because Saul's pride will not let him seek God, his friendship with David ends.

Jonathan warns David, and their friendship grows.

He wants to keep trusting his father, but each time, he learns that this demon that possesses him is too powerful.

Politicians

Saul was Israel's first king. It's the first taste of a politician.

He lies to their faces and then attempts to kill them at the same time.

Those close to him, his son Jonathan and his daughter Michal, both love David.

The more Saul tries to destroy him, the more they protect him.

These insecurities tear this family apart.

Moving away from insecurity, we read of another good point.

Positive Influence

When a person is on a mission for God, those around them will be too.

We read Saul keeps sending men to capture David.

David was with Samuel. Each time the men got near Samuel, they began prophesying.

Saul goes to him, and he gives him a prophecy.

The job of every Christian is to be like Christ.

To have a positive impact on the world, so that others will emulate us.

We must be on fire, and fan those flames so the fire spreads.

Jonathan, still trying to have hope for this father, made a covenant with David. (v 20:14) He would have to keep that pact, even though it would cause Saul to attempt to kill him. (v 20:33)

The problem is that they resort to lies and deceit. Sin is never the way to defeat sin.

You can only overcome evil with good. (Rom 12:21)

We all have relationships. There are friendships and romantic alliances. We also have casual acquaintances.

In all these, we must be careful and not allow others to be abusive toward us. It starts small but will always escalate.

First to higher forms of abuse, and to sin.

If something doesn't seem right, ask a friend to help you look at the situation.

Like David asking Jonathan, leaning on others to get to the truth.

Tomorrow, we will read 1 Samuel 21-24.

Day 84: 1 Samuel 21-24: A Man After God's Own Heart

Good morning, today we read 1 Samuel chapters 21-24.

According to 1 Samuel 13:14, David was a man after God's own heart.

This does not mean David was perfect or without sin.

Only Jesus fits that description.

On Mission is Not Perfect

We see in our opening verse today that David goes to a priest in Nob. He lies to him about being on a secret mission.

Christians should all be on a mission for God. This should never be a secret.

We should be like a city on a hill (see Matt 5:14-16), a light to those around us.

Persecution awaits us (see 2 Tim 3:12), but God will be with us. He will bless our perseverance. (Matt 5:10-12)

Lying is a sin. (Ex 20:16) We should never deny our allegiance to Jesus Christ. (Matt 10:33) Here, we see David lying to a priest.

He compounds this sin by eating the consecrated bread. Anyone other than the Levites (see Matt 12:3-4) should not eat this.

His story signifies we can pursue God with all our hearts. We can be a shining example of a person whom God loves. Yet, we still will not be perfect.

Like most creative people, I'm a perfectionist and harder on myself than others are.

Sunday morning, when I play my guitar, I am cringing on the inside. All I hear are the missed notes and mistakes.

Perfection awaits us, but not in this life.

We will all fall short (Rom 3:23) and disappoint the Lord.

He still loves us and has already forgiven those transgressions.

People try to be "good enough" to enter the Kingdom of Heaven. We never achieve this. If you think you are that good, you are deceiving yourself and calling God a liar. (1 John 1:8) That would make him equally culpable for the wrongful execution of Jesus. He is not.

We all sin constantly. Sins of commission and omission. Intentional sins, and unintentional sins. Sins of action and of thought.

You know you are saved when you experience the same pain from those sins that Jesus felt at Calvary.

Usefulness of Our Past

When I was an atheist, I reveled in my sins. I thought they were entertaining and even fun. It was not unusual for me to boast about them.

We see segments of our society that like to flaunt their sins today.

The story here in 1 Samuel 21 shows us that God is not seeking perfect goody-goody people to follow him.

Jesus came to save the sinners. David's story shows us he sinned often.

He shows restraint, however. David and his men refrained from having women when they were on missions.

Then, he takes the sword of Goliath. This is a reminder that we all have pasts.

Relics of our past can be useful.

I frequently recount stories and make confessions about my life before my salvation. These help others connect.

This should not become a celebration of the sin, but a mourning over it.

David finds this emblem of his past and takes it to use for his future.

Centered on God

He also protects his past by hiding his parents in Mizpah.

It is important that we protect our families. This includes our biological siblings and our brothers and sisters in Christ.

While going on the run and into battle, David continues to bring the ephod with him. This is keeping God at the center of all he is doing.

It is easy for our circumstances to overwhelm us. We focus only on the situation at hand.

David remains centered.

He is to be king but still shows respect for Saul. God had anointed Saul, and David, therefore, bowed to him and refused to harm him in the cave in chapter 24.

Respect Authority

I did not appreciate the last administration, but I respected their authority.

Knowing God appoints rulers to accomplish His purposes, I didn't like the man, but I respected the office.

This was what David showed in the cave. He could have killed Saul and taken the kingdom by force. God had already anointed him. Even there in the cave, God was delivering Saul into his hands. But he had respect and spared his life. This led to the ending God had planned.

David will be king, but not by treachery.

How are your actions showing the world around you that Jesus is your Lord?

Are you visibly demonstrating the love of Jesus when you deal with your enemies?

Seek the Lord and ask Him for the strength of character that He gave David.

Tomorrow, we will read 1 Samuel 25-27.

Day 85: 1 Samuel 25-27: Wisdom and Deception

I hope your week has been productive.

Today, we read 1 Samuel 25-27.

Marriage

We will meet another of David's wives, Abigail.

Polygamy was a customary practice in those times and within that culture.

I have had four wives, but never more than one at a time. A man can only deal with so much.

The thought of multiple wives is more than I can comprehend.

My current wife has been married to me for 32 years.

She is the only one I was married to in the presence of a pastor.

We have learned to worship the Lord together and made God a central focus of our lives.

This separates our marriage from the previous ones.

When you live for the Lord, the daily challenges are easier to manage. Temptations and your own desires become less pressing.

Wisdom

We read how Nabal disrespected David and his men.

To keep face and show his men he supported them, David was going to massacre all of Nabal's family and servants.

Abigail was Nabal's wife. Verse 25:3 describes her as beautiful.

It's her intelligence and wisdom that impress me.

Her compassion towards her people is also clear.

She overrides Nabal's' actions, which is a risky move.

Society did not afford women the same respect as men in those days. He could have put her away, and no one would have stopped him.

God was with her. He led her to intervene and dispel the threat that David and his men presented.

How We Present Ourselves

Nabal was gruff and insulting.

Treating people with respect and diplomacy is important.

Others often describe me as grumpy. One of my past coworkers admitted to being afraid of me.

This is not the image I seek to portray. I hope that when people look at me, they see Jesus.

Instead, because I wouldn't smile, they always assumed I was mad.

I love people and never get mad. My wife jokes about how even-keeled I am.

Even when someone does me wrong, I try to pay back good for evil.

This was not Nabal. He paid back evil for good. (v 25:21)

Abigail brings a peace offering and smooths things over.

This must have impressed David.

Ten days later Nabal dies. (v 25:38) David asks her to marry him. (v 25:40)

Demons Persist

We learn Saul had given Michal, David's wife, to Paltiel. (v 25:44) Marriage was much different in that culture.

Along with giving away David's wife, Saul has had another change of heart. He is back to pursuing David.

My worst traits never leave me. I am obsessed about things which happened long ago.

I forgive, I try to forget, but in my mind, they play on a loop.

To drive them out, I tell myself to stop thinking about them. That just makes me think about them.

Saul needed to move past his animosity toward David. It could have cost him his life in the cave.

But he doesn't. He can't.

He gathers up three thousand men and sets out to find him again.

This time, David sneaks into his camp, and instead of slaying him, he takes his water jug and spear.

Demonstrating that he could have killed him again but didn't. He convinces Saul to call off the search.

Violence

Then David goes to Gath and begins raiding the other tribes.

There was little else for people to do in those times, so they fought.

We have become so consumed with activity in our culture that it is hard to fit anything else into our schedules.

Although wars and conflicts remain in the headlines, Americans live in peace.

There is still conflict, but we have made violence into entertainment.

The practice of conquering kingdom after kingdom has subsided. This gives us hope for a future.

God wants us to have peace. He gives us His peace. (John 14:27)

It is not His desire that we live in fear. The news tries to keep us there, anyway.

Inspired by Abigail's wisdom and beauty, we must be fearless in our actions.

Seek peace with those around you for the sake and safety of your household.

Show kindness and love your enemies. (Matt 5:44) Tomorrow, we will read 1 Samuel 28-31.

Day 86: 1 Samuel 28-31: The Witch and The Warrior

Good morning. I hope you are all doing well today.

Today, we finish reading 1 Samuel, covering chapters 28-31.

Tomorrow, we will continue this story as we begin 2 Samuel; the separation occurs as Saul and his sons' lives end. We will get to that more in a moment.

An Unexpected Alliance

We begin in an unusual place. David supports Achish and fights in support of the Philistines.

They remember how he killed their champion and multitudes of their soldiers. He is a legendary foe of theirs. So, they do not feel good about him bringing up the rear.

It feels like he could ambush them. So, they sent him away.

Today's opening verses seem to present everything as reversed. David wants to support the Philistines. Saul has driven the mediums out of Israel. It's all upside down.

Saul's Desperate Plea

After the Philistines dismissed David, Saul viewed their army and felt terror.

He was doing what was right, but his heart was still not with God. So, he calls on the witch of Endor. (v 28:6-7)

This happens in churches today.

People will know they need God. Their lives are not making sense, so they accept an invitation to attend a service.

God has put eternity on our hearts. (Ecc. 3:11) Therefore, an unsaved person senses a void.

The preacher shares a message of hope and love. It all tickles their ears.

The coffee was free; the donuts were fresh. So, they come back the following week.

They're never confronted with genuine issues.

They have a sin problem, and Jesus is the only solution.

Then trouble shows up on the horizon.

Like Saul, they turn to their idols.

Their lips say they trusted Jesus. Actions say they are still trusting only in themselves.

They miss a few weeks while putting in overtime. Thinking more money will fix their problems.

Soon, they are out of the habit of attending.

When someone asks why they stopped coming, their answer is deceptive.

"We weren't being fed," they will say.

This is true. They were eating donuts, not the Gospel.

The Gospel requires you to confront your sin.

The Downfall of Saul

The Medium conjures up the spirit of Samuel.

This tells me that those ghost stories we like to think of as myths could contain truth.

Samuel asks why Saul is disturbing him. He is in heaven with the Lord. (v 28:15) His thoughts are not on the things of this world.

Saul is looking for cheap grace.

Changing nothing within himself, he wants Samuel to tell him God will fight for him.

Instead, Samuel tells him he and his three sons will all die the next day. (v 28:19) They do.

David's Victory at Ziklag

Meanwhile, the rulers of the Philistines turn David away.

People like to believe that others can't change. This is not accurate.

I was always a liberal Democrat until I examined the issues. My salvation led to God convicting my heart. I could no longer support a party that supported so much sin. I had to have that old nature stripped away. Like David's troops found when they reached Ziklag, everything they valued was gone. So, they wept.

Then, they find an Egyptian who the Amalekites had kept as a slave. He had gotten ill, so they left him behind to die.

Feeling abandoned and discarded, we change our allegiances.

This slave will help David find the enemy's camp.

David can overcome them with only four hundred men. A subgroup had fallen behind because of exhaustion.

Because those troops were not with them for the fighting, David's soldiers didn't want to share their spoils. David made it an ordinance that all would share in the plunder.

A Call for Unity

There are people today who continue to fight against our current administration.

When our economy recovers, everything is prosperous again. It would be natural to want to prevent them from sharing in the recovery.

This would only hold the country as a whole back and continue to breed division.

We must take the coming improvements as an opportunity to share the Gospel and mend fences. Let's pave a path to a brighter future by embracing the hurts and offering an olive branch.

Even today, we can start by opening lines of communication.

Resist the urge to fight back.

Learn to share in our hope for the future.

Tomorrow, we will read 2 Samuel 1-3.

Conclusion of 1 Samuel

Now that you have read the ninth book of the Bible, take a moment to reflect. How have the events in 1 Samuel mirrored lessons in your own life? Do you feel yourself growing in knowledge? Are you also growing in faith?

For fun, here are five questions I want you to answer (I will post some brief answers at the back of the book).

1. Who was Hannah, and what was her special prayer about?
2. Who was Eli, and what were his sons like?
3. How did God first speak to Samuel, and what important message did He give him?
4. Who was the first king of Israel, and what was he like initially?
5. How did Saul's feelings toward David change over time, and what did Saul try to do to David?

Chapter 9: Footnotes

1. **Health of Pastors in Africa** Odhiambo, Janet. "Discipleship Amidst Crisis and Health Implications: A Case Study among Pastors in Kenya." *Pan-African Journal of Health and Environmental Science*, March 24, 2025.
https://www.ajol.info/index.php/ajhes/article/view/291442..

    This study explores the physical and emotional health challenges faced by pastors in Kenya during the COVID-19 pandemic, including burnout, stress, and the shift to online ministry.

2. **Restaurant Portion Sizes and Health Conditions** American Heart Association. "Portion Size Versus Serving Size." *American Heart Association*, December 18, 2023.
https://www.heart.org/en/healthy-living/healthy-eating/eat-smart/nutrition-basics/portion-size-versus-serving-size.

3. Albert Barnes, *Barnes' Notes on the Old and New Testaments* (London: Blackie & Son, 1884).

4. The Personal Growth Project, "The Role of Isolation in Abuse," accessed July 1, 2025, https://www.thepersonalgrowthproject.com/blog/the-role-of-isolation-inabuse.

Chapter 10:
2 SAMUEL

Day 87: 2 Samuel 1-3, Leadership and Loss

Congratulations, we now have reached the tenth book in the Bible. By now, this should have become a habit.

The desired progression is from task to chore to habit to hunger.

We get deeper into the realm of King David, which is everlasting because of Jesus.

His descendant will be on the throne forever.

Therefore, we should develop an insatiable passion for spending time with the Lord.

Saul's Death and David's Grief

As we begin 2 Samuel, King Saul is dead, and this Amalekite risks his life to tell David.

Matthew Henry asserts the soldier's undeniable guilt for taking Saul's life, despite extenuating circumstances.[1] He had confessed because he believed God would justify him.

We all like to justify our actions.

Knowing they violate God's Law, we think that applying our rationale will alleviate the guilt. It does not.

Taking food because your children are hungry doesn't make it not stealing. Nor does taking from someone with excess.

Lusting after someone who dresses provocatively, even if that was their intention, is still adultery (see Matt 5:28).

Accidentally killing someone may get you a sentence of manslaughter, but it is still violating the sixth commandment (Ex 20:13).

Romans 6:26 tells us the wages of all sin is death.

David may have been acting out of resentment for the Amalekites, or vengeance, or grief. Either way, God justified him in doling out the judgment.

David's Kingship and Dependence on God

Then, in chapter 2, we see David seeking the Lord in all his decisions.

This is what I am praying our current leaders will do.

David was king over all of Israel.

People would follow his edicts. The people loved him.

Still, he would not even go up to Judah without speaking to the Lord. (v 2:1)

Conflict and Reconciliation

Dropping to verse 2:14, we read that Abner and Joab decide to have a dozen of their men fight each other. Benson says this was for recreation and entertainment, much like boxing or cage matches would be today.[2]

It served a purpose, however, in eliminating the need for greater bloodshed or causing either of them to lose face.

Boxing was called the Sport of Kings.[3]

I recall watching great boxing matches when I was younger.

My friends and I would put on gloves and go for a few rounds with each other. We were still friends, but for some unknown reason, we enjoyed trying to knock each other out.

The Cost of Unfocused Ambition

My third point of interest today is this example we have, culminating in 2 Sam 2:23. Asahel was fast and focused. He was chasing Abner and refused to give up.

Ignoring the warnings Abner gave to him, he continued until it cost him his life.

There are times when I will have my mind set on obtaining something.

I justify my coveting.

I've worked hard and provided for my family (the Lord had provided), but I feel I have earned it.

So, I make it my mission to accomplish the task. To achieve the prize.

I can even twist the scripture to say that I'm running the race, fighting the good fight, keeping my eye on the prize.

We forsake other areas of our lives: Time with family, Projects at work, Service to God. All while pursuing the goal we have.

Years later, we can't remember the object of our affection.

Did we obtain our goal? Or not?

Did it live up to our expectations? Or did we just tire of it?

I loved camping, but with my disability, I knew it would be easier to sleep in an RV.

Knowing I was of little help to my wife when we had to pack for a lake trip, I justified the expense. She wouldn't have as much to do. It would all be ready when we wanted it.

After years and glorious memories, we had a nice used motor home. It was rotting on the side of our house. We sold it to a friend.

This is an example of how we justify our sin (coveting), lose focus on God, and end up with nothing.

We were more fortunate than Asahel, who lost his life.

What are you working toward right now that is drawing your energy away from what is most important?

Are you content with what God has given you?

Will your sacrifices be worth it?

God sacrificed His absolute best so you could have fellowship with him. Are you using that time well?

Or are you running away like Abner or chasing something that is wrong, like Asahel?

Tomorrow, we will read 2 Samuel 4-7.

Day 88: 2 Samuel 4-7:
Uzzah's Disobedience and God's Covenant

Today, after enjoying your time with the Lord, I would encourage you to get outside and appreciate the day He has given us.

Let's start by reading 2 Samuel 4-7.

The Impact of Leadership

In chapter four, we read that without their leader, Abner, all of Israel loses courage. (v 4:1)

I have encountered individuals who excelled in acquiring promotions and advancing to managerial positions. They interview well, are charismatic, and have excellent organizational skills. Some of them have proven to be superb managers.

There is a difference between being a manager and being a leader. A leader has a quality that inspires others to follow.

Some people lead from the front, others from behind.

Regardless of position, they know how to motivate and enable.

Harvard Business School lists six characteristics of an effective leader.

They are influencers. This allows them to steer the work and direction of others. A manager can track that performance, but a leader will create it.[4]

Transparency is another trait required. People will not follow if they are not sure where the leader is going.

The death of Abner left the Israelites too afraid to take risks. Ishbosheth instilled fear in them.

A powerful leader encourages risk-taking.

A powerful leader will exhibit integrity and accountability as well.

These traits are essential for anyone to feel confident that their efforts will matter.

Weak leaders change priorities and flip-flop on their position.

I have worked hard to finish projects that were then unnecessary. It is demoralizing.

Uzzah's Disobedience

God displays this characteristic when He strikes down Uzzah in 2 Samuel 6:7.

This is a confusing passage for people. They assume Uzzah acted out of concern for the ark.

It may have even been an instinctual response.

Numbers 4 instructed the Levites to avoid the uncovered ark. They could not look at it, and in Num 4:15, Moses told them that touching it would cause death.

The Lord's anger burned because Uzzah disobeyed His command. Uzzah lacked faith that the Lord would protect the ark.

This also showed the fifth characteristic of leadership.

The Lord acted decisively.

Weak leaders stall, hoping someone else decides or that circumstances change, and they get off the hook.

God's Covenant

Resilience is the last trait that Harvard lists.

David wanted to build a house for the Lord. The Lord told him He would have his descendants build that house.

We could consider Solomon, the builder of the Temple.

The true everlasting dwelling place of the Lord, however, is our hearts.

This was David's descendant, Jesus Christ. He is the one who is forever on the throne.

Lord of Lords, King of Kings. God's people have found a home in Him where the wicked can no longer oppress them. (v 7:10)

For this reason, God told David that He would establish His kingdom. (v 12-13)

I love David's statement in verse 7:22, "How great are you, Sovereign Lord? There is no one like you."

As we read this history of David, we will continue to see God's leadership.

We will see David stumble.

Then, we will witness God's unfailing love and forgiveness.

Take a moment to just notice God's creation and humble yourself to thank Him for all He does for you.

Tomorrow, we will read 2 Samuel 8-11.

Day 89: 2 Samuel 8-11: Victory and Temptation

I like to block out worldly noise on Sunday.

Prior to Jesus coming into my life, it was a day for football and watching races on TV or going to the lake in the summer.

Now, I start by reading my Bible, writing my post, and then going to church.

I follow that by working on my next book.

Family events are the only exception. Otherwise, I remain focused on God all day. This makes Sunday a perfect day.

Today, we will read 2 Samuel 8-11.

There is a saying in marketing, "sex sells." It is why we see so many scantily clad young men and women used in ads for everything.

Therefore, the temptation would be to jump to chapter 11 and discuss David's dalliance with Bathsheba.

I am going to hold that for tomorrow.

The Fruits of Patience

Instead, let's start with our first five words, "In the course of time." (1 Sam 8:1a) The Bible lists patience as a fruit of the Spirit.

This means it is not part of the natural man. It is something that God imparts to us when we accept the gift of salvation.

This is one proof I have that God is real. It's how I know I am saved.

Before I knew God, I had a temper. It led me into fights and arguments.

I needed everything immediately.

Instant gratification is a part of our culture.

When I didn't get that gratification, I became irritated.

Most Christians I know will tell you never to ask God for patience. He develops that in us by teaching us to wait.

Now, I am always calm and even keeled.

This was not always the case.

Seeing how God has given me the skills to work with others who might not always accept my instruction and remain under control is miraculous.

Measuring What Matters

David measures off the Moabites and slaughters two-thirds of them.

This made me think of how we measure ourselves.

Is what we weigh or how tall we are important?

People obsess about these things. They build our self-esteem or destroy it. The problem is we don't always have control over these factors.

Do we measure ourselves by our bank account balance or by the title next to our name?

There are people who achieve great worldly success but will spend eternity in hell. How can we affirm their success? (see Matt 16:26)

Do we measure our children by the grades on their report cards or whether they make the first team?

What matters in this life is that we know Jesus and grow in our relationship with Him.

There is more value in leading a friend to Christ than in getting a promotion or a raise.

Acknowledging God's Provision

In the sixth verse we read today, it says, "The Lord gave David victory wherever he went." (2 Sam 8:6, NIV)

We must acknowledge our success isn't from our skills, talents, and dogged determination. Those might be characteristics the Lord has blessed us with, which contribute.

But all we have, and all we are, comes from God. That context should humble us.

I know I do not give Him back anywhere near what I should.

He's earned every bit of recognition he receives, which we see in 2 Sam 8:11 when David dedicates all the nation's silver and gold to the Lord.

Kindness and God's Grace

The Bible says David was a man after God's own heart. (1 Sam 13:14) Not because he was sinless. We have seen flaws already and will talk about more tomorrow. It is because he understands that even the king of all Israel is nothing without God.

We see another display of this when David shows Mephibosheth "God's kindness." (v 9:3) Kindness is another fruit of the Spirit. (Gal 5:22-23)

None of us deserves God's grace more than Mephibosheth. We all deserve God's wrath.

Following the Spirit enables us to show these characteristics to others (Eph 2:3). We claim to see fruit in a Christian when these traits are present.

Tomorrow, we will include chapter 11 in our discussion because this is our sinful nature. This is the battle that we are all in.

Even a valiant warrior like King David struggles against this foe.

Today, we should just focus on recognizing areas where we can see God in our lives.

If you are not seeing these fruits. If following God has not changed you.

Pray that He would manifest Himself in your life for others to see.

Tomorrow, we will read 2 Samuel 12-14.

Day 90: 2 Samuel 12-14:
Sin, Consequences, and Forgiveness

Today, we conclude studying the Bible for the third straight month.

You need to celebrate this accomplishment.

A Lifeway study found 87% of Americans own a Bible but only 11% have read the entire book.[5]

I hope these devotionals motivate you to continue.

Today, we are going to talk about Chapter 11, which we read yesterday, and then 12-14, which we read today.

I didn't jump into the story of David and Bathsheba because it is like the story of Amnon and Tamar and even of Absalom and the woman from Tekoa.

All these incidents, happening in succession, teach us three important truths.

God is Omniscient

People act according to their own impulses in each of the three cases. The lust of the flesh and access to power cause them to act selfishly.

They believe they can get away with their actions because they are above the Law.

Their actions are impulsive. Because of this, they have left gaps.

My wife and I watch too much television. Absent of quality, we will find shows on Netflix or Prime and binge one series after another. One of our favorite genres is detective shows.

One common thread runs through every plot.

The criminal, no matter how clever, always makes a mistake that the detective figures out.

This leads to their arrest and conviction.

A statistic compiled by The Sleep Judge points out that while most crime happens during the day, murders, rapes, and robberies happen more frequently at night.[6]

John 3:19 teaches us that men love darkness. They believe their actions will remain hidden.

Darkness does not prevent God from knowing our actions.

He sees what David does from the privacy of his rooftop.

He uses His messenger, Nathan, to expose the action.

Amnon believes getting Tamar alone in his bedroom will hide his raping her.

It does not, and her brother takes vengeance for her.

Her brother, Absalom, thinks he can have his brothers conduct this punishment and then flee.

God is aware of all of it.

Absalom cannot return to his father's house, but Joab uses this woman from Tekoa to expose the error.

People may escape earthly retribution for their actions, but a judge will condemn them.

God always knows the truth. (1 John 3:20) God is the truth. (John 14:6)

Actions Have Consequences

The second truth we see in these situations is there are always consequences.

Because God knows what we have done, He will hold us accountable.

This may happen after our death. (Heb 9:27) Thinking you can get away with it that long, there are two things you must know:

After you die, there is no way to repent. Forgiveness is no longer an option. You will spend eternity in hell. Throughout your life, you may miss the fellowship and blessings God offers.

Living with guilt prevents us from grasping all that God intended for us.

There have been times in my life when I have lost that closeness with God.

I am working harder than ever. I am running hard but getting nowhere.

God removes obstacles for me daily. When I am not walking with Him, those obstacles are endless.

Sin creeps into our lives, and we avoid confronting it.

Denying sin happened does not make it go away.

All we do is drift for a season.

Our salvation is not in question if we have trusted Jesus.

That daily connection to the blessings of God can be.

The overarching narrative of the Old Testament centers on Israel's cyclical pattern of sin, estrangement from God, repentance, and subsequent restoration.

The same thing happens to us.

This has been one of the "proofs" I know God is real. I have seen what His presence and absence look like in my life.

It is like watching leaves on a tree. When the wind blows, even though we can't see the wind, we know it is there because the leaves move. As the wind ceases, the leaves stop moving.

Forgiveness is Possible

The third lesson we can take from these situations is that, with repentance, forgiveness is possible.

Repercussions continue; although David survived, Israel remains at war. Absalom returns, but not to full fellowship with his father.

While we have breath in our lungs, we must repent and place our trust in Jesus. We can ask for forgiveness and know we receive salvation. 1 John 1:9 tells us that if we confess, we have the assurance of forgiveness.

I hope you haven't murdered, committed adultery, raped or robbed anyone.

In the Sermon on the Mount (Matt 5-7), Jesus teaches that hatred is murder and lust is adultery. Taking a grape from a grapevine may not seem important, but without permission, it is still a robbery.

We all have sinned. (Rom 3:23) Therefore, we all need a Savior.

Have you confessed your sins to God and asked for His forgiveness?

Have you trusted Jesus has paid the penalty for your sins?

Tomorrow, we will read 2 Samuel 15-17.

Day 91: 2 Samuel 15-17: Absalom's Deceit, David's Humility

Good morning. Welcome to a new month. I am not sure about the rest of the world, but in America, we have a strange tradition on April 1st. We call it April Fool's Day. A day where we lie about things.

Lying is a sin, but we find it funny to prank someone.

Of course, you need to come clean and confess the lie. Otherwise, it's just mean.

Today, we read 2 Samuel 15-17.

Lies and Manipulation

What an appropriate storyline for this day.

We have Absalom sitting by the side of the road (v 15:2), lying to the people.

Like modern-day politicians, he would kiss the people and put on a good show.

He would then plant the idea in their minds that he should help them with their complaints.

Winning the hearts of the people with deception has been around for a long time.

Other leaders would use force and brutality, but Absalom used cunning and deception.

Within four years, what we have set out as a presidential term, he had won the people over to his side.

Then, he lies again and goes to Hebron, setting up the plan to become king.

He was David's son. He had been around power his whole life. Power corrupts. It is addictive. People who have power and lose it will do anything to regain it.

We see this every year throughout the world.

Our Secrets

People will lie, cheat, and steal to get the things they want.

I have always had an endless work ethic. My IQ is remarkably high, and I think fast on my feet. This combination has served me well.

There have been times I tried to take a shortcut. We call them get-rich-quick-schemes. I have never been rich, at least not by worldly measures.

Everyone's secrets will be revealed. (Luke 8:17)

More impressive than Absalom's plan is David's response.

He gathered all the tribes loyal to him, including the newly arrived Gittites, and embarked on a journey through the Kidron Valley.

Though he is a king, God's anointed leader of Israel, he knows his sinfulness.

He humbles himself, walking barefoot and weeping.

The whole countryside weeps with him.

The countryside's love for David was so strong that Absalom's attempt to steal their hearts failed.

Leaving it in God's Hands

David then sends the Ark of the Covenant of God back to Jerusalem.

We had always seen Israel's strength was having God with them. Now, he separates from the ark.

There have been times, knowing I had sinned, that I allowed God to be distant from me. I missed the closeness.

Longing for fellowship and thirsting for restoration, I would attempt to fix my problems on my own.

Not because I didn't think God could or even would. He has always been faithful, even when I am not.

Guilt has led me to allow a gulf to form, because I didn't think God should have to fix the mess I had made.

Knowing I was not doing His will, I took my chances and failed. I didn't feel worthy of His love.

Fortunately, God's love for us is not based on our feelings. It is not determined by our worthiness. We are never worthy.

God's grace is because of His character. It is who He is, not who we are.

Therefore, our works are like filthy rags. (Isa 64:6)

David doesn't play his God card. He didn't remind God of the promise of an eternal throne, nor did he claim to be the anointed one. Absalom, after all, was his son.

Instead, he allows that separation to exist. He leaves the ark behind, trusting in God's will. If it is His will, he knows God will bring him back to Jerusalem. If not, he is getting what he deserves.

When Shimei, son of Gera, curses him and throws rocks and dirt at him. He does not retaliate.

The king's men want to cut his head off, but David knows he is a murderer. What Shimei is saying is true.

We must accept our wrongfulness and trust in the Lord's forgiveness.

There is nothing we can do that will earn us salvation.

Only God, by His mercy and through the atoning blood of Jesus, can bring us back to His presence.

David does not deny his guilt. He doesn't leverage his position or standing. It is not by his strength or reputation as a fighter, but only by the grace of God, that he will return to Jerusalem.

Do you feel a space between God and yourself?

Are you wearing yourself out trying to get back into His graces?

It is time to admit your sins and accept His mercy.

He wants you to come back to Him.

Salvation is a gift for you to accept. (Eph 2:9-10) Stop walking barefoot away from God.

Repenting means turning around.

Instead of heading into the wilderness, seek God and trust in His worthiness.

Tomorrow, we will read 2 Samuel 18-19.

Day 92: 2 Samuel 18-19: Loss and Leadership

Good morning. This year keeps moving along whether we are ready for it or not. I hope you are growing in the Lord as we read. Today, we look at 2 Samuel 18-19.

These are the three themes I will speak about today: Even kings don't always get their way all the time; nature can work against us; and we must not worship ourselves.

You Can't Always Get What You Want

Not even the great King David always gets his way. He had men killed, had his way with women who bore him sons, conquered giants, and ruled over all twelve tribes of Israel.

He goes to battle and wants to be with his men. A good leader likes to lead by example.

He loves his troops. Therefore, he wants to ride with them as he has always done.

A good leader also develops others and takes advice from those in his inner circle.

They tell him it is too risky for him to be in battle; he agrees. In verse 18:4, he answers, "I will do whatever seems best to you."

People with power will sometimes behave arrogantly. The adage: my way or the highway, comes to mind. This is not always wise.

A smart leader with power will trust his advisors.

President Trump's ongoing practice of praying with spiritual leaders at the White House is a source of immense joy to me.

This was my prayer that he would seek God. Let's hope this persists.

David gives one command, "Be gentle with the young man Absalom for my sake." (v 18:5) Joab does not honor this request.

It's Only Natural

Verse 18:8 tells us the forest swallowed up more men than the sword.

This includes Absalom getting his hair stuck in a branch. He dies hung in a tree.

I'm from the generation that would let our hair grow long as a sign of freedom.

Here, it condemns Absalom.

In our understanding, Galatians 3:13 refers to Jesus, who redeemed us from the Law's curse by becoming a curse for us. As it is written: "Cursed is everyone who is hanged on a tree." (NASB)

That passage is found in Deuteronomy 21:23.

Joab and ten of his men thrust their spears into Absalom's body, foreshadowing when the centurion pierces Jesus.

It's Not About Us

Absalom, as we spoke of yesterday, had been conniving and deceitful. His treachery contributed to his demise.

We read in verse 18:18 that he made a monument for himself.

This is a problem today.

People choose not to attend or support a church. They will say that the people are hypocrites.

Often, they recount an experience where something or someone at the event offended them. They use this as a justification for not attending again.

If they are committed to God, they may find another church. The issue is the same.

They are creating for themselves a religion based upon themselves.

It is a blessing to gain something from a service. That is not why we should go to church.

The purpose of attending church is to join others in worshipping the Lord. It is about Him, not us.

It's not about getting; it is about serving.

The Bible tells us to gather (Heb 10:25) to praise God. He has earned our respect and admiration.

People will claim they aren't being fed.

First, it isn't about being fed but about feeding others.

Second, when we are feeding others, we have food in our hands. We starve ourselves by refusing to eat what God provides.

David, though he is king, cannot even grieve for his son.

With unwavering support, he boosted the morale of his discouraged troops.

He understands and respects that others have needs, too. So, he does what is necessary.

We could all take this attitude, and we would see our faith grow.

The reward of serving others would be a blessing to us. Joy would come from giving.

When you attend, are you there for you? Or are you there for the person next to you who may need your support?

A tree draws from the soil, but it gives more of itself to the world around it. That is what growth is.

Are you growing?

Tomorrow, we will read 2 Samuel 20-22.

Day 93: 2 Samuel 20-22: Troublemakers, Justice, and the Song of David

Good morning! I hope this has been a wonderful week for you so far. The best is yet to come.

Sometimes, it feels like we're Sisyphus pushing a rock up the hill only to have it roll down again.

I digress. Let's open the Bible and read 2 Samuel 20-22 today.

Sheba's Rebellion

We start with verse 20:1, speaking of a troublemaker named Sheba. Replicas of Sheba remain today.

I have been trying to build my social media following on all the different platforms.

My book has not sold enough for it to make sense to invest in advertising or marketing for it. That is all right, I didn't write it to become rich and famous. My goal is to spread the Gospel.

To increase my base and my following, I reach out and follow people who have profiles that align with my values. This is not foolproof.

Along the way, I have met females who think I want to go into private apps so they can be "friendly." I refuse and use the opportunity to explain why this is inappropriate.

When they persist, I block and delete them.

There are others with Illuminati scams and crypto cons, and people warning the banking industry is about to collapse.

The bottom line is there will never be a shortage of troublemakers. Sheba's descendants have multiplied.

Moral Integrity

I will ask them if they know Jesus Christ as their Lord and Savior. The vast majority will answer they are atheists.

Like Sheba, they have no share in David. (v 20:1b) I share with them this heritage, but explain God changed me.

At this point, most will stop bothering me. I hope they see my posts and God works on their hearts.

It is not my role to convert them.

Jesus commissions us to share the Gospel and witness to them. This is telling them what God is doing in our lives.

The rest is up to the Holy Spirit.

I mention the women who want to get me alone to be "friendly" with me because, in verse 20:3, we read when David returned to his palace, he treated his concubines with kindness.

It was not their fault Absalom abused them. They were, however, defiled, and so David never had sexual relations with them.

Maintaining moral standards is important.

He was the king, and they were his servants. He could have done with them as he wanted. No one would have been able to suppress him.

He did the right thing.

This is integrity, doing the right thing when you have choices.

What I find shocking on social media outlets is the blatant deception: People claiming to be Elon Musk or even his son, just to con you. Misrepresenting who they are and what they believe to steal your identities.

A friend of mine is part of the Cybercrimes division within our police department. She has provided me with enough knowledge to know how to protect myself.

God's Justice

If we pay attention, we can see their daggers hanging out of their belts like Amasa should have when Joab reached for his hand. (v 20:8-9)

Instead, he ignores the blade, and his guts spill out.

People will attempt to disarm you to encourage you to spill your guts. To divulge details of your life which they can exploit.

I have also met wonderful people on social media.

They have read the devotionals I share. The Word of God is spreading.

This encourages me to continue, but I can't ignore the warnings in scripture.

We live in a treacherous world, and sin will always look for a way to destroy us.

Protecting ourselves requires not giving the devil a foothold. (Eph 4:27) The righteous also deserve our help.

The woman in verses 20:16-22 understands her city faces destruction because of Sheba's wickedness.

Undeterred, she fearlessly took a stand, using her cunning to eliminate Sheba.

Her actions saved their city.

Chapter 21 begins with a famine.

God will hold us accountable. He pours out His wrath against Israel because of how Saul and his people killed the Gibeonite.

Even though David was fighting Saul, he wasn't denying the debt.

It would be easy to say, "I was trying to kill Saul and did!"

That would not have righted the wrong. As the leader of Israel, he takes the action to correct this injustice.

The Giant

Toward the end of this chapter, we read about an enormous man with six fingers and six toes. Descendant of Rapha. Related to Goliath.

When reading the Bible, my mind becomes distracted by non-biblical knowledge.

All I could think about as I read this paragraph was the six-fingered man in "The Princess Bride." A silly movie about vengeance.[7]

This fits the narrative of this chapter, although I know it's unrelated.

My guess is that you are now reciting in your minds, "My name is Inigo Montoya. You killed my father. Prepare to die!"[7]

We experience things in life. Sharing those that glorify God is important.

Enjoying the parts God has blessed you with honors Him.

Avoiding the dangers which are ever-present. Watching out for troublemakers. Paying attention to details, like daggers falling out of a belt, is crucial to survival.

Atonement

Trusting in the Lord to protect us when we slip up. To hold us accountable even when we were not the perpetrators helps us to grow in our faith.

What are the warning signs you see around you today?

Are there people in your life who would take your head off?

Are you pursued for actions you, or someone else, took?

How can you repent and atone for these transgressions?

The greatest news of all is even when we can't do anything about them. Jesus will remove that debt from us.

He paid for all our sins on the cross. Holding on to them will cause the debt to remain on the road. It will block your progress. Giving it to Him will remove it and allow our life to move forward.

Are you ready to hand it all to God and seek His salvation?

Special note: Chapter 22 is all about the Song of David. Just like the Song of Moses in

Exodus 15, this deserves its own discussion. If you have read my book, Moving Ahead: How to Make America Godly Again, you know that Psalm 144 became a seven-week sermon series and is the basis of a book. The Song of David deserves the same attention.

Tomorrow, we will read 2 Samuel 23-24.

Day 94: 2 Samuel 23-24: David's Last Words and the Census

I can't believe we are finishing 2 Samuel reading chapters 23-24 today.

Last Words

This is the end of King David.

Sure, we will hear more about him in Kings and Chronicles and, of course, Psalms.

The title of chapter 23 in the NIV says David's Last Words.

So much of the Judeo-Christian faith centers on this shepherd who rose to lead Israel.

God established his throne forever. (2 Sam 7:13-14) His descendant is Jesus Christ. (Matt 1:1)

Morning Light

The first line that captured my attention was 23:3-4. "The one who rules the people with justice, who rules in the fear of God, is like the morning light when the sun rises." (NIV) I have mentioned my wife, and I have lived in the same location for over thirty years.

Before our son was born, we bought a house from a client of mine. He helped us obtain the down payment and secure affordable terms.

It was a mobile home, which had been set on a foundation and added onto. This made it triple-wide.

It had a spacious yard, room for gardens, lush trees, and a swimming pool.

At the time, it was what we could afford while I was working at the newspaper.

As the years passed, my income increased.

We resisted the temptation to move to a newer, bigger house. It had all we needed.

The one downside was it was not wheelchair accessible.

I could walk on a cane and, later, crutches. So that was not a problem.

We knew it would become a problem.

After a series of surgeries on various limbs, we needed to tear down that home and build an accessible site-built home.

We've been living in that home, at the same address, for over two years now.

The first morning in our new home, my wife walked into the living room, and the gorgeous morning view shocked her.

The sun coming up over the Catalina mountains, an array of colors in the sky.

Our backyard now has a wall around it, and our pool has a sidewalk.

It continues to take our breath away, even after seeing it daily for over two years.

We had waited to build until we had enough money saved to pay for it.

Debt is something we avoid as much as possible.

The economy had taken a bad turn when we began the project, with inflation driving the cost of everything up.

Enduring Faith

Now, we have a new president, and prices are dropping.

This didn't happen overnight. We won't fix it immediately, either.

God has provided, so I am not worried about prices.

I am in prayer that our current administration will continue to "rule with the fear of God." The last one had little regard for the Lord, from what I could see.

Later, in verse 23:16-17, we read about the characteristics of good leadership.

David will not drink the water his men bring him, because they should not need to risk their lives for his pleasure.

Building a Legacy

I pray our leaders keep our troops out of the wars that are going on. We have become involved with sending arms and support. So far, that has not included soldiers.

We have no business in those conflicts.

I support our president using whatever leverage he must to seek a peaceful resolution between those nations. If it does not escalate to placing our people in harm's way.

The chapter concludes by listing thirty-seven men who were leaders with David.

The key takeaway for me is that leadership is never a solitary pursuit.

Good leaders surround themselves with good people and allow them to contribute.

They also allow them to receive recognition for their contributions, as we see in this chapter.

Costly Mistake

As we move to the closing chapter of 2 Samuel, we see the sin of pride.

David is placing his faith in the number of troops he has. He is counting on himself.

It was the Lord who gave them victory and preserved his men. David ignores that and orders the census.

Therefore, God's anger burned against Israel. (v 24:1) We must learn from this the delicate nature of following God.

Avoiding all sin, especially pride, is difficult.

Choosing Sacrifice

Because of it, the Lord gives David three hard choices: three years of famine, pursuit by enemies for three months, or three days of plague.

The first would cause long-term suffering. Pursuit by the enemies would cause losing men closest to him. A plague would cause the death of his people.

David would rather fall into the Lord's hands, so he rejects the second option.

Instead, he watches as the angel unleashes a plague on Israel. Hearing the wails and seeing the death toll rise, he asks the Lord to punish him, not his people.

This is the final characteristic of a powerful leader. He makes policy, but he puts his people first.

You may oppose the America First agenda. To me, this is the strong leadership shown by David.

He sacrifices for the people. But he is not willing to accept the objects of that sacrifice for free.

A sacrifice must cost something to have value.

For God, He sacrifices His Only Son for us.

We had a debt to pay, and He paid it with the highest possible price.

We must not take that for granted.

Our sacrifice needs to have value.

There is no cheap grace.

Are you willing to repent?

Can you turn from doing things your way, enjoying making your own rules, to following the Lord's commands?

Tomorrow, we will read 1 Kings 1-2.

Conclusion of 2 Samuel

Now that you have read the tenth book of the Bible, take a moment to reflect. How have the events in 2 Samuel mirrored lessons in your own life? Do you feel yourself growing in knowledge? Are you also growing in faith?

For fun, here are five questions I want you to answer (I will post some brief answers at the back of the book).

1. Who succeeded Saul as the king of Israel?
2. What was David's relationship with Bathsheba?
3. What is the significance of David's bringing the Ark of the Covenant to Jerusalem?
4. What role did Nathan the prophet play in David's life?
5. What is the overall message or theme of 2 Samuel?

Chapter 10: Footnotes

1. Matthew Henry, *Matthew Henry's Concise Commentary on the Whole Bible*, s.v. "2 Samuel 1," accessed July 1, 2025, https://www.biblehub.com/commentaries/mhc/2_samuel/1.htm.

2. Joseph Benson, *Benson Commentary on the Old and New Testaments*, s.v. "2 Samuel 2," accessed July 1, 2025, https://biblehub.com/commentaries/benson/2_samuel/2.htm.

3. Adrian Russell, "Lamenting the Days When Boxing Was the Sport of Kings," *Irish Examiner*, September 23, 2011, https://www.irishexaminer.com/sport/arid20166942.html.

4. "6 Characteristics of an Effective Leader," Harvard Business School Online, accessed July 1, 2025, https://online.hbs.edu/blog/post/characteristics-of-aneffective-leader.

5. "Americans Are Fond of the Bible, Don't Actually Read It," Lifeway Research, April 25, 2017, https://research.lifeway.com/2017/04/25/americans-are-fond-of-thebible-dont-actually-read-it/.

6. Cody Nie, "When Do Most Crimes Happen?," Deep Sentinel, February 16, 2024, https://www.deepsentinel.com/blogs/home-security/when-do-most-crimeshappen.

7. *The Princess Bride*, directed by Rob Reiner (1987; Twentieth Century Fox).

Chapter 11:
1 KINGS

Day 95: 1 Kings 1-2: Discipline and Deceit

Thank you for joining me to read our next book, 1 Kings. Today, we read chapters 1-2.

There are three lessons we will examine from these chapters: discipline, the dangers of sin, and the peace that Jesus offers.

Discipline

The Bible mentions at least eight of David's wives.[1]

They would move from town to town in battles and on foot and horseback.

It was common to be absent for prolonged periods of time.

God designed marriage to be one man and one woman (Gen 2:24). Jesus confirms this in Matthew 19:8. Most civilized countries practice this today.[2]

I love my wife. We have a great relationship that has lasted through 32 years of marriage. But marriage is challenging work.

A relationship requires commitment and sacrifice from both parties.

I could not imagine why a person would want to maintain multiple households.

David was old, and they could not warm him. They bring him this virgin Abishag, and he does not defile her, (v 1.4) even though she is beautiful. This is one example of his discipline.

Even in that culture, he knew that adultery was a sin against God. Therefore, he restrained himself.

Dangers of Sin

We see Adonijah, who is misbehaving, but it says, "His father had never once reprimanded him." (v 1:6)

When a parent refuses to discipline their children, they grow up with no respect for the rules. (Pro 13:24)

This lack of discipline shows up in how Adonijah attempts to circumvent David's authority and take the crown away from Solomon. He throws a banquet to celebrate himself. (v 1:19)

Sin is the root of his problems. Conceited, he felt his appearance and shrewdness guaranteed his kingship.

This backfires, and David has Solomon anointed. (v 1:28-40)

Adonijah, conscious of his wrongdoing, trembled in the presence of Solomon.

I remember when I was in my early twenties and living with my cousins. Although I cannot remember what I had done, I knew when my uncle came home I was going to get the belt.

They lived in a territorial-style house with a parapet wall around the roof. I climbed up and hid on the roof for so long that I fell asleep.

When I awoke, I could tell it was late. They were all outside, calling my name and looking for me. Knowing I wasn't allowed on the roof and had already misbehaved, I realized I was in serious trouble.

Like a six-year-old might do, I cried.

My weeping gave away my location. I got the belt and then additional punishment!

Adonijah knew his guilt, and it condemned him.

David instructed Solomon and all of us to walk in the way God demands. We must follow His commands, ordinances, and decrees. (v 2:2-3) When we don't, trouble will follow.

Sin rules Adonijah. Pride had caused him to celebrate the lie of being the king when he was not.

Then, lust caused him to ask for Abishag as his wife. (v 2:21)

This results in his death. (v 2:25)

Peace

God wants His children to have His peace. Peace from the Lord (v 2:33) means not fearing retribution.

We all have sinned (Rom 3:23) and deserve that punishment.

But Jesus did not come to condemn the world (John 3:17) but to give us His peace. (John 14:27)

Unfortunately, we all have trouble maintaining our obedience.

As with Shimei, we can follow the Lord's commands for a time. When circumstances arise, we take it upon ourselves to bend those rules.

Shimei dies, which is consistent with Romans 6:23, "For the wages of sin is death, but the free gift of God is eternal life in Christ Jesus our Lord." (NIV) Have you accepted the gift Jesus is offering you?

The knowledge of your wrongdoing haunts you, doesn't it?

Give that fear to Jesus and ask Him to save you today.

Tomorrow, we will read 1 Kings 3-5.

Day 96: 1 Kings 3-5: Solomon's Wisdom

I pray the Lord finds you in good spirits.

Today, we will continue reading 1 Kings, advancing through chapter 5.

A King's Request

We are now transitioning from David to Solomon.

David had walked before the Lord and served with faithfulness, righteousness, and integrity. (v 3:6) The reward for this was God gave him a son to sit on his throne after him.

Solomon was young. Like all of us, he was making mistakes.

In verse 3:3, he was following the statutes as his father David had done. He was also sacrificing and burning incense in high places, which is idolatry. There must have been something about this which bothered him.

I have had times when I was active for the Lord. Reading my Bible daily and serving in as many ministries as I had the capacity to. But I could still sense I was not "right" with the Lord. Though I couldn't put my finger on it, I knew the struggles I was facing daily resulted from my not being in step with God.

After careful examination and praying to God for guidance, I realized that while I was busy, I wasn't engaged. I was going through the motions, but with half a heart. My service was an obligation, not a passion.

I have been on fire for the Lord. Blazing hot and eager to be effective. We can't sustain that kind of heat. It will consume us.

So, we cool down. Being honorable, we keep the commitment. Only without our hearts in it are we not effective.

I think Solomon may have felt that way.

When God offered him whatever he asked for, Solomon requested wisdom to guide his people. (v 3:9)

The Value of Wisdom

Notice in verse 3:12 that God does not give him a beautiful mind. God did not fill him with knowledge. He does not begin spouting off geometric equations like the scarecrow in The Wizard of Oz.[3] Knowledge alone has led to our current problems. We know what, but not why. From that, we figure out how and believe when is always now.

In truth, we know extraordinarily little. Only after trial and error do we realize our hypothesis was wrong.

Wisdom is knowing what and when to apply how to solve the problems we encounter. It is seeking and doing God's will in all areas. Waiting on His timing and trusting in His provision.

A smart man may think he has a better way. A wise man knows God's way is always best. He made the universe and all that is in it. Only God can see across time, so He knows the outcomes before the test begins.

Anyone who thinks he is smarter than God is a fool. (1 Cor. 1:25, 1 Cor. 3:19)

So, God does not give Solomon a clever mind. He gives him a discerning heart. All the wisdom in the world is useless if we don't apply it with love. (1 Cor. 13:1-3)

We have already seen that not all of David's sons were following him. Each may have inherited certain characteristics. They were valiant warriors, handsome, or persuasive.

Solomon had that heart, which caused him to ask for wisdom. Therefore, God gives him wisdom and much more.

Prosperity Through Peace

He displays that wisdom by judging with the heart in the case of the prostitutes who were fighting over the baby. (v 3:16-26)

More so when he built his cabinet and surrounded himself with priests and spiritual advisors. (v 4:1-6)

Because he was seeking the Lord with all his heart, his people were living in prosperity. (v 4:20) They could prosper because they had peace. (v 4:24)

Solomon used his wisdom to discern what was important. Though God gave him more wealth, fame, and power than anyone in history, he focused on teaching. (v 4:32)

He taught economics and philosophy but also focused on biology. (v 4:33)

When his advisors guide him to build the Temple, he sets up trade agreements with leaders of nearby nations who have more resources and skilled labor than he did. Most nations lack essential resources. This makes them form alliances and be co-dependent upon each other, which helps them maintain peace. When you are counting on your neighbor for food, you don't withhold your oil from them. This would be foolish.

Modern Applications

America is in a different situation. The Middle East was a bunch of small kingdoms that relied on each other. America is a group of states that, combined, have all the resources they need. But no one state has it all.

You need the farmland states to provide food but states like Wyoming, Texas, and Pennsylvania have the oil and coal. There are states that have water and others that have livestock. They all need each other.

That cooperation is based on respect for God and each other. When one tries to impose control over another, it weakens the whole.

We all need to apply the heart-driven, God-centered wisdom of Solomon to how we move forward as a nation.

Tomorrow, we will read 1 Kings 6-7.

Day 97: 1 Kings 6-7: Building God's House

I like to start every day by asking what I can do to make this one better than the last. The answer is to spend more time connecting with God and learning to apply His will to more areas of my life.

Today, we will learn lessons from 1 Kings 6-7.

Building for God

The church I am a member of, Sandario Baptist Church, in Tucson, AZ., is undergoing a building project. We have been worshipping in an old mobile building. The maintenance and upkeep were becoming restrictive. Years ago, we began praying about it. After years of praying, we felt God telling us it was the right time.

We had been looking at moving to a different location to build. There have been communities spring up nearby. Being closer to them would benefit us.

God had a different plan. He clarified we needed to remain where we were. After years of resistance, the family that owned the land next to our building sold the property to us at a very reasonable price.

We went through a year of church votes and negotiations. The time came to meet with an architect and begin the project.

Facing Delays

This has been over two years ago, and it is difficult to maintain enthusiasm when things drag on.

We read in 1 Kings 6:1 that it had been four hundred and eighty years since Israel had left Egypt. They had been carrying around the Ark of the Covenant of God for almost five centuries.

Every time it moved, they had to break everything down and then set it up. They followed every rule and obeyed each commandment and ordinance of God.

David wanted to build the Temple, but God told him he couldn't. (1 Kings 8:17-19) We will read more about that tomorrow.

Solomon knew that because David had killed so many people, God had determined his son would build it. However, he had been the king for over four years and still hadn't started the Temple.

We can relate to his frustration. Being on fire for the Lord, you want to get things finished. Not to feel good about what you did. You want everyone who sees the result to say, look what God did.

Children can be very impatient. Our culture demands instant gratification. If a commercial comes on our television set, we switch the channel.

Solomon was only sixteen years old when he became king.

I remember being sixteen. The most important thing for me was getting my driver's license.

I worked extra hours to afford a car. It is inconceivable that a person of that age would be ruling a nation.

God had given him wisdom, and he used it.

Now, at twenty years of age, he began building the Temple.

The craftsmen finished each brick at the quarry. There were no metal tools used at the construction site. (v 6:7)

The entire complex was enormous, but the Temple was only about ninety feet by thirty feet wide. Compared to the size of modern churches, this was not exceptionally large.

It took eleven years to complete the construction of the Temple.

There is a saying, "You can do it right, or you can do it fast." The builder who has pride in his work, wants to do it right. The people who want the job done want it fast. This creates tension.

Today, you also need to factor in inflation. The longer a job takes, the more the job will cost. Keeping within your budget when a job lingers is a challenge.

Even though Solomon's Palace and the one he built for his wife are larger than the Temple, (see chapter 7) God was still blessing them.

God's Presence

As parents, I know we always want our children to have more than we had. I don't think God was unhappy at all that Solomon gave himself such lavish living quarters.

God is omnipresent. (Psalm 139:7-10) A building does not contain him. (Acts 7:48) His dwelling place of choice is in our hearts. (Eph 3:17) But He will not force Himself in. You must have faith and make room in your heart for Him to dwell.

God will not exist in a sinful environment. So, you must repent, leaving your sinfulness behind and trusting Him to fill the space it opens.

When you do, you will see God manifest Himself in your life in undeniable ways.

I pray you do that today.

Tomorrow, we will read 1 Kings 8-9.

Day 98: 1 Kings 8-9:
Solomon's Prayer and God's Promise

Today, we read 1 Kings 8-9, and here are my thoughts on these verses.

The Ark of the Covenant of God

Solomon has finished building the Temple, and he calls for the priests and Levites to bring in the Ark. (v 8:4) He places it between the cherubim and dedicates the Temple. (v 8:6)

We have seen wherever the Ark was, God was there with them. It is true here as the cloud and the glory of the Lord filled the Temple. (v 8:11) We are to worship God, not the Ark.

Men like to find relics and give them spiritual significance. Relics exist, including the famous Shroud of Turin, the spear of destiny, the crown of thorns, and pieces of the crucifixion cross.

The Ark was nothing more than a box. Even its contents, the stone tablets Moses brought down from Mt. Sinai, were just tablets. It is a symbol of people's obedience. They followed the directions given to Moses by God.

We read today of a tremendous offering Solomon and the people made to the Lord. "Twenty-two thousand cattle and a hundred and twenty thousand sheep and goats." Fourteen days of festivities.

God does not want our festivals (see Amos 5:21-24). He wants our hearts.

Solomon's Prayer

In 1 Kings 8:12, Solomon prays to the Lord. He opens with praise, acknowledging who God is and what He has done. God has been faithful to Israel and the house of David. He continues to be faithful to all His people.

We read in verses 8:17-19 that David wanted to build the Temple, but God had planned for Solomon to do it. The Lord always keeps His promises.

Then, after acknowledging how he was fulfilling the Lord's plan, he spreads his arms toward heaven and begins his Prayer of Dedication.

I would encourage you all to read this prayer more than once. There are specific parts, and we can validate each one throughout the scripture.

The consistent theme throughout is that terrible things happen in life. He has a list; we will have neighbors betray us, lose battles, have droughts, famines, and plagues.

Each one requires God to forgive us first, and then to restore us.

This tells me that all our misery results from sin being in the world. God promised this to Adam in the Garden of Eden. (Gen 3:17-19)

All of us sin and draw God's anger toward ourselves. (v 8:46)

God Promises Forgiveness

1 Kings 8:47 tells us that when a country reconsiders and repents, calling out to God. Confessing their sins to Him. God will hear our plea and uphold our cause. (v 8:49) He will forgive His people (v 8:50) and show us mercy.

He doesn't do this because of who we are. Though it states, He singled Israel out from all the nations. If He has called you to faith in Jesus, this is you too! We are nothing other than what God enables us to be.

It is because of who He is that He does this. His character is absolute and unwavering. He cannot be involved in sin. It is against His nature. When we persist in sin and refuse to repent, He permits us to follow our own path. (Rom 1:24)

This is the story we see in the Old Testament and New. His people sin, suffer, and repent. He is always faithful to forgive. God wants our fellowship. Sometimes, I don't even like being around myself. But God wants us to be close to Him.

God Answers Prayers

When we humble ourselves and repent, turning our hearts toward God and seeking His ways, He gives us the strength to follow His decrees and commands. (v 8:58) Then, we can celebrate and enjoy all the fellowship He offers.

Solomon prays this long prayer, and then God answers him. This is only the second time he hears God's voice.

God puts His Name, which is Jesus, in the Temple. It is not the place; it is the Name. His eyes will always be there, on His Name. (v 9:3)

We need to heed verse 9:4. Allow me to paraphrase: "As for us, if we walk before Him faithfully with integrity of heart as David did. Keeping His commands and obeying His laws. He will establish us forever."

However, we see Israel could not do this. Neither can we.

So, God, having promised never to forsake us, does the very best thing. He provides the atonement for our sins.

Jesus Christ, who knew no sin, took our sins onto Himself. On the cross, He paid the price we could never pay.

If we wish for God to judge us by our own life, and many people want to be "their own man," we need to look at the cross and realize that is the price we will have to pay.

We can only restore ourselves to a place of fellowship with God by giving Him Lordship over our lives, repenting of our pride, and trusting in His sacrifice.

The sacrifice of one hundred forty-two thousand heads of livestock could not keep the people of Israel from returning to their sins. Don't be foolish enough to think anything you can do will be strong enough.

Trust in Jesus today.

Tomorrow, we will read 1 Kings 10-11.

Day 99: 1 Kings 10-11: Wisdom and Idolatry Today, we will discuss 1 Kings 10-11.

Relationships

There was a time in my life when I was what one may call "a player." It was not by design. It just turned out that way.

I have always loved women. All women! My first wife was a couple of years younger than I was. My current (real) wife is nine years younger than me.

Both my second and third wives were older than I was. Age didn't matter.

I dated women of other races and cultures. My third wife was Jewish.

Having three older sisters and witnessing the deep hurt men inflicted upon them shaped my love for women. I have always had empathy. I never wanted to be like those men, even as a child.

Every woman I dated, I wanted to be monogamous with. I was always looking for a longterm, serious relationship. It just turned out that I would not meet my proper wife until I was thirty-two. We have been together now for half my life.

Chapter 10 begins with the Queen of Sheba. We learn in chapter 11 that Solomon had a thousand wives. We picked up one of his secrets in verse 10:2. When she came to talk to him, he listened! He heard all that was on her mind.

The problem I have with social media is the shallowness of conversations. We live in sound bites. We count people as "friends" whom we never know.

There are people who have the same relationship with the Lord. They know they don't want to go to hell, so they trust Him to be their Savior. But they never get to "know" Him.

God wants to have a personal relationship with each of us. We are His bride.

I don't know how Solomon kept up with a thousand wives.

God differs from us. He can have a deep, meaningful relationship with billions of people. Unlike us, He faces no limitations.

Leadership

Solomon's wisdom and wealth impressed the Queen of Sheba. She felt this way because he had taken the time to hear all that was in her heart.

God has far more riches and much greater wisdom. We learn this when we take the time to talk to Him. He is a superb listener and wants us to tell Him all that is in our hearts.

According to an article I read online, the average length of a man's prayer is ninety-seven seconds.[4] Although people may accuse women of talking too much, their average prayer is only seventy-six seconds.

We assume that God already knows everything, which is true. (Heb 4:13) But think about your relationship with your children. Just because you know they are going through something, don't you still want them to tell you about it?

The Queen of Sheba was like us. Until she sat down with Solomon and poured her heart out to him, she didn't believe the reports she had heard about his wisdom. (v 10:7)

In verse 10:9, we learn the responsibility of leadership. She says to Solomon, "Because of the Lord's eternal love for Israel, he has made you king to maintain justice and righteousness." (NIV)

Consequences

Over the last few decades in America, we have forgotten this. We have focused on equality instead of justice.

Equality suggests everyone deserves the same reward. Being fast enough to win the race shouldn't mean you get the bigger prize.

Justice would differ. It says each of us deserves what we have earned.

We don't want justice because the wage of sin is death! (Rom 6:23) We want mercy.

To gain mercy, we need righteousness. None of us are righteous, not one. (Rom 3:10)

God wants us to bring this to Him. To talk about, or confess, that we are not righteous.

He will take our sinfulness and replace it with His righteousness. (2 Cor. 5:21)

We see the reasons Solomon received God's punishment in chapter 11. God tells him not to intermarry with women from other countries. They would bring their gods. While adept at hearing women's concerns, his spiritual attentiveness was lacking. Because of this, he did not walk in the footsteps of David. Therefore, God tore Israel apart and took it from his son. He left a remnant from which He provided Jesus. God's mercies never fail.

We may want justice from our leaders. From God, we need mercy.

Is God your leader? Have you sought His righteousness? He is waiting to hear from you.

Tomorrow, we will read 1 Kings 12-14.

Day 100: 1 Kings 12-14: The Kingdom Divided

This is our 100th day of reading the Bible, and things are about to get hot for Israel in 1 Kings 12-14.

Failed Leadership

David had united the twelve tribes of Israel, but because of Solomon's idolatry, God was about to split the kingdom up.

Rehoboam was David's grandson and ruled over Judah, but the ten tribes of Israel had made Jeroboam, son of Nebat, their king. Neither of these men walked with the Lord.

The people were about to make Rehoboam their king, (v 12:1) but he faced a challenge because they demanded better conditions. This is like a modern-day labor dispute or strike. Jeroboam asks Rehoboam to require less of them. (v 12:10)

Rehoboam received advice from the elders, (v 12:13) but he rejected it. He prefers to follow the advice of his younger friends.

Like Pharoah increasing the burden on the Israelites in Egypt, Rehoboam decides the best way to deal with the complaining is to pile on. He increases the demands, and the people revolt.

The interesting thing about the situation is God orchestrated it. (12:15) This was from the

Lord and part of His plan. For this reason, there was a separation between the house of David, Judah, and later the followers of Jesus, and the rest of Israel. (v 12:19)

Then the word of God comes to Shemaiah, saying the two groups should not fight with each other. (v 12:24)

Idolatry

Jeroboam tries to win the people over by letting them worship idols in the high places. He appointed his own priests instead of the Levites. (v 12:31)

Then he throws a party for everyone to celebrate. (v 12:32)

Nothing like a festival to make everyone happy. While they rejoiced, God's displeasure was palpable. He has a prophet calling Jeroboam out for his wickedness.

He tells him that Josiah will sit on David's throne.

Jeroboam tries to stop the prophet, but God makes his hand shrivel up. (v 13:4)

This is my concern for America. Solomon did not listen and married women from foreign countries and embraced their idols. (chapter 11) This splits the country.

Our country is more divided than I remember in my lifetime.

There was a similar chasm in the days leading up to the Civil War. The press and other leaders were against Abraham Lincoln.[5]

Lincoln stayed the course, but he humbled himself and went into the Oval Office, dropped to his knees, and prayed for God's intervention.[6]

If President Trump will do likewise, we can reunite and prosper.

Jeroboam and Rehoboam did not take that path. They sat up in high places, made golden calves, and let the people commit idolatry.

They put on a good show. King Jeroboam asked the man of God to intercede for him. God restores Jeroboam's hand because of his intercession. This does not change the course of his actions. (v 13:33)

Consequences

It is not only the responsibility of leaders. They trick the man of God into eating and drinking in the land God had warned him against. Because of this, a lion eats him.

The prophet tells Jeroboam's wife that when she walks into her city, her son will die. (v 14:12) What mother would still return to that city? She doesn't take the word to heart, and when she returns, her child dies. (v 14:17)

The people of Israel and Judah did not listen. The kings refused to change their ways. Their sins surpassed those of their predecessors, provoking greater divine wrath. (v 14:22)

Repentance

People carried off the temple treasures to Egypt (v 14:26) because of their refusal to repent. The Israelites did not find peace. (v 14:30)

We will face a similar fate if each of us, as individuals, as people of God, and as leaders in our nation, do not repent and seek the Lord.

The word of God is useful for teaching, rebuking, correcting, and training in righteousness.

(2 Tim 3:16-17)

We must learn from what happened to them and correct our path. Time is running out!

Tomorrow, we will read 1 Kings 15-17.

Day 101: 1 Kings 15-17:
Righteousness and Rebellion

Good morning. I hope you are all ready for a roller coaster ride. Today, we read 1 Kings 15-17.

Set The Example

We had established in 1 Sam 13:14 that David was a man after God's own heart. He was not perfect, and neither will we be. David was as flawed as any of us. Jesus set the bar we should all strive for.

Chapter 15 begins by looking at Jeroboam and how he committed all the sins his father had done before him. (v 15:3)

I have done foolish and sinful things in my life. I have told some of them to my son, as a cautionary tale. Others I have not mentioned because I didn't want to glamorize the sin.

God is so faithful to David, even with his sins, that for his sake, he continues to protect Israel, and three thousand years later, they persist.

That is the role model we should be. Not claiming perfection, our kids will not buy it anyway, but showing that steadfast love for God. Establishing God as our priority and letting our children see that.

Even when we do this, it is no guarantee. Jeroboam did not walk with the Lord the way his father had. David had already established the standard.

When Asa comes along, we see he follows David's example (v 11) in Judah.

Sin Increases

Meanwhile, in Israel Nadab, is doing the evil his father had done. He's killing off families and worshipping idols. God is not pleased with him. (v 30)

He only reigns for two years, and then Baasha comes along and does worse things.

We have seen in our times how sin has increased. As a child of the sixties, I learned the value of obedience and duty. We were latchkey kids whose parents both had to work. After we finished our homework when we got home from school, then went out to play.

If we didn't, we would face consequences, including spanking, going to bed without supper, grounding, and losing privileges. My parents never sent me to a timeout.

People may claim this behavior harms our self-esteem. I would be a narcissist if I had any more self-esteem. What it did was build character. I stopped doing wrong because I knew it was not in my best interest.

We see how Baasha followed the ways of Jeroboam.

Elah comes along and only rules for two years.

Next comes Zimri, who kills Baasha and his whole family (v 11) because of the sins of Elah and Baasha. Zimri only reigns for a week (v 15) before he sets fire to the citadel and dies in the fire.

We then see early signs of democracy in Omri and Tibni opposing each other. The one with the most support becomes the ruler. But Omri sinned more than all those before him. (v 25)

It continues to escalate as Ahab, his son, does evil more than any of those before him. (v 30) They were setting up altars for Baal.

This is the nature of sin. Sin wants to be our master. If you steal a cookie, you cover it by lying. People catch you lying, you get in a fight. It always ratchets up.

God Provides

But then, in chapter 17, we meet Elijah, one of the great prophets.

God is tired of escalating sin. He's about to bring the people back to Himself.

Then he sends a prophet to warn him of the coming 3-year drought. (v 17:1) Even in the toughest of times, God provides for his servant.

I have seen how birds feed their young, so I am not sure if I want ravens to bring me bread and meat. But if that is God's plan, I would be fine with it.

Then he has Elijah help this poor woman who is waiting for her and her son to die. They have so little, all they can do is wait for the inevitable. God intervenes, as He has in my life, and makes what she has last.

There is more than one way God can provide for us. Because I worked in an industry that rewarded my performance, sometimes I would have a great quarter and know that my bonus check was going to be larger.

This was not for my enjoyment because I would have a car problem or an AC unit in my house would burn out. The purpose of the blessing was to enable me to bless the mechanic or technician.

I have everything I need, so I was fine with that. This taught me not to get excited and run out and buy things, thinking I was about to have a windfall.

The other way is without a change in my income, or even with a drop, I would go months, even years, with no unexpected expenses. God knew my income and made it cover my needs.

This is what He does for this woman. Her oil and flour never run out while she is with Elijah.

Our Biggest Need

There is one need only God can provide.

This woman is faithful, but her only child gets sick and dies.

Sometimes dreadful things happen, even to believers. The Bible does not tell us having faith will make all our problems go away.

The opposite is true. Jesus tells us in John 16:33 that in this world, we will have troubles.

Then Elijah prays and stretches himself out. This may have been an odd ritual; I think it is symbolic of stretching our faith. He does it three times, not giving up.

Elijah restores the boy's life. He lives, just as Jesus lived when He rose from the grave.

We all need to have this life. He will give you that same gift if you stretch your faith to believe in Him.

This doesn't start after we have died, like with the boy. At that point, it is too late.

The life Jesus gives us manifests itself the moment we trust in Jesus.

"Confess with your mouth that Jesus is Lord, and you will be saved." (Rom 10:9, NIV) Tomorrow, we will read 1 Kings 18-20.

Day 102: 1 Kings 18-20: Elijah's Courage, Jezebel's Wrath

I hope you are enjoying your time with your loved ones. Today, we are going to discuss what we have read in 1 Kings 18-20.

These are exciting chapters, and it is hard to not write about Elijah and the prophets of Baal. It is such a comical yet tragic scene. I'm assuming you have heard that story, and I am sure I will write more about it myself in the future. That is the story that most people preach from these chapters. I want to look at something different.

Listen

We open today with Elijah in hiding, and God telling him to show himself to Ahab. Wouldn't we all like getting explicit instructions from God? I pray for God's will. Then, I read the scriptures and seek understanding. Trying to be still so I can hear the Holy Spirit's guidance.

I often feel immobilized. Stuck doing nothing because I am not sure what God wants me to do.

Does God not answer us? Or are we not getting the answer we want?

Are we hearing God, but we don't like or trust the message?

Have you ever said, "I know I should have done this years ago, but…" and we have an extensive list of excuses.

Elijah had a great ear to hear the Lord. God tells him to go present himself to Ahab. Ahab has been seeking him for years, wanting to kill him. (v 18:1)

He goes to Obadiah, and he doesn't want to get involved because it will mean death for him too! (v 18:9) The difference between us and Elijah is he did what God told him. Even though he didn't like the idea.

Ahab calls him a troubler of Israel. (v 18:17)

In antiquity, Plutarch, Sophocles, and later Shakespeare, all taught not to blame the messenger.

Ahab felt the drought Elijah had warned them was coming because their idolatry was his fault.

We All Must Choose

Even when we don't make a choice, we have made a choice. We chose not to make a choice.

I was once an atheist. I thought I believed in nothing. What I believed in was my belief system, which was flawed.

Elijah calls out the nine hundred prophets of Baal and Asherah and asks the people how long they're just going to stand there and not make a choice.

Alexander Hamilton said, "Those who stand for nothing will fall for anything."[7]

Like us, at the end of verse 18:21 – "the people said nothing." (NIV)

Then, we have the famous scene where Elijah taunts the prophets. After they cannot produce results, he stacks the odds against himself. He knows nothing is impossible for God.

From here, he goes to the mountaintop to watch for a change in the weather.

There have been times I knew what God wanted me to do. So, I did it. Then, nothing happened.

We have a loved one who is sick, so we pray for them, and they don't improve.

When we're out of work, we pray and continue to fill out applications, but the bills keep coming, and there are still no job offers.

I've experienced this countless times. Wondering if my prayers are bouncing off the ceiling while I lie in bed pouring my heart out.

Elijah's servant keeps looking for the change. He is doing so because his master is telling him to "Go back." (v 18:43)

When Jesus is your Lord, He is your master. We should not be weary when He tells us to go back. Instead, we need to keep faith.

Discouragement

After it rains, even when God had provided, Jezebel still wants Elijah executed. He runs for his life. (v 19:3)

At work, I will complete a task and research the results and show how successful I was in delivering what the teams needed. In my mind, I used to fantasize that I would get a raise, no raise. An award? No award. Will I get a mention in the bulletin or a pat on the head? No, instead, someone has a complaint. We've all been there.

Elijah sits under a bush, giving up. He wishes God would just pull him from the starting lineup. (v 19:4) What more could he do?

He hides in a cave, and then God asks, "What are you doing here?" (v 19:9)

In a comparable situation, Jesus asked the men in the boat, "Where is your faith?" (Luke 8:25)

In a scene more violent than the Sea of Galilee, Elijah stands on Mt. Carmel as God tears the mountain apart. The key word is he stands; he does not flee.

God isn't in the noise and tumultuous activity around him. He is in the whisper.

Which leads us back to the opening question. Is it that God isn't answering or that we aren't hearing?

Is there too much noise around us?

Are we expecting a thundering voice, and He is answering in our hearts?

Tomorrow, we will read 1 Kings 21-22.

Day 103: 1 Kings 21-22: Desire, Deceit, and Discernment

I hope you take the time to contemplate the bravery and compassion of Jesus Christ. Jesus foresaw his own crucifixion. (Matt 16:21-23) Even though He knew this, and that we would be sinners, (Rom 5:8) He still entered Jerusalem with festivities. There was no attempt to slip into town unnoticed.

Today, we finish looking at 1 Kings. The final two chapters focus on three topics: Desire, Deceit, and Discernment.

Desire

King Ahab had his palace. Servants addressed his needs and provided food for him. Through his inheritance, he had land, and all public land was his.

He saw Naboth had a nice vineyard, and it was close to his palace. His desire for the land caused him to devise a scheme to get it.

Coveting is a sin. When we covet what someone else has, it becomes an obsession. We conceive ways to get what they have.

This can involve getting others to help us plan (v 21:6) how to bring this to fruition.

We may even get others to help execute the plans. (v 21:13)

Sin always escalates. Therefore, coveting becomes deception, which leads to murder.

Coveting is an internal emotion. God knows our hearts. (Jer 17:10)

People may think, what harm is there in wanting what someone else has? This is the first step in disobeying God.

Deception

When you get outside of His will, the next step is easier. Lying, in this case, telling someone else to bear false witness and claim "Naboth cursed both God and the king" (v 21:13) may seem insignificant.

I always instructed my son he would get into more trouble for lying about something he did than he would for whatever the deed was. The only spanking I ever gave him was for lying. When someone lies to you, they lose trust. This damages relationships.

Here the lie leads to stoning and the theft of the property. (v 21:19)

We may wield power to escape earthly retribution, but God's judgment is inescapable.

Ahab humbles himself before God and avoids the immediate punishment. But his son will have to deal with those consequences. (v 21:29)

As we move into chapter 22, peace has existed for three years between Aram and Israel. (v 22:1) Because of coveting, greed, or boredom, the kings of Israel and Judah decide to fight Ramoth Gilead. We don't have reason to believe they needed the land or what it contained. There was no sign of provocation of any kind.

Jehoshaphat has the discretion to first seek the Lord before going into battle. (v 22:5) We should always see God's will in all we do. This has been a practice at our house for decades. I will not say we are perfect in following this practice. When we are planning on a large purchase or a life-changing move, like when to retire, we always pray about it.

The problem is when it seems like a day-to-day decision: do I buy this pair of shoes? What program should we binge on Netflix tonight? We leave God out of the conversation.

Assuming He is too busy to bother Him with such mundane things.

God loves us and wants to be a part of all our decisions. By always seeking Him, we avoid letting things into our lives that shouldn't be there.

We watch a TV show and then have images of evil in our hearts. Those shoes become an obsession and an idol. Therefore, we must always seek God first in all we do. (Matt 6:33)

Discernment

These kings seek God, but they don't want an answer which opposed their plans. They call on the four hundred false prophets who will lie and tell them what they want to hear.

People choose religions and churches in this same way. If a pastor is always preaching about sin, they choose the one who only preaches on hope. A Gospel that does not address sin is not the true Gospel of Jesus Christ. (1 John 1:8)

Ahab didn't want to hear from Micaiah because he didn't like the truth. (v 22:18) True to form, Micaiah foretells Ahab's death, which happens in verse 22:35.

We must seek God's direction, and then we must heed the advice. When we don't, the circumstances can be fatal.

Too many times, even when we prayed first, we still went with our original plan. When it failed, we could only blame ourselves. If we thought God was too busy to bother him with minor aspects of our lives, how do we expect Him to have time to clean up our messes?

Tomorrow, we will read 2 Kings 1-4.

Conclusion of 1 Kings

Now that you have read the eleventh book of the Bible, take a moment to reflect. How have the events in 1 Kings mirrored lessons in your own life? Do you feel yourself growing in knowledge? Are you also growing in faith?

For fun, here are five questions I want you to answer (I will post some brief answers at the back of the book).

1. What is the significance of David's defeat of Goliath?
2. Who was Solomon, and what was his role in 1 Kings?
3. What is the significance of the building of Solomon's Temple?
4. What was the significance of Solomon's wisdom?
5. How did Solomon's reign differ from David's?

Chapter 11: Footnotes

1. Unless otherwise noted, scriptural references and commentary regarding David's wives are based on the author's own biblical interpretation.

2. **2.** Stephanie Kramer, "Polygamy is Rare Around the World and Mostly Confined to a Few Regions," *Pew Research Center*, December 7, 2020, https://www.pewresearch.org/short-reads/2020/12/07/polygamy-is-rare-around-the-world-and-mostly-confined-to-a-few-regions/.

3. **3.** *The Wizard of Oz*, directed by Victor Fleming, et al. (Metro-Goldwyn-Mayer, 1939).

4. "General Conference Prayer Length," *Zelophehad's Daughters* (blog), July 13, 2020, https://zelophehadsdaughters.com/2020/07/13/general-conference-prayer-length/.

5. Harold Holzer, *Lincoln and the Power of the Press: The War for Public Opinion* (New York: Simon & Schuster, 2014), 237–245.

6. Abraham Lincoln, quoted in William J. Federer, *America's God and Country: Encyclopedia of Quotations* (Coppell, TX: Fame Publishing, 2000), 370.

7. Alexander Hamilton, in a letter quoted in John C. Fitzpatrick, *The Spirit of the American Revolution as Revealed in the Public Statements of Political Leaders of the Period* (Washington, D.C.: U.S. Government Printing Office, 1924), 92.

8. Kendrick Onganya, "How Many Wives Did David Have in the Bible?" *GodsVerse.org*, September 12, 2023, https://godsverse.org/how-many-wives-did-david-have-in-the-bible/.

9. **Lincoln and Opposition from the Press and Political Leaders** Holzer, Harold. *Lincoln and the Power of the Press: The War for Public Opinion.* New York: Simon & Schuster, 2014.

10. **Lincoln's Prayer for Divine Intervention** Bowling, Karen. "Celebrating President's Day With 5 Prayers From the Oval Office." *Nebraska Family Alliance*, February 20, 2017. https://nebraskafamilyalliance.org/celebrating-presidents-day/..

11. **Eadie, Gordon A.** "The Over-All Mental-Health Needs of the Industrial Plant, with Special Reference to War Veterans." *Mental Hygiene* 29, no. 1 (January 1945): 101–109.

Chapter 12:
2 KINGS

Day 104: 2 Kings 1-4: Integrity in Life

Today, we will begin another book, 2 Kings, reading the first four chapters.

Elijah and Elisha have always been two of my favorite prophets. We will discuss them both.

First, we should contemplate the question the king asks in 2 Kings 1:7, "What kind of man was it who came to meet you?"

Based on the physical description and message relayed, he knew it was Elijah.

Integrity

A mark of integrity is that people should know who you are in any circumstance. This was not always something I could claim. People I worked with knew a serious, somber guy. My family knew a goofball with a strange sense of humor. Other people knew me as an athlete or as a musician.

I was always a chameleon of sorts. In high school, I drove a hotrod car. People thought of me as a motorhead. My after-school job aided this reputation. I worked at a gas station doing oil changes and tune-ups. Others knew I was a musician and that my friends were "stoners." I didn't enjoy marijuana, but it didn't bother me to be around them. Few knew I was on the honor roll and would get straight As. Those that did weren't familiar with my friends. I played sports but had few friends on the football team. On game days, I wore my jersey, and it always shocked people I owned one.

In "The Breakfast Club",[1] there is a narration at the end. They realize that although people see them each as a specific thing, the truth is they all had all those characteristics.

Being Christlike

Later in life, when I ran into someone from work with my family, I wasn't sure which way to act. Thom at church differed from who he was at the office. Both differed from the dad my son knew.

We run into this complexity of the human condition when we try to understand the Trinity. How could God the Father be Jesus the Son and the Holy Spirit? I have no problem with this, having been many, yet one, myself.

Since becoming a Christian, I have tried to be the same person in all situations. It has freed me from confusion about how to act in those awkward times.

My goal is that people never see me, or how I act. I hope they only see Jesus and how He acts, through me. He loves; He forgives. If you are sinning, He will call you out on it and even take whips and drive you from the temple if necessary.

Foreshadowing

This identity confusion is common. Remember, in Mark 8:27-29, Jesus asks his disciples, "Who do people say I am?" They replied, "Some say John the Baptist; others say Elijah; and still others, one of the prophets."

Why would they say He was Elijah or one of the prophets? We will see the answer in today's verses.

After we ponder that question about the prophet, we see this scene where the king sends three captains and their fifty men to a cave. Elijah is in the cave. God protects him by sending a fire to consume the first two groups. When you follow the world instead of God, there are consequences.

Replicating Miracles

The third captain knew his fate and asked for mercy. He confesses that there is only one God in Israel. God gives him grace.

People ask Elisha if he knows the Lord will take Elijah that day. (v 2:3 and 2:5) As Christians, we celebrate Easter. We know Jesus will die. He went to the cross to pay the debt we owe. Elisha did not want to fixate on the knowledge he was about to lose his master. We should acknowledge the crucifixion so that we understand the price He paid.

Easter is not about Jesus' death; it is about His resurrection. He defeated death for us. He will resurrect us with him. (Rom 6:5-6)

The other thing to know is how Elijah replicates the miracle of Moses and Joshua, proving he has the strength of God with him. He stops the Jordan River so the two men can cross on dry ground. (v 2:14) Elisha takes his cloak and does the same thing.

Jesus performed the miracles of God by trusting in the Lord for the power. He quoted the scripture and glorified the Father. We are to take that same scripture and do likewise. As Elisha used the cloak of Elijah, we are to use the Word of God. By doing so, we can do miracles, too.

An example is that Elisha purifies the water by the power of God. Jesus turns water into wine with that same power. These verses all foreshadow the work Jesus will do.

Elisha feeding a hundred men with twenty loaves of barley bread was foretelling when Jesus would feed five thousand men and their families with five loaves and have baskets full left over. (told in all four gospels, including Luke 9:10-17)

The story recorded in 2 Kings 3:27-28, where the king offered his son as a sacrifice, is a foreshadowing of God giving His only son for our salvation.

We read of Elisha raising the Shunammite woman's son from the dead. It started with God giving them a son, echoing when Sarah and Abram had Isaac at an old age.

Let us all remember these are not tall tales or legends. This is the history of these people. Historians outside of the Bible have corroborated much, and archeologists continue to find other proof. We can know these things happened and trust that the Bible is true.

Have you placed your faith in this hope?

Tomorrow, we will read 2 Kings 5-7.

Day 105: 2 Kings 5-7: Faith, Pride and God's Judgment

It's never fun to pay taxes, but I try to focus on God and not worry about money. It isn't always easy to do. Jesus tells us we can't serve God and money. (Matt 6:24) Whenever I focus on finances, I become anxious and worry if I have enough. By keeping my eyes on Jesus, I never worry, and I always have enough.

God can meet all our needs. (Phil 4:19)

Today, we'll examine chapters 5–7 of 2 Kings.

Naaman's Bath

We begin by looking at Naaman. The text describes him as a great man in the sight of his master. (v 5:1) I have one master, Jesus Christ. There's no desire for Him to see me as a great man, only a loyal servant. I hope that my lack of greatness magnifies His grandeur.

For Naaman, he was great because the Lord had given victory to Aram through him. (v 5:1) He was a vessel. You become a vessel by submitting to God and seeking His will instead of your own. Allowing the Holy Spirit to fill you.

Even prominent men have problems. Naaman had leprosy. This wasn't a minor issue. In those days, it was a death sentence. Because of it being contagious, they put you out of camp. Others would cast you out and reject you.

Elisha told him that for healing, he needed to bathe seven times in the Jordan River. (v 5:10) He took offense to this because he expected something more spectacular than taking a bath. (v 5:11)

Tempering Expectations

We like to project our expectations on God. My disability began thirty-nine years ago. I had been involved in a vehicle rollover.

In September of 2023, I preached a sermon on miracles. My legs had been gaining strength while collaborating with a physical therapist. I felt God telling me I was going to walk again. I know this is true. Whether here on earth or in heaven, I will walk again.

The point of the sermon, however, was that I, this wretched sinner, have that promise of heaven because He saved me. God forgave my sins, and they no longer hold me back.

Think of a person with paraplegia who experiences a miracle. Picture them jumping out of their wheelchair, doing somersaults, and landing a backflip. Why wouldn't God make it spectacular so that everyone could see and know it was an act of divine healing?

Sometimes, God does things this way, like with the paralytic at the pool in John 5:1–9.

Usually, God stays away from the parlor tricks. He's God. He doesn't need to put on a show. We should believe in Him by faith. Faith is believing without seeing. (Heb 11:1)

Challenge Yourself

Naaman's servant challenges his thinking about his response. (v 5:13) Pride can prevent us from hearing those who serve us. Naaman was great because he listened to his subordinates.

We assume because of our position in society, we're greater. Everyone is equal, but there are separate roles that need to be filled. Each of us has a part to play in the grand scheme of things.

Sometimes, we think we can change our station. Nothing tells me Gehazi had this intention when he went out and took payment from Naaman. He may have thought he could get away with it.

Elisha was in communion with God. The Lord is watching everything we do. Elisha learned of Gehazi's actions, uncovering his secret.

God unveils all our actions. (Luke 8:17)

Owning Our Problems

Naaman's leprosy afflicts Gehazi because of his transgression.

Our troubles in life are often trials that God gives us to develop character. Others are problems we bring on to ourselves. Actions have consequences.

In chapter six, we see another foreshadowing of Jesus. Elisha makes the ax-head float. (v 6:6) This reminds me of Jesus walking on water. (Mark 6:45–52)

Later in this chapter, we receive the assurance that we're never alone. In verse 6:17, Elisha prays for God to open his eyes. The servant realizes they are surrounded by hills full of horses and chariots.

If Jesus had summoned his angel army, they could have prevented his crucifixion. They could have wiped out all the Roman soldiers and the Jews who condemned Him.

Grace

He knew we'd only have salvation if He paid the price we owed. His sacrifice was the only thing that saved us. We should be eternally grateful. John 10:18 tells us that no one took Jesus' life; He laid it down. It was His gift to us.

Our sinful nature makes us all evil, every one of us. An example of this is in 2 Kings 6:21. "When the king of Israel saw them, he asked Elisha, "Shall I kill them, my father? Shall I kill them?" (NIV) You can hear the bloodlust in his voice.

I hear a child asking for a piece of candy located near the cash register at the grocery store. "Can I have a piece, Momma? Can I, have it?"

Elisha tells the king, no. Instead, foreshadowing Jesus' teaching from the sermon on the mount, he tells them to love their enemies and do good to them. (Matt 5:44) Elisha tells the king to give them food and water.

Because he takes this action, they stop raiding Israel's territory. (v 6:23) We can have peace if we follow God's commands.

Are you impetuous? Eagerly seeking your will instead of God's?

Does peace elude you?

I urge you to consider the cross and think of what God gave up for you.

Tomorrow, we will read 2 Kings 8-10.

Day 106: 2 Kings 8-10:
Heroes, Villains, and Choices

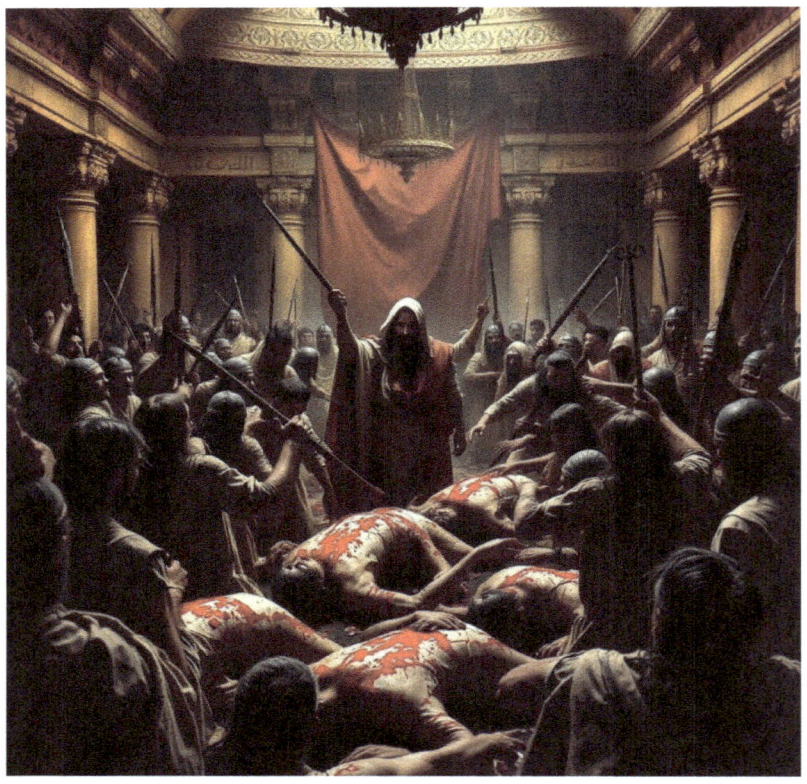

Good morning. I hope this day finds you in good spirits. Today, we will read 2 Kings 8-10.

Sometimes, it is hard to decide if someone is a hero or a villain. People will show you a smile while hiding a dagger behind their back. Therefore, we must always be cautious.

The Woman's Wisdom

Chapter 8's opening verses reintroduce the Shunammite woman whose son was raised from the dead, by Elisha.

I like Matthew Henry's comment on this verse. He states, "It is well to foresee an evil, and wisdom, when we foresee it, to hide ourselves if we lawfully may do so."[2]

My sphere of influence is small. To reach more people with the Gospel, I have been using social media.

God has put me in a unique mission field. He didn't send me to a foreign land, physically. Instead, He has provided a way for me to reach all lands digitally. This blessing of the modern age requires careful handling.

A friend at our church is a member of our police force's Cyber Crimes Unit. She has discussed how to protect yourself and exposed the dangers of the technology we all use.

Therefore, I have a policy. I will follow and befriend most people on all the platforms I use. There are people I'm developing a genuine connection with.

I will not, however, leave those platforms to have "private conversations" on the apps that have higher levels of encryption. People use those apps to share inappropriate content or request personal information.

As a teenager, I threw large parties. I had figured out how to make a profit by charging a cover charge. We had three enormous parties in the desert. The next one was at a friend's house in town. Taking three hundred dollars at the door, we made a nice profit. The beer we bought only cost us around one hundred and fifty dollars. I was always looking for business opportunities in life.

Someone put something into the drink of my best friend's girlfriend. I was sober, so I drove her to the hospital.

We could blame the person who did that. They are culpable. This does not change the fact that we are also responsible. If we had not been at that party, they could not have drugged her. While we were with her at the hospital, the police responded to a call about the party and arrested or sent everyone else home. They got in trouble because of where they were. If they hadn't been present, the police would not have arrested them.

Because we were not there when the police arrived, we escaped punishment. I am not telling you this as a justification for having the party. This is only an example of how we assume risk when we place ourselves in certain situations.

Staying out of those isolated areas will keep me from seeing inappropriate material.

Elisha told this woman, who had shown him kindness, to leave Israel because a famine was coming. She left and avoided suffering.

Joram's Downfall and Jehu's Rise

When she returned, there was no loss. The king, Joram, had all her land restored, including the profit it had earned.

Because of his mother Jezebel's witchcraft, Joram would die at the hand of Jehu. (v 9:24) If he had not met him in battle, this would not have happened.

Responsibility and Avoiding Danger

Jehu then invites all the worshippers of Baal to an event. They all come thinking they can revel in their idolatry. Because they are all in the same place, it is possible to have them all executed at once. They would not have died if they were not there?

We always want to blame circumstances, but we need to take responsibility.

People who cheat on their partner will claim they were at a friend's house. They say one thing led to another, and they started fooling around with each other. They will claim they didn't mean for it to happen.

Adultery is never an accident. It would not have happened if they had not been alone with each other in that situation.

We taught our son that nothing good ever happens after midnight. If he was out with friends, he needed to avoid the temptation to go to the next destination. When his friends would tell him how they had gotten into trouble, he could know he wasn't among them.

Removing yourself from a situation, or better yet not putting yourself into it at all, is your best defense.

The worshippers of Baal should not have been part of that culture. Even though they were, they could have escaped death had they not gone to the event.

We all sin (Rom 3:23). Therefore, we have all put ourselves into a situation where we deserve punishment for those sins. The only way to avoid that punishment is to remove ourselves from that place.

Jesus has paid the price for us to excuse ourselves before the retribution comes. We need to look at our situation and realize it is time to remove ourselves before the punishment comes.

Hebrews 9:27 teaches that people are destined to die once and then face judgment. (NIV) What is happening in your life that you know, in your heart, you should not be a part of?

Ask the Lord, and He will deliver you from that sin.

Tomorrow, we will read 2 Kings 11-14.

Day 107: 2 Kings 11-14: Restoring a Fallen Kingdom

Today, we will read 2 Kings 11-14.

Reading these chapters each day has created in me a desire to research and author a book with more depth about each of the kings. That is not the purpose of this devotional; it is to share enough details to help you all enjoy reading the Bible. You have made it a great distance already. It only gets better!

A Righteous King

As chapter 11 begins, it is not a king but a queen that rules Israel. Athaliah was viscous. The death of her son, Ahaziah, broke her heart, and she ruled with a vengeance.

They hid Joash, his nephew like they hid Moses from Pharaoh. Joseph will also hide Jesus from Herod as a baby. It is important to notice patterns in scripture.

We have read about many evil kings. There are forty-two kings described as rulers in Israel and Judah in the Old Testament. Only five were good. Five righteous kings in four hundred years.

This makes Joash one of the few. Though only seven years old, when he becomes king, (v 11:21) he does what is right in the eyes of the Lord. (v 12:2) But the next verse informs us they did not remove the high places.

My concern for America and President Trump is that we try to make things better, by human standards, without making them right in the eyes of God. It is not enough that we overturn Roe v Wade. We need to help people proactively understand the evil of abortion. Only God can change their hearts.

People get offended, so we tolerate their sins. Freedom can become an idol. It is important to protect liberty. We can't tolerate sin. When faced with what is lawful by man and what is Godly, we must choose God.

Joash did the right things, but he left the high places. The people continued to offer their evil sacrifices.

Restoring the Temple

People will give to a cause they believe in. As mentioned, our church is in a building program. It becomes discouraging when people give, and nothing moves forward. Sometimes, there is activity, but it is not visible.

Cappadocia, Turkey, shows how we can protect hidden things.[3] Under the mountain, there is an entire ecosystem that thrived in ancient times.

Joash had ordered they rebuild the temple. Twenty-three years later, priests were still collecting money, but repairs were not happening. We can get bogged down in planning. The priests were trying to do the repairs themselves. God gives each person unique skills and gifts. If we try to do work we're not meant for, it will distract us from our own objectives. We lose efficiency.

With the money, King Joash hired skilled workers to make the repairs.

Embrace Honesty

According to 2 Kings 12:15, "They acted with complete honesty." Honesty is a quality lacking in our culture. We have become accustomed to politicians and reporters lying to us. Lying is Satan's native language. He lied to Eve in the garden. (Gen 3:4) He is the father of lies. (John 8:44) When we tolerate lies, we are giving Satan a foothold, which we should not do. (Eph 4:27-29)

Our culture has made lying a high place. We defend a person's right to claim an identity, race, or gender, which is not real. This is where we need to not only change laws but educate people on the dangers of not returning to God.

Joash deviated from God's will. God will not tolerate this from a leader. Therefore, his officials assassinated him. (v 12:20)

This allowed another evil king to replace him, Ahaziah. He allowed idolatry to proliferate. (v 13:6)

Touched by the Lord

In 2 Kings 13:20, Elisha dies.

The following verse tells of a dead man thrown into Elisha's tomb. Touching the bones resurrected him. This is another miracle foreshadowing Jesus. He replicates so many of Elijah and Elisha's miracles, but always much larger. Jesus did not stay in his tomb, as Elisha had. We are not thrown into it either.

The apostle Thomas needed to touch Jesus to believe. (John 20:24-29) We just need Jesus to touch our hearts so that we have faith. Faith is believing without seeing. (Heb 11:1) Has Jesus touched you?

When you think of what He went through on Calvary, does your heart cry out?

No one can throw you into the bones of Jesus. They aren't in his tomb. Only you can throw yourself into Him and seek His mercy.

Tomorrow, we will read 2 Kings 15-17.

Day 108: 2 Kings 15-17: Leadership, Idolatry, and the Ultimate Kingship of Jesus

Today, I want to talk about Good Friday. That term used to confuse me.

As an atheist, I understood it referred to Jesus' crucifixion day. Could this be something positive? It made me wonder what was wrong with Christians that they considered this good. As a believer, I now understand. If He had not died for me, I could not rise with Him.

Today, we will read 2 Kings 15-18.

Righteous Kings

We meet another king who started out doing what was right in the eyes of God named Azariah. (v 15:3) Just a little older than Joash when he became king, he was sixteen.

At sixteen, I went to school, worked in a fast-food restaurant and later at a gas station, and was learning to date girls. My biggest concern was keeping my grades up and my car running. I did not know what I wanted to do with my life.

Azariah was ruling God's chosen people. He would do so for fifty-two years. That is hard to comprehend.

I have been living with a disability for thirty-nine years. Azariah lived with leprosy for his whole life. (v 15:5) This meant he lived in isolation.

We learn three things about leadership: you don't have to be old, being a leader won't protect you from troubles, and you don't even need to be popular.

Azariah did not, however, remove the high places. He did what was right but let the people have their sins. This would be the downfall of Israel. King Azariah also goes by the name Uzziah. The influence of the people overtook him, and he worshipped Baal.

When he died, Jotham would become another one of Judah's righteous kings. (v 15:34)

Reign of Evil

Meanwhile, there was a line of evil kings in Israel. One was Menahem, who would tax wealthy people to pay tribute to the Assyrians. Instead of trusting in the Lord for protection, he bowed to Tiglath-Pileser III and invited the Assyrians and their gods into Israel. This would end up creating the oppression which we will read about in the book of Isaiah.

Then, we hear about Pekahiah. What was interesting to me about this little-known king is the sentence in 15:26. "The other events of Pekahiah's reign, and all he did, are written in the book of the annals of the kings of Israel." (NIV)

With all the other kings, it always asks, "Are they not written in the book...." (v 15: 21) Why is this different only for Pekahiah? I don't have an answer; therefore, we must read our Bibles closely. Find anomalies and then investigate them. One day, I will have an explanation for this one.

Even with the righteous king Jotham, we read he does not remove the high places. When you let the devil have a foothold, he will make his presence known.

While God never gives up on Israel, He never allows lasting peace, either.

The Downfall of Israel

With the door open, the enemy comes in, and we get to King Ahaz. At just twenty years of age, he becomes king and does evil. He even sacrifices his son in the fire. (v 16:3)

Then, he makes a deal with the Assyrians, who will turn against Israel. Meanwhile, King Ahaz allows them to pollute Israel with their gods.

Today, we have so many cultures worshipping sin and evil in our country. We must look upon these chapters as a cautionary tale.

This happens when we allow idolatry to remain. Even if we make positive changes, leaving sin unhindered will expose us to dangers. In verse 16:16, we read that even Uriah, the priest, did as Ahaz ordered. The spiritual leaders must push for the changes we need to see. There will never be peace if we don't.

Just as evil proliferated in Israel after King Ahaz, with Hoshea, (v 17:2) I believe it will do so in America if we don't apply this warning.

Idolatry in America

We can't do the things which are displeasing to God, in secret. (v 17:9) God will observe our actions and judge us. The Lord says, "You must not do this," (v 17:12) because idols fill our land.

The Lord removed His presence from Israel, (v 17:23) and the Assyrians took them captive.

He sent lions to feast on them. (v 17:25) "They would not listen, however, but persisted." (2 Kings 17:40) Even the people who seemed to worship the Lord were serving their idols. (v 17:41)

Why bother with all this history about kings?

Above Jesus on the cross, as he died, someone placed a sign reading "Jesus of Nazareth, King of the Jews."

They wrote it because he was their king, but they did not recognize him. He still is our King whether we recognize Him or not. He will forever be the King.

Do you recognize Him?

Tomorrow, we will read 2 Kings 18-20.

Day 109: 2 Kings 18-20: Obedience in Faith

Good morning. I hope you are all feeling blessed.

Today, we read 2 Kings 18-20.

The Obedient King

Today, we read about Hezekiah. The Bible says, "There was no one like him among all the kings of Judah, either before him or after him. (v 18:5) Unlike the last three righteous kings, not only did he do what was right in the eyes of the Lord, (v 18:3) but he also tore down all the high places, Asherah poles, and idols. (v 18:4) This proves a leader can remove all those sins from a land. By doing so, he had outstanding success. (v 18:7)

There are still those who oppose him, like the field commander. (v 18:19-20) I'm not suggesting he was perfect. Only Jesus can claim that. He sold off or gave away the articles from the temple. He even handed over the gold from the doors. But he was seeking God and trusted in Him alone.

The Humble King

He calls on Isaiah, who gives him guidance.

With confidence, he knows the Lord will protect Judah. (v 18:32)

In verse 19:1, Hezekiah enters the temple dressed in torn clothing and sackcloth. He was humbling himself before the Lord.

I have seen online debates about people dressing too casually at church. There should be a reverence for God, and we should bring our best. This can be a problem, however, if people are trying to be "good enough" on their own. We can polish the outside up but still be a cesspool on the inside. (Matt 23:27) Bringing God our best is not about appearances but about bringing God an open and clean heart. (1 Sam 16:7)

The Human King

King Ahab left Hezekiah a mess. He did not decree that all the people should shape up. Instead, he led by example and submitted himself to the Lord.

The intensity and aggression of his opponent was frightening. Sennacherib was a brutal killer. He had already conquered Israel and taken the people captive.

Israel was ten tribes, Judah only two.

When possible, they would build their towns on hills to make it harder to attack.

Sennacherib would build siege ramps, and he had a large army. The people could see them approaching from far away. Sennacherib assumed since they had destroyed all the idols, which he thought were their gods, they had no one to save them.

Hezekiah had destroyed those idols because he knew the hand of man did not make God. God was God and He could save them.

All of this will not protect Hezekiah from personal trouble. We would like to believe that, as Christians, we don't have to deal with illness and heartache. Jesus assures us we will have trouble in this life. (John 16:33)

Hezekiah was about to die. Isaiah had even told him this would happen. (v 20:1)

The Trusting King

When we trust in the Lord, we will have trouble, but we can turn to Him and He will carry us through those times. Hezekiah prays, and the Lord extends his life for another fifteen years.

It would be comforting to know the time we all had left. Making financial decisions, planning retirement, and choosing career paths would all be easier if we knew the years we had to plan for.

God knows if we had that knowledge, we would procrastinate before we live for Him. This would be a waste of life. I wish I had not lost so many years living for my own desires. The days I have left to live for God will not be enough.

So, God, in His infinite wisdom, wants us to prepare now.

None of us know the number of days we have. We must use all our days to bring honor and glory to the Lord.

Tomorrow, we will read 2 Kings 21-23.

Day 110: 2 Kings 21-23: The Hope of Salvation

This morning let's discuss Easter. My family always celebrated Easter, even though we rarely attended church. It was eggs, bunnies, and chocolate. What child wouldn't love that holiday?

For me, it was the unofficial beginning of waterski season. We would have a three-day weekend and spend it at Apache Lake.

As a Christian, it saddens me I was so oblivious to the significance of this day. I thought it had something to do with the day Jesus died, which was Good Friday. Jesus defeated death that day. Satan thought he had the perfect way to stop God's plan. He lost. He played right into God's hand and gave him the one thing he needed: an atoning sacrifice.

With that sacrifice complete, Jesus could secure salvation for all who would believe in Him.

When He rose, it provided us all with the opportunity to rise with Him.

Today, we are going to talk about 2 Kings 21-23.

Evil is Everywhere

The focus of these chapters is one of the greatest earthly kings, Josiah.

Preceding him was a king named Manasseh, who took evil to its highest level. (v 21:15-16) Like Satan thinking he was defeating God, Manasseh added evil to evil to lead Judah astray. He built altars to other gods and to the stars in the temple! (v 21:5) Practicing divination, he had mediums and spiritists seek omens. (v 21:6)

As I read about his actions, I think of the people I know who consider themselves "more spiritual than anything else." They think this is a good thing. It is not.

This is Satan's game plan from the beginning. The devil will cause people to substitute evil for good, even within the church, to make it feel like they are earning their way to heaven. Instead of getting people to join his church, he will deceive the people within the temple to worship the wrong gods.

Hope Exists

Just when it looks like God should give up on Judah, a new king appears, the child – Josiah. He followed the ways of his father, David. He even had all the evil Manasseh had done removed. Instead of leaving the high places, he had them destroyed.

During the destruction and cleansing of the temple, Hilkiah finds the Book of the Law. (v 22:8)

Jesus is the fulfillment of the Law. (Matt 5:17-18)

I see a parallel image of destruction, leading to the cleansing. Just as Josiah destroyed all the sins of Manasseh, Jesus, by allowing them to destroy Himself, cleansed us of all our sins.

Wrath is Coming

God was still not happy with Judah. (v 22:16-17) He was still going to punish them.

He is not pleased with us either. He will still pour out His divine wrath on the earth. We have rejected Him. We worship idols and practice sin without end. There is a day coming, I believe, soon when He will stop protecting us.

We Found the Answer

Josiah reads the scriptures to the people. (v 23:2) Faith in Jesus comes by hearing the Word of God. (Rom 10:17)

The punishment is still coming. Megiddo is where Josiah dies in battle. (v 23:29)

Armageddon is coming. This is the last battle between good and evil. The name Armageddon means Mount Megiddo.

God let Josiah die to protect him. Because he had turned from evil. He had humbled himself and tore his robe and wept. (v 22:19) His heart was receptive, ensuring that God would spare him from witnessing the impending devastation.

I believe God will rescue His children, those who are in Christ, before that battle happens.

Josiah sees the tomb of the prophet and leaves it untouched. I believe that when that battle happens, Jesus' burial will leave Christians unharmed.

Revelation 20:2-3 says Satan will rule for one thousand years before Christ casts him into outer darkness. This is reminiscent of Jehoahaz bringing evil back to the land after Josiah had cleaned it up. Those who were in the tomb remained safe, but those in the world returned to evil. We know from the empty tomb Jesus defeated death and rose. If we are in the tomb with Him, we will rise with Him.

My question to you is, are you ready to die to yourself and live with Christ, or will you risk staying in the world?

Tomorrow, we will read 2 Kings 24-25.

Day 111: 2 Kings 24-25: New Beginning

Good morning.

We have celebrated Jesus rising from the tomb. He will walk around for forty days, and over five hundred people will see him before his ascension into heaven.

Today, we will finish reading 2 Kings, chapters 24-25.

Rebellion

I remember my arrogance before my salvation. My wife insisted on taking our son to church. I went along to dispute what they taught him. Like Jehoiakim in v 24:1, I was rebelling. Because of the sins I clung to, I refused to accept the idea of God.

God was merciful toward me. First, He preserved my life when I was in an automobile accident. Then, He brought me into a church where I heard the Gospel, and He opened my heart to receive it. This changed my life and my future.

Judah was holding onto the sins of Manasseh. Verse 24:4 says he had shed "innocent blood, and the Lord was not willing to forgive." (NIV)

America has allowed abortion for fifty years. There is nothing more innocent than an unborn baby. We have blood on our hands. If Jesus had not paid the price for us, I don't see how God would forgive our nation. It would contravene what we read here.

We must never return to that practice. I know people who still think of it as a right.

Retribution

For those sins of Manasseh, God punished the entire nation of Judah. He allowed Nebuchadnezzar to take them captive. (v 24:14)

My sins held me captive. Their logic didn't ease the pervasive emptiness and sadness I felt.

We will read more about the captivity in Isaiah, Daniel, and the other books of the prophets.

The actions of the kings we have read about led to God giving them over to the Babylonians. They didn't come in and take Israel from God, "He thrust them from His presence."

I can live with my disability. My failures are something I will own. Heartaches come and go. I would not want to live one moment without having God in my life.

The Bible describes hell as a place without His presence. (Thes 1:9) Even if I were not there, life without God would feel that way.

Verse 24:17 says that they named Mattaniah king but gave him the name Zedekiah. He rebels against the King of Babylon and brings about the fall of Jerusalem. (v 24:20) Zedekiah would become blinded and suffer the loss of his family. (v 25:7)

I think of the movie "The Princess Bride," where Westley, the Dread Pirate Roberts, threatened to inflict pain on Prince Humperdinck.[4]

Westley tells him they are going to fight "to the pain." Imagine knowing your loved ones are suffering, and yet you must continue to live? This was the meaning of "to the pain." I think Zedekiah knew this pain.

Redemption

When we put our faith in Jesus, we become a new creation. (2 Cor. 5:17) We should now have a new identity. I once rebelled against God. This brought about my fall. Through Jesus, I have risen again to be that new man.

Whereas they blinded Zedekiah, I now see. (John 20:29)

We concluded 2 Kings by seeing Jehoiachin eating at the king's table. The king provided him with a daily allowance for the rest of his life.

As we move on, let us all put our faith in Jesus. We can then eat at the King's table. He is our daily bread.

Tomorrow, we will read 1 Chronicles 1-2.

Conclusion of 2 Kings

Now that you have read the twelfth book of the Bible, take a moment to reflect. How have the events in 2 Kings mirrored lessons in your own life? Do you feel yourself growing in knowledge? Are you also growing in faith?

For fun, here are five questions I want you to answer (I will post some brief answers at the back of the book).

1. What was the significance of Jeroboam's setting up golden calves?

2. Describe Elijah's contest with the prophets of Baal on Mount Carmel.

3. What was the significance of the Assyrian invasions?

4. What was the role of the prophets in 2 Kings?

5. What is the overall message or theme of 2 Kings?

Chapter 12: Footnotes

1. *The Breakfast Club*, directed by John Hughes (1985; Universal Pictures).

2. Matthew Henry, *Matthew Henry's Concise Commentary on the Whole Bible*, s.v. "2 Kings 8," accessed July 1, 2025, https://www.biblehub.com/commentaries/mhc/2_kings/8.htm.

3. "The Story Behind Turkey's Underground Cities," The Culture Trip, last modified March 8, 2021, https://theculturetrip.com/europe/turkey/articles/the-story-behindturkeys-underground-cities.

4. *The Princess Bride*, directed by Rob Reiner (1987; Twentieth Century Fox).

Chapter 13:
1 CHRONICLES

Day 112: 1 Chronicles 1-2: Family, Fighting, and Forgiveness: A Journey to Unity

Congratulations! Though it is impossible to know what percentage of people never make it through twelve books of the Old Testament, you are a part of the minority. It is important to ponder what you have already learned along the way.

Today, we begin 1 Chronicles, reading chapters 1-2. I will warn you but encourage you: these next two books can be challenging.

Authorship

Most scholars attribute these books to Ezra. Ezra likely wrote them during Hezekiah's reign, around 450 BC, after the Israelites' return from exile. The Biblical Archaeology Society Library suggests Chronicles, Ezra, and Nehemiah may have been one book.[1]

Another website points out that while they repeat a lot of the history we have already covered, they are not just a repeat, but a retelling, looking at the history through a different lens.[2] They are an important pivot point in our journey because from them, we see that the story of Israel is not over.

Let's examine a few points from today's two chapters.

In verse 1:1, you may have noticed there is no mention of Cain or Abel. Abel died without having descendants. All of Cain's heirs perished in the flood. Though Adam and Eve may have had other children, tracking their descendants would be futile since God eradicated them. The Bible Project also examines the possibility that some of Cain's descendants, the Kenites, may have survived along with the Nephilim.[3]

What Really Matters

These points are interesting to ponder, and I feel we should. However, they are not salvational. They will not determine your eternal destination. Salvation is by grace alone, through faith alone. (Eph. 2:8–9)

We believe that the entire Bible is true. (Prov. 30:5) But we encounter these other tribes, and we should meditate on God's Word. That means contemplating all these things.

The interesting point in today's reading is verse 1:4. This passage omits mention of Adam and Eve's other descendants, focusing only on those before Noah and, in this verse, those exiting the ark. According to Ellicott,[4] Ham means black or sunburnt, and Japheth is fairskinned. He points out that Shem likely meant brownish.

Race should not matter. While the Bible teaches that heritage and culture are important, the color of a person's skin is not. God made all of us, and we all descended from Noah.

Family

All the Judges we read about, as well as the kings, descended from these seventy tribes. We are all family. The problem, which we have already seen, is that families like to fight with each other.

I have one brother. We don't see each other as often as I would like, but we are close. But this doesn't mean we didn't fight. I remember one occasion growing up when he was picking at me, and I had had enough. We were standing in my mother's kitchen, and I lowered my shoulder, grabbed him around his waist, and drove him into—no, through—the wall into the bathroom. My mom had planned on remodeling her house, so we expedited the need. I still stood with him at his wedding. There was never a moment when I didn't love him.

Brothers fight with each other. Sisters too!

Tribal Tension

We see the same dynamic in God's children. While they all branch out from Noah, they squabble over who the chosen family is. Who can claim God is their God? God chose Israel, and this made them the tribe the others despised.

Faith Unites

Through Jesus, we can all reunite. Faith reunites us all with our heavenly family. The various churches and denominations continue to fight with each other. They get hung up on traditions and interpretations.

Therefore, God gave us a clear guide, the Bible. If it isn't in the Bible, God didn't say it, and therefore, we should not be standing on that principle.

If you are in a family that is fighting, maybe you have an estranged sibling. Ask yourself, what would it take for you to be the bigger person? For you to extend the olive branch and reunite? If you have a friend or neighbor, maybe someone who left your church to attend another, what can you do to mend that fence?

As we move forward, let's renew the hope that God wants us to all have: the hope of reunion in heaven. Why wait until we are there? Make the effort now and enjoy the blessing.

Tomorrow, we will read 1 Chronicles 3-5.

Day 113: 1 Chronicles 3-5: How Jabez Can Inspire Our Walk with God

Good morning. We've reached the middle of another week. I hope God has blessed you and your household today. We are now going to look at 1 Chronicles 3-5.

David's Sons

Chapter 3 is about the lineage of David. There were no surprises in these verses. However, when I read 3:9, it says, "besides his sons by his concubines." (NIV)[5] We read of the many sons of David. Several had become kings. David was God's anointed king. I can only guess how many people went through their lives knowing David was their father but not being able to lay claim to it, because their mother was a concubine? Did any of them rise to fame, having the genetic makeup of a great warrior? Were they people of faith? Or did they follow the evil paths of some of their half-brothers? We will never know, at least not here. I wonder if in heaven we ever find these answers. We have eternity. Will we even care?

Sorrow and Pain

Then, in 1 Chronicles 4:9, we read of Jabez. Many of the commentaries at BibleHub.com[6] draw attention to this man. I will draw from Matthew Henry's Concise Commentary.[7]

The verse says his mother named him Jabez because of his painful birth. (NIV) Was it his mother's pain? Or his? Perhaps it was the pain of all of Israel? We don't know. Other translations use the word sorrow. This conjures up images of Jeremiah, the weeping prophet. He cried out because of the sins of Israel. Or even of Jesus, who we read: "He was despised and rejected by mankind, a man of suffering, and familiar with pain. Like one from whom people hide their faces, he was despised, and we held him in low esteem. Surely he took up our pain and bore our suffering, yet we considered him punished by God, stricken by him, and afflicted." (Isa. 53:3–4 NIV)

Jabez's Prayer

Our text in 1 Chronicles says Jabez was more honorable than his brothers. The chronicler considered him more honorable because he cried out to the God of Israel. Knowing the idolatry of the people, he was crying out to the true God. Much like Jeremiah, lamenting the people's sin.

He asks for four specific things from God: that He blesses him, enlarges his territory, has

His hands on him, and keeps him from harm—easing his suffering. (v. 4:10) A blessing from God is a gift or talent. God gives some people gifts of prophecy, teaching, or healing. This tells me that Jabez was not taking credit for his own accomplishments but giving glory to God for all he had. When we do anything with our own strength, we highlight our weaknesses. This allows God to get the glory when He provides His strength. Territory determined a man's wealth in those times. I think it refers to more than land in this case. He is talking about his reach.

Modern Application

I am seeing more clearly how writing is my mission field. In Marana, Arizona, I might one day preach in front of a couple of hundred people. Combine observing the webcast; perhaps if I gain notoriety, I might reach a few thousand. Publication ensures a book's lasting availability, often becoming more significant. George Orwell's books had some popularity during his lifetime. Now, seventy-five years later, as we see so much of what he wrote in 1984[8] or Animal Farm[9] coming true, they deserve another look. Through the written word, I may share the Gospel with untold numbers of people, now and in the future.

God's Will

Having His hands on us has several implications. When I preach or write, I ask that it be God's words, and not mine, that people hear. I know I am nothing, and all I can do is through and for Him. So, praying that God has His hands on me would give all control and dominion to Him. This was Jabez's prayer. He was not seeking for God to magnify himself. He was asking God to be his Lord. His name suggests pain and suffering. Having this removed would be important to him. Matthew Henry points out he was not asking for personal healing in this prayer. This mirrors Jesus's prayer in Matthew 5. He is asking God to keep him from evil.

Remember, Jabez suffered because of the surrounding evil. He was empathetic and knew Israel suffered for their sins. The verse says he is more honorable because he is not seeking his own glory. Many other kings were calling on idols, hoping to enlarge themselves. Jabez was seeking the will of God. This makes him more honorable.

Are you familiar with suffering? Is it your own sin or that of others which bothers you the most? Do you cry out only for yourself, or are you seeking God's will for everyone?

Tomorrow, we will read 1 Chronicles 6.

Day 114: 1 Chronicles 6:
The Sacred Duty of Music in Worship

Good morning. Today, I have a message for you that is dear to my heart based on 1 Chronicles chapter 6.

Musical Memories

I have been a musician since my earliest memories. We lived in an apartment that had a hallway with a door, a small space, another door, and then another apartment. I was six years old, so I didn't understand the architecture. Somehow, I had a plastic toy guitar, and I would go into that breezeway and close both doors, which would set up some interesting acoustics, and make up songs. Then, I would play those songs for my siblings and mother.

Later, when I was ten, we lived in a house and had a neighbor named Kevin. He was a retired session musician from New York who had played with some recording artists I was familiar with. His son, Sean, was only five, so he was too young to learn much. Kevin liked to teach me chords and scales and let me play his custom guitars. I was hooked. Kevin moving away left me with a deep and overwhelming sense of loss. My mother could see how much I had enjoyed learning to play. That Christmas, she bought me an electric guitar and an amplifier combo from the Spiegel catalog. Money was always short, but she made that a priority. Fifty-four years later, I am still playing. These days, it is in the church's praise band.

Temple Musicians

What does this have to do with 1 Chronicles chapter 6? Let's look…

In these verses, we read about the genealogy of the Levites. This would include Aaron and all his sons. We have met many of them throughout the previous books. Then, in 6:31, we hear about the Temple Musicians. These were the men whom David put in charge of the worship music. Some were singers, others perhaps songwriters. In verse 33, we hear of Heman, the musician. Verse 6:48 says, "Their fellow Levites were assigned to all the other duties of the tabernacle." (NIV)[10]

Sacred Duty

These were sacred duties, as we have discussed. It also implies that music is a sacred duty. This is how I have always approached playing in the praise band. A prophet would not tell prophecy without consulting the Lord. If someone is a preacher, they would study the scriptures and allow the Holy Spirit to guide them. Teachers would never attempt to instruct a classroom without learning the lesson first.

Unfortunately, I have seen, if I am being honest, even been, a musician who has taken part in worship because I enjoy playing music. They will approach this duty to make attending church more fun for themselves. There is nothing wrong with enjoying your service to the Lord. We all should have a desire to do what we do.

A problem can arise when a musician does not ask God to improve their skills. Nor will they push themselves to learn more than they know. I used to tell people I didn't know how to play bar chords. They were hard to play, and I had resisted learning them for three decades. I knew this held me back as a musician, but I was only doing it for fun, so what did it matter?

Now, I understand that being a part of the praise band is a ministry. That like these Levites, I had to approach it with the same decorum as I approach preaching or teaching; I had to accept that challenge. If I am preaching a Bible verse that God puts on my heart, like 6:31, I would never say I don't know what it means. I would study and research until I do. There is a gentleman at our church who likes to ask me what various passages mean. When I don't know, I tell him I will find out. Then I research and learn. This is a responsibility I accept. (2 Tim. 2:15)

Making the Effort

A praise band musician or choir singer needs to look at this as a duty and put in the same effort. When they do, they will not only sound better and have more fun, but they will feel the Lord working through them, using them as His instrument in reaching hearts. (2 Chron. 5:13)

Has a song stirred powerful emotions in you? That is God working through the hands and voices of the praise team, through their instruments, into your ears. He is doing this for your benefit, not the musicians. He is blessing them with the ability to do what they are doing. Then God is making it all sound the way He wants it to sound. He is opening your mind and heart to respond to it. (1 Sam. 16:14–23). Days later, when a song is stuck in your mind, that isn't just a catchy tune. This is the Holy Spirit helping you recall something He taught you. (John 14:26). It is God talking to you.

Are you listening or just humming along? What is He saying to you?

Tomorrow, we will read 1 Chronicles 7-8.

Day 115: 1 Chronicles 7-8:
God's Love Extends to Each of Us Through Faith

Good morning. I hope you have enjoyed the week. Today, we read the next two chapters of 1 Chronicles 7-8.

Recognition

When going through genealogies, it is easy to get lost. Name after name, many we recognize, others we don't. What is the point of all of this? God is economic. He never wastes resources. Even though He is eternal, He would not waste our time if there wasn't an important lesson to teach. Therefore, when I race through names, I must remind myself to slow down. Then ask myself, "What am I supposed to learn from this?"

Many of these people play no significant role in the overall picture of the Bible. None are insignificant. Not all of us are called to have notoriety. Many of us will live our quiet lives unnoticed. For most of us, this is our preference. We enjoy when those close to us appreciate what we do. It's always good to hear, "Thank you." Even that is more than we are seeking. There are times I am noticed for doing something, and I am embarrassed. What I was doing needed to be done. I was fortunate to have the opportunity.

What I see in these pages is that God knows every one of us. None of us are just names on a page to Him. He sees everything we do. When we help someone, we are showing His kindness to them. This makes our Father happy. Think of how you feel when you see your child display a sympathetic character. It is humbling to know that a God who has millennia of names and faces to remember does not find this a challenge.

What Is Missing?

Then I ask, "What am I missing?" In these chapters, as I read through the commentaries, I find this note from Matthew Henry: "7:1–40 Genealogies. – Here is no account either of Zebulun or Dan. We can assign no reason why they only should be omitted; but it is the disgrace of the tribe of Dan, that idolatry began in that colony."[11]

He goes on to remind us, "Men become abominable when they forsake the worship of the true God, for any creature object." This should cause us all to hit the brakes for a moment. Are we worshipping God or the god we have created? Have we forsaken the creator for the creation? What have we allowed to become idols in our lives?

We will all stand before God at the Judgment seat of Christ. "For we must all appear before the judgment seat of Christ, so that each of us may receive what is due us for the things done while in the body, whether good or bad." (1 Cor. 5:10 NIV) On that day, it will not be genealogies that are judged, but our actions. How we used the life God gave us.

For those who were not worshipping Jesus, there will be one initial test. Is our name written in His book? "And I saw the dead, great and small, standing before the throne, and books were opened. Another book was opened, which is the book of life. The dead were judged according to what they had done as recorded in the books." (Rev. 20:12 NIV)

Are You Listed?

My prayer is that everyone who reads my words and is reading His Word will place their hope in Jesus. It is only through that faith our names will be there. Do you know your name is there now? Maybe you think you are too sinful to have hope?

In verse 7:21, we read of the men of Gath. They were driven out of Aijalon before being driven out by Beriah and Shema. (v 8:13) Why is this important? The men of Gath, or the Gittites, were the tribe that Goliath came from. This tribe was David and Israel's enemy, but God still records them in His book.

We all sin and are enemies of God. (Rom. 5:10) Therefore, we all have earned death. (Rom. 6:23) Through the Grace of God, we can all receive life. Repent and seek His forgiveness and have your name written in the Book of Life.

Tomorrow, we will read 1 Chronicles 9-11.

Day 116: 1 Chronicles 9-11:
Reflect on the Legacy You're Building Every Day

Looks like another beautiful day. I hope you are enjoying all that God gives us. Today, we read 1 Chronicles 9-11.

Records

As stated, we believe Ezra wrote this book. He may have been a person whose job was to keep the chronicles. This may have been a position, like a secretary, which was handled by many people. They had scattered and incomplete records. Ezra, if he was the author of this book, gathered all these records and compiled this history. Because of this, we have a lot of duplication.

Today, we read about Saul and how he and his family died. Then, we read about how they anointed David as the king of Israel. It's easy to rush past these stories; we just read them. But when God repeats something in the Bible, He has a reason. This is something we need to know. Our first verse today, 9:1, states that Babylon took them captive because of their unfaithfulness. God has much more to show us. We must be faithful to meditate on all of it.

We know of kings and judges, but here we read of priests, Levites, and gatekeepers.

Everyone has a job to do. That is God's will for humanity. None of us are here to just take up space and consume resources. Each has a purpose.

Ceremonies

At the AWANA ministry, we start with three children being assigned the special task of taking part in the opening ceremony. One will hold the American flag, one the AWANA flag, and the third the Bible. The group will say a pledge to each of these three objects. I remember how special it felt when I was young to be chosen to do one of these duties.

Though I was not in AWANA, there were similar situations in clubs and school programs.

Then we read about a Levite named Mattithiah. I'm sure we all know who Matt is, right? Probably not. People have recognized him as the Korahite responsible for baking the offering bread (v. 9:31) for over 2,600 years. Shallum, his father, must be very proud. He might also be the same Mattithiah who stood by Ezra while he read the law in Nehemiah 8:4 or that David will appoint to minister before the ark in 1 Chronicles 16:5.

No Minor Jobs

There is an unlikely possibility that he is the Mattithiah listed in the genealogy of Jesus in Luke 3:26. I say unlikely because that Mattithiah was the son of Semein.

Every day, we all get up, get dressed, and go to work. Sometimes, it feels meaningless and demeaning. Here is a man who served God. We know nothing more about him, but we know he served the Lord. There are no minor jobs. Everyone is important.

If someone writes about me in the distant future, I hope they say I served the Lord in some context. What will be your legacy?

Tomorrow, we will read 1 Chronicles 12-15.

Day 117: 1 Chronicles 12-15: Finding God's Guidance Amidst Life's Changes

Good morning. I start each day with the belief that it is going to be a good one. This goes against logic. Some days will not be pleasant.

I have been with my company for over two decades. You have heard me reference my day job in these pages. Yesterday, like many people in companies around the world every year, my company laid me off. Today, this is the lens I will be looking through as we read 1 Chronicles 12-15. From these chapters, I see hope, comfort, and caution.

Hope

David was a shepherd whom God chose to lead Israel. In verse 12:17, he says, "If you have come to me in peace to help me, I am ready for you to join me." David was seeking peace. Jesus gives us His peace. (John 14:27) After we read of David's desire, we read that, day after day, men came to help David. (v. 12:22) This is the hope I believe I can count on. God had chosen David, and He was bringing to him all the help he would require.

Comfort

I have felt God saying to my soul, "Your work is with me." Many times, I have written about trusting in God, not in our employers. Each day, as I tried to fit serving God around doing my job, I have felt hypocritical for not living the values I preach.

Change is hard. Walking away from a job God had given me was a risk. I didn't do it.

Instead, I kept praying that God would make clear to me what the next move should be. There was no doubt about what He wanted me to write. It was never a matter of what I needed to do. The question was when. Was that steady income enabling me to do the things I do to share the Gospel? Or was that job preventing me from taking the next step? David was seeking peace while building an army. The dichotomy is rich.

Caution

Why did he pursue both? He knew they were not keeping God's commands. In 1 Chronicles 13:3, he says, "Let us bring the ark of our God back to us, for we did not inquire of it during the reign of Saul." When we live our lives next to God instead of in Christ, we allow sin to widen that separation. Soon, we realize God is not even with us.

Return

He never leaves us, but we leave Him. God's patience is unwavering. (2 Pet. 3:9) He waits for us to return. David is seeking peace, watching the army grow, seeing battles flare up with Saul and the Philistines. He looks around and considers his situation and realizes they are trying to do this all without consulting God. They had lost the habit and discipline of seeking God. So, he says let's get the ark and return to the Lord.

There were very strict protocols on how to move the ark. They would place the poles through the rings, lift the ark onto their shoulders, and march with it. Specific Levites, the Kohathites, were to carry the ark. (Num. 3:29–31) Instead, they put the ark on a cart and had oxen move it. In their excitement, they were playing music and singing and dancing. I picture the circus rolling into town. This was not the way to move the Ark of the Covenant of God. Therefore, oxen, being the clumsy animals they are, stumble, and Uzzah reaches out to steady the ark.

I have always wondered why would God punish Uzzah for protecting the ark? He wouldn't. God's anger was not based on Uzzah protecting the ark; it was on them not following the laws He had given them on how to move it. If they had been carrying it on poles and marching with it, the ark would not have teetered. We had spoken in Numbers 4:15–20 about how only a limited group of Levites could even look at the ark. They kept it covered. It was sacred. Uzzah was treating it like common luggage.

When we have reverence for God and seek Him, He provides clear guidance. In verse 14:14, He tells David how and where to attack the Philistines. He even tells him when to make the move. This is the comfort we can take when we go through changes in our lives. Whether they are employment disruptions, health concerns, relationship issues, financial struggles, etc., if we seek God, He will provide us with guidance through the Holy Spirit. We just need to stop the chaos around us and listen to His voice.

When we don't listen to God and try to make our own path forward, we can find even our best intentions will cause us to suffer. We can't be half-hearted. God does not want lukewarm worshippers. (Rev. 3:15–16) We attempt to optimize tasks, such as using a cart, and expect God's joy at our circumvention of His will. We say, "We will do this our way," and expect God to bless us for it. Instead, we must commit to doing God's will. How does He want this done?

I encourage you to look at all the areas of your life. Where are you pursuing your path, hoping God will join in? How does God want you to do whatever it is you are doing? If you don't know, be like David. Bring God back into the picture and seek His guidance. He will give you the victory.

Tomorrow, we will read 1 Chronicles 16-19.

Day 118: 1 Chronicles 16-19: Provision, Responsibility, and Salvation

Good morning. Today, we read 1 Chronicles 16-19. Our themes today will be provision, responsibility, and salvation.

Provision

People ask why I use a wheelchair. I tell them how I was involved in an automobile accident and broke my neck and back. Since the time I was twenty-five years old, I have had trouble walking. They respond with pity, saying, "I'm sorry that happened to you." I would respond the same way to someone who told me that story. This is because we rarely understand the whole story.

My goal when I was young was to live fast, love hard, and die young. I never wanted to live past thirty-five. Being an atheist, I thought all there was to enjoy was the life we had. I looked at people over thirty-five, and they had so much responsibility they didn't seem to have time or money for fun. The assumption was partially correct. My death in the car wreck would have sent me to hell, where I would have longed to die. We are eternal. That suffering would never end. God, in His mercy, kept me alive and brought me to salvation.

We see in 1 Chronicles 16:3 that David provided food for every person in Israel. God provides all we have. We may think it is our labor, or the money in the bank. It is not. These things are the tools we use. We would have no job if God didn't provide it. He provides all our needs (see Phil. 4:19). I worked in sales, and part of my income was commissions. There were some months I would have a large commission check, but I would need every penny, because my car, air conditioner, or refrigerator would break. Other months, I would have a little commission. Somehow, I had no expenses. God knows our needs before we do. He provides.

Responsibility

With that provision also comes responsibility. He will not provide a way for us to sin or live in a fashion that does not glorify Him. It is meeting our needs, not our wants. Verse 17:12 highlights his greatest provision. God tells David that He will provide One who will build the house for God. In Him, He will establish His throne forever. The verse is not referencing Solomon building the Temple. This is Jesus, creating in our hearts the actual house for God.

This is where He dwells now. It says, "I will be His father, and He will be My Son."

With this provision, He also gives us responsibilities. Verse 16:4 tells us that David appointed some Levites to minister before the Lord's ark. The responsibility of ministering included extolling, thanking, and praising God. Ellicott uses the word record, instead of extol.[12] To record meant chanting during the offering. This would commemorate the sacrifices given to the Lord. They would also thank the Lord. This recognized Him for all He had done and provided. Even the offering they gave was from Him and for Him. Then praising, as it is today, was singing songs and hymns, playing music, and celebrating their love for God. This was their assignment. It is still ours today.

Verse 8 says, to "Give praise to the Lord, proclaim His name; make known among the nations what he has done." (NIV) When the praise band sings and plays for the Lord, there is a humbling sensation that comes over me. I misused the talents God gave me, pursuing sin. He now uses them to praise Him.

Salvation

The chronicler gives us a Psalm starting in verse 16:8. It tells us all we are to praise God for. Then, in verse 16:23, we are to proclaim his salvation day after day. In 16:35, it explains that we should cry out, "Save us, God our Savior."

The Lord saved me when I cried out, asking for His salvation. He saved me long before that when He kept me alive during my car wreck. Even before that, when I was only five years old, a truck hit me. God has been saving me my whole life.

What is God doing in your life? Have you recorded all He has done? Do you thank Him, or are you taking Him for granted? Today, remember to praise Him for the love He shows us.

Tomorrow, we will read 1 Chronicles 20-23.

Day 119: 1 Chronicles 20-23:
Spring, Satan, Solomon, and the Son of God

Good morning. I pray that God will guide my words today. Some Pastors, including one I respect, Dr. David Jeremiah, like to use alliterations when constructing their sermons. I typically don't. Today, when looking at 1 Chronicles 20-23, I stumbled upon a pattern. We will speak of Spring, Satan, Solomon, and the Son of God.

Spring

Springtime in Tucson, Arizona, is not really a defined season. Our winters are so mild that we don't see the snow ending, like in other parts of the country. We will see some cool nights and unseasonably cool days. Our summers are brutal. We often exceed one hundred degrees. I have seen those temperatures hang on throughout the nights. Spring is psychotic. We can have nights in the low forties followed by days in the nineties.

One of the common characteristics of spring is love. It is a time of renewal and fresh starts. Romance and hope. For David and his men, verse 20:1 implies that it was a normal situation, that kings would go to war in the spring. They had been cooped up all winter, getting on each other's nerves. Now, everything was thawed out, and it was time to go fight. What a strange dichotomy: smell the flowers, look at the green grass, make love to my wife, go kill people.

During this tumultuous time, we meet a familiar character. For the first time, we hear his name.

Satan

Ellicott states, "When the adversary, the enemy of mankind, is meant, the word takes the article, which it does not here."[13] In other words, he is claiming this is not the person of Satan, but the wrath of God. Benson interprets this more to be a similar situation as in the Book of Job.[14] Satan stands before God, asking that David would be tempted to do evil.

We know that God does not tempt us to do evil (see Jas. 1:13). Therefore, I see that some evil force or being is granted permission to tempt David to do this deed. What is so evil about taking a census? Taking a census is looking at your own strength instead of counting on the power of God. It's springtime, and David is contemplating who he wants to fight. The proper way of doing this, as we have seen, would be to inquire of the Lord. God would have said, go against the Ammonites, and I will deliver them into your hands, for instance. Instead, David is saying, "Go count my troops so I can determine my odds of victory." This is Pride, and that is a sin. For this, God's anger is poured out, and David needs to choose one of three punishments.

As a child, I hated when I had to choose my punishment. "You can get a spanking, do extra chores for a week, or go to bed without dinner." I would always be thinking, just do whatever you are going to do and get it over with.

Solomon

We had already learned that David, because of all the blood he shed, would not be allowed to build the Temple. (2 Sam. 7:1–17) Now, he is told his son, Solomon, would have that honor. David is old; he knows his days are numbered. So, he begins the preparation for Solomon. Solomon, we remember, asked for wisdom. (1 Kings 3:9) God provided him this wisdom and more. He is also a foreshadowing of Jesus. (1 Chron. 28:6)

The temple is a building. God does not dwell in buildings made by human hands. (Acts 17:24) He dwells in human hearts. (Eph. 3:17) This does not happen when we "invite Jesus into our hearts." That phrase does not appear in the Bible. What the Bible does say is that by God's grace, through faith, He will forgive our sins. (Eph. 2:8–9)

God is holy and cannot even be in a sinful heart. Before He could dwell there, atonement must be made for our sins. The "temple," that is our hearts, must be cleansed. That atonement was made when Jesus died for us. The cleansing happens when we have faith and confess Him as our Lord. (Rom. 10:9) All of this happens because of what He did. If He is not living in you, it is because you are resisting giving Him Lordship over your life. You are holding on to sin, and your heart remains inhospitable to the Lord.

We all have demons inside us that, like Satan, tempt us to do things that displease God. These demons are driven out by prayer. Admit that you have a sin you are holding on to, and ask God to remove it. Then, trust that Jesus has removed it by paying the penalty for it. This prepares a place for Him to dwell.

Tomorrow, we will read 1 Chronicles 24-26.

Day 120: 1 Chronicles 24-26:
Every Person Matters: Find Your Purpose

Matthew Henry, in his Concise Commentary, writes, "When everyone has, knows, and keeps his place and work, the more there are, the better. In the mystical body of Christ, every member has its use for the good of the whole."[15] This is regarding the twenty-fourth chapter of 1 Chronicles, which we read today, along with the two chapters after it. (25 and 26)

Roles

We begin by looking at the order of the priests who ministered in the Temple. They set the order in which families would serve. Within the families, who would perform which duties were determined by lot. We like to use seniority, qualifications, or specialization to determine the order of things. This fosters a system that elevates some above others. Christ is the head of the body. The rest of us serve at His mercy.

Therefore, I am pleased to serve by teaching, preaching, playing music, or being a webcast specialist. It is not about me or what I feel qualified for. God will provide the talent when we make ourselves available. He does not show partiality among men. (Acts 10:34)

Priests

Therefore, when the priests came to the temple to serve, they just drew their assignment and performed the duty ascribed. This was no small thing, either. There were twenty-four clans who served as priests. A priest wasn't just the man at the front preaching the sermon. It was anyone involved in conducting the rituals of the sacred offering. From building the fires, lighting the lampstand, sprinkling the blood on the altar, etc. Even releasing the scapegoat. All these duties required someone to do them and in a specified manner.

Those of us who serve on Sunday morning think of our particular niche role. We have singers; that is all they do. Each week, someone volunteers to bring snacks, which we put out at a welcoming table. One of the most dedicated people in our church has the role of handing out the day's program and greeting people. He is the face everyone encounters as they enter the sanctuary. He also helps count the offering one week a month. My wife watches the babies in the nursery and oversees counting the offerings and getting them to the bank on Monday.

In ancient Israel, it took one thousand men a full week to perform the duties necessary. Whatever their normal occupation was, it didn't matter. For that week, they served in the temple. One may have wished, "I hope I get to clang the cymbals. That is easy and fun." Another may have responded, "Not me, it's too loud! I hope I get to light the lamps." A third possibly added, "Oh no! I always burn my fingers. Let me wash the basins." All the jobs were important. The person doing them needed to humble themselves and realize their importance wasn't in doing what they liked to do, but in doing their best for God. It is a blessing to be part of the service.

Musicians

Chapter 25 moves on to the musicians David assigned. Most musicians I know, including myself, play music because we love it. We learn at a young age, and it's not just what we do, it's who we are. I don't play the guitar; I'm a guitar player. Several jokes about drummers come to mind. You may have one sleeping on your couch right now?

Within the temple, this was a sacred duty. It is a blessing to serve God, but we should not judge these individuals by our standards. We should not say, "Only so and so can sing because the others are off-key." This is performing for the congregation. Worshipping is giving our best to God and for His enjoyment. As a world-renowned pianist, Sam Rotman always says he plays for "an audience of One." God will hear our hearts, not our voices. We may hear every missed note. He only hears our love.

If we perform to gratify others and glorify ourselves, He will hear it and probably will not impress Him. For this reason, a music minister should never deny someone the opportunity to praise the Lord. It isn't about impressing the people who listen to it on YouTube. It is the sincerity of the individuals and their motivation toward the service.

Gatekeepers

In chapter 26, we examine the gatekeepers. We must protect the temple and the people in it. When people are worshiping, they should not need to keep a hand on their weapon. We should be able to focus on the Lord, not keeping an eye out to protect our families. Therefore, God ordained men to stand guard and watch the gates.

It is important to keep danger out of the temple. More important, however, is protecting the hearts and minds of the people. The greatest danger to our modern church is the messages we are hearing from the pulpit. Watered-down messages that tolerate sin will not help people come to the right relationship with God.

As we look at all the masses of people who served in the temple, we need to ask, are we doing our part? Is church an activity? A ritual? Or is being a part of a congregation a blessing we must honor with our full participation? We cannot assume someone else will do the work. When we do, we cheat ourselves out of blessing God.

Tomorrow, we will read 1 Chronicles 27-29.

Day 121: 1 Chronicles 27-29: Making God Laugh, How to Deal with Change

A new month begins. First, we have three chapters left in 1 Chronicles. Today, we will read them 27-29.

Changes

Life can deal you unexpected cards. I had worked for a company for over two decades. Last week, I was told that my services, along with those of many of my coworkers, were no longer required.

I am known as a champion of change. Every year, we would have new programs, new features, new compensation plans, and new leaders. My colleagues would panic! How can we hit those quotas? Am I going to make less money? What will our customers say when we tell them about the new prices? Anxiety lives next door to change. They hang out in the backyard, barbecuing courage on Saturday afternoon.

I would assure the newer members of the team that the company always takes care of its people. Not to stress. If it isn't working, we will figure out a way to make it work. With these changes in my life, I needed someone to say those things to me.

Everything is Temporary

God does that in these chapters. He tells me in 27:1 that each of the army divisions was on duty for one month. Change is part of God's plan. We don't like it, but everyone we know gets older. We all will die. (Heb. 9:27) God knew this; He ordained it. This is the way it is supposed to be. We are not supposed to live in our comfort zones. He will move us out of them to help us grow. The wind that knocks it around strengthens a plant.

When we get too comfortable, we think we can make the rules. This happened with David when he ordered the census, and 27:24 reminds us that "God's wrath came on Israel" because of it.

Different Roles, Different Roads

Then, verses 26-31 tell us the names of all the men who were in charge of various duties. This tells me we all have different roles to play. If God blesses us with a particular skill or talent, He will use it according to His will. We see this in verse 32.

I can trust God has equipped me for the road ahead. It may be new to me, but He knows what is there. The destination is the same, but the path has changed. My son and I were hunting on Aspen Peak one spring and headed home. We found the road was closed because of the weather. He pulled up his phone map and found a new direction.

Make God Laugh

Years ago, my wife taught me a funny but true saying: If you want to make God laugh, show him your plans.

David had made plans. He wanted to build God a temple. God laughed and said, "Not with those blood-stained hands." (paraphrasing v. 28:3) In verse 28:1–3, David brings everyone together to show them the plans but lets them know his son Solomon will be in charge of building it. David did not fight God on this. He didn't whine or bargain. Instead, he gives direction to Solomon to obey the Lord. (v 28:9–10)

Everything is His

Everyone gave all they could. They praised God for giving them all they had. Everything in this world, other than sin, belongs to God. (v 29:14) We must humble ourselves and ask, "Who am I, and who are my people, that we should be able to give as generously as this?"

David didn't get everything he wanted the way he wanted it. He was thankful for everything the Lord had given him. He trusted in the changes God made. I will move forward now, trusting God, too.

Tomorrow, we will read 2 Chronicles 1-5.

Conclusion and questions for 1 Chronicles.

Now that you have read the thirteenth book of the Bible, take a moment to reflect. How have the events in 1 Chronicles mirrored lessons in your own life? Do you feel yourself growing in knowledge? Are you also growing in faith?

For fun, here are five questions I want you to answer (I will post some brief answers at the back of the book).

1. What important religious object did King David bring to Jerusalem, which was a major event in 1 Chronicles?

2. What great project did David intend to build for God, but was told he would not be allowed to, though his son would?

3. 1 Chronicles emphasizes the importance of a particular tribe for worship and serving in the Temple. Which tribe was this?

4. What did David provide and prepare extensively for the building of the Temple, even though he wouldn't build it himself?

5. Why does 1 Chronicles spend so much time on the details of the Temple and its worship services?

Chapter 13: Footnotes

1. "Did the Author of Chronicles Also Write the Books of Ezra and Nehemiah?," Biblical Archaeology Society Library, accessed June 1, 2025, https://library.biblicalarchaeology.org/article/did-the-author-of-chronicles-alsowrite-the-books-of-ezra-and-nehemiah/.

2. "Chronicles: Not Just a Repeat," The Bible Project, accessed June 1, 2025, https://bibleproject.com/articles/chronicles-not-just-repeat/.

3. "Why Do Cain's Descendants Show After the Flood?," The Bible Project Podcast, accessed June 1, 2025, https://bibleproject.com/podcast/why-do-cainsdescendants-show-after-flood/.

4. Charles John Ellicott, *Ellicott's Commentary for English Readers*, s.v. "1 Chronicles 1:4," accessed via Bible Hub.

5. *The Holy Bible, New International Version*, 1 Chron. 3:9.

6. "1 Chronicles 4:9 Commentaries," Bible Hub, accessed June 1, 2025, https://biblehub.com/commentaries/1_chronicles/4-9.htm.

7. Matthew Henry, *Matthew Henry's Concise Commentary on the Whole Bible*, s.v. "1 Chronicles 4:9," (Nashville, TN: Nelson, 1997).

8. George Orwell, *Nineteen Eighty-Four* (New York: New American Library, 1981).

9. George Orwell, *Animal Farm* (London: William Collins, 2021).

10. *The Holy Bible, New International Version*, 1 Chron. 6:48.

11. Matthew Henry, *Matthew Henry's Concise Commentary on the Whole Bible*, s.v. "1 Chronicles 7:1-40," (Nashville, TN: Nelson, 1997).

12. Charles John Ellicott, *Ellicott's Commentary for English Readers*, s.v. "1 Chronicles 16:4," accessed via Bible Hub.

13. Charles John Ellicott, *Ellicott's Commentary for English Readers*, s.v. "1 Chronicles 21:1," accessed via Bible Hub.

14. Joseph Benson, *Benson's Commentary of the Old and New Testaments*, s.v. "1 Chronicles 21:1," accessed June 1, 2025, https://biblehub.com/commentaries/1_chronicles/21-1.htm.

15. Matthew Henry, *Matthew Henry's Concise Commentary on the Whole Bible*, s.v. "1 Chronicles 24:19-31," (Nashville, TN: Nelson, 1997).

Chapter 14:
2 CHRONICLES

Day 122, 2 Chronicles 1-5:
Seeking God's Purpose Over Self-Gain

Good morning. I can never grow tired of watching how God provides.

Today, we will begin 2 Chronicles, reading the first five chapters.

Our Motivation

Solomon is now king in Israel and God tells him he can have anything he asks for. Do not mistake God for some genie who grants your wishes. God anointed Solomon to lead Israel. He knew his heart before He chose him.

James 4:2 says we don't have, because we don't ask. He declares it is because we ask with the wrong motives. Solomon asks for wisdom to lead God's people. Because of that, God makes him wiser, richer and more honored than any king before or after (see v 1:12). When we focus on what God wants from us, success will bless us. Too often, we start out that way, but success comes in and we focus on maintaining the success. Because the church experienced growth, they invested in a building. Their priority is now paying for the building, not God. They try adding programs, putting out food, hiring better musicians. Nothing works, because their focus is wrong.

Confidence in God

This I remind myself, when no one buys my book, or only reads the free edition. It isn't about money. Those who make it about having enough money will never have enough (see Ecc. 5:10). God's word is reaching people through my ministry. I am assured God will take care of me. Chapter 2 reminds us that God is not limited to buildings (2:5). He is everywhere, and the building is there for burning sacrifices for Him. We are here to serve God. Anything we want God to do to make us greater than we are is futile, unless it enables us to serve Him better. Our service "must be large and magnificent" (2 Chron 2:9). The chronicler is talking about the temple, but we are the temple. Our hearts are where God dwells. If we are asking to build ourselves up, He can, but we must build our hearts up to worship Him more. It has to be about our capacity to serve Him.

Patience

Notice in verse 3:2 that it took over two years to even get started. David had already gathered the materials and conscripted the labor. He completed the plans. God could have just made the temple appear. He did not. We appreciate the things we work for. Labor builds our hearts up. Time and sweat, keeping the faith, make the result sweeter. We saw in

1 Kings that the construction took seven years. When the construction was complete, Solomon filled the temple with the treasures his father had given him (v 5:1). Where we keep our treasure is where our hearts will be (see Matt 6:21). Worldly concerns will worry us if we focus our hearts on them. Therefore, we must remain steadfast and focused on God. He will not move. When our treasure is Him, it is always safe and abundant. Then we can celebrate like the entire assembly of Israel does in 2 Chron 5:6.

Tomorrow, we will read 2 Chronicles 6-8.

Day 123, 2 Chronicles 6-8:
From Darkness to Light: Finding God's Healing

Good morning, and may God bless you for reading His Word today. My normal routine is to wake up, shower, come out to the living room and read the Bible while my wife makes breakfast for me. Yes, I am spoiled by her. I won't deny it. I read the Bible on my phone and highlight passages that speak to me. Later in the day, I will go back and read the highlighted verses and recall what the Lord had placed in my heart. Then I bring up this document and write. I felt an overwhelming sense of urgency and power from the Word this morning. So I am writing this while many people are still having their morning coffee. We will read 2 Chronicles 6-8 today.

Darkness and Light

This was the blessing Solomon gave at the dedication of the temple. We begin in verse 6:1, which says, "The Lord has said that he would dwell in a dark cloud." (NIV) Ellicott gives us this added detail, "The thick darkness.—'Araphel, which is explained as caligo nubium, "gloom of clouds." (Ellicott 1954, 2 Chronicles 6:1) The greatest dichotomy of all time was that moment when Jesus hung on the cross. It was the darkest event in history. We murdered an innocent man, who was also the Lord. If I were God, praise the Lord I am not, I would have just wiped humanity from existence at that very second. When Jesus said, "It is finished" (John 19:30), I would have ended everything. This would have been the thick darkness, the gloom of clouds. But, it was also the brightest moment in history, because we didn't kill Jesus. He laid His life down for us (1 John 3:16). It was at this very instant that Jesus defeated Satan, and all who placed their faith in Jesus won the victory.

The Nature of Sin

We start today in this dark cloud because we all are sinners (v 6:36). When we sin, God becomes angry with us and allows sin to take us captive. One sin sends me down the rabbit hole again, even though I focus intensely on God and strive for a clean life. It is like when you are diligent in your diet and are avoiding sweets. After a while, you don't even want them. You can look at a donut and all it looks like is grease. You may go along for weeks, months even, and feel great. No cravings, good energy. Then you see a chocolate-covered Bavarian creme-filled donut, and you cave. You enjoy the gooey sweetness, thinking – it's just one donut, no big deal. Suddenly, you are craving many carbohydrates. Not only sweets but snacks, chips, French fries, bread! I am not saying eating is a sin, though gluttony is. Sin works the same way. When we indulge, it is hard to stop. With the diet, you put on some pounds. Your energy drops. Even though you love going to the gym, you want to skip a few days. Your clothing gets tighter and doesn't look as good on you. With sin, you realize you are working harder. Nothing seems to go as smoothly as it had been. Your health declines. Even your boss is not happy with the quality of your work.

The Importance of Repentance

Take that up a level, and if you look at this on a national scale. Famines, plagues, natural disasters. The economy tanks, and strife increases everywhere. Where harmony once filled the land, anger and hatred now reign. This is what Solomon was talking about in verses 6:36-38.

He tells them, when this is happening, they have a choice. They can turn away from their sin. This is what it means to repent. But that is only the first step. When you do this, all you are is a sinner standing in no-man's-land, not sinning. Like a guy standing at the snack table looking at the donut but not eating it.

Then, in verse 37, it says you must admit your sinfulness. Accepting that what you are doing is wrong. Until you see it as evil, it will not offend you enough for you to resist it. This is that moment when you decide not to take the donut, but you don't walk away. In your mind, you are trying to justify that it's just one donut. You ate little for breakfast. Lunch is a long time from now. If you walk away, you might be okay. But you don't. You just stand there with your back to the table. Temptation is still within reach.

The Pathway to Salvation

Verse 38 tells us we need to move. Turning back to God. Heading in a different direction. It is not enough to admit that you were wrong. Now, you must do what is right. God does not dwell in a temple made with human hands. He dwells in our hearts. We must pray to that temple, to Jesus dwelling in our hearts. This is how we open our hearts to let Him change them.

When we are going through the struggles of life, we must realize the problems that result from our sinfulness. Verse 7:13 tells us these things are to be expected. Then verse 7:14, which is what inspired me to write this, says, "If my people, who are called by my name, will humble themselves and pray and seek my face and turn from their wicked ways, then I will hear from heaven, and I will forgive their sin and will heal their land." (NIV)

God didn't leave us here to do this alone. He knew we would sin, and Jesus paid for that sin. He gave us a way to come back to God. This means realizing our wrong, turning away from it and moving toward Him. You don't need to suffer. It doesn't matter if you don't have the willpower. He has done it for you. All you need to do is walk away from the sin and go to the Lord.

Tomorrow, we will read 2 Chronicles 9-11.

Day 124: 2 Chronicles 9-11: Overwhelmed by God's Glory

Good morning. Let's begin by asking God for wisdom as we look at 2 Chronicles 9-11.

Overwhelming

The queen of Sheba wasn't just impressed with King Solomon. All he possessed and their way of conducting affairs overwhelmed her (2 Chron 9:4). She was a queen. The opening verse said she arrived with a very great caravan. We can assume she had traveled and met other dignitaries. Nothing compared to all she saw when she met Solomon.

Things have impressed me, but only one overwhelmed me. Around 2009, I took my wife and son to New York City for Christmas. We were only there for three days and went to see the Statue of Liberty. The cab driver dropped us off near the site of the twin towers, which were brought down by terrorists in 2001. The site was under construction, but workers had excavated it. I have seen the Grand Canyon, so the size of the pit did not strike me. But the heaviness of the grief was palpable. An ominous sadness filled the entire job site.

My employer sent me to Chicago in 2003 to train employees of a partner company on all our products. This was a six-month assignment. I grew up in Tucson, Arizona. During my childhood, it was a town of one hundred thousand people. When I was seventeen, they built the Bank of America Plaza. It was our tallest building. It stood two hundred-sixty-two feet tall. My company rented me an apartment in the Presidential Towers, which are four hundred sixty-one feet tall. I lived on the forty-eighth floor. Less than a mile away is the Willis Tower, then called Sears Tower. It stands one thousand seven hundred twenty-nine feet. When I stood at the base and looked up, I felt dizzy. It impressed me with its magnitude.

While I was living in Chicago, theaters released the movie, "The Passion of the Christ" (Gibson 2004). I attended it alone. As the actor Jim Caviezel portrayed Jesus, it was almost more than I could watch. Each time he was being beaten and tortured, I could only think of how casually I had taken sin in my life. Each time the hammers struck the nails, which were being driven through his hands, I felt like crying for causing Him that pain. While I knew this was a cinematic portrayal, I also knew it happened. This was God. He could have stopped it. He should have. I am not worth it. To Him, I am. That overwhelmed me.

In verse 9:6, she says, "I did not believe what they said until I came and saw with my own eyes." Thomas, the apostle, had to see the holes in Jesus' hands, and put his finger in His side, before he would believe (see John 20:27-31).

666 Talents

The yearly rate of 666 talents of gold in verse 9:13 troubled me. This is the sign of the beast in Revelation 13:18. Gold is money. Jesus said you can't love money and God (Matt 6:24).

So, I assumed there was a connection. I have researched this and found no connection. The Cambridge Bible for Schools and Colleges claims there was a numbering system used at that time by the Assyrians, which would suggest this is a round number (Kirkpatrick 1907).

Things are not always what they seem.

Discernment

Therefore, we must be discerning. If we hear someone quoting scripture, this does not make them a man of God. Remember, even demons believe in God (Jam 2:19). They believe, but they don't know Him.

We see other false prophets throughout scripture. In 2 Chron 11:14-15, Jeroboam puts his own priests in place. They worshiped the goat and calf idols he had made. This was a sin. Like many today, he preferred to hear a message that tickled his ears. Any gospel that does not cause you to confront your sin is not the Gospel of Jesus Christ.

What overwhelms you? If it is your troubles, you are not focusing on Jesus. If it is not how Jesus would take the punishment you deserve, then you haven't understood how sinful you are.

Tomorrow, we will read 2 Chronicles 13-17.

Day 125, 2 Chronicles 13-17:
Seeking God Leads to Lasting Peace

One Million two hundred thousand men, ready to fight. Today, we begin by reading 2 Chronicles 13-17. We will talk about soldiers, salt, serenity, and salvation.

Soldiers

The size of this battle is staggering. The current US Active Duty Military, as of September 2023, with all branches combined, has 1,290,000 active members. Therefore, this one battle was almost equal to our entire armed forces. In those days, men approached each other with swords, spears, and bows and arrows. They held shields, but as we have seen depicted in movies, a battlefield was a bloodbath. Now scale that up and imagine the amount of blood flowing from a battle of this magnitude.

Abijah, though not devout, worshiped the God of Israel. He would only reign for three years.

On the other side, with twice the personnel, was Jeroboam. He had driven out the Levites and replaced them with his own priests. This made him an idolater, and God was against him. Abijah knew this and trusted in God for deliverance.

Salt

He reminds Jeroboam that God has "a covenant of salt" with the family of David. Salt is a preservative. They used salt to prepare the sacrifices they offered God. They considered a "covenant of salt" a permanent, sacred, unbreakable agreement. Because of it, Abijah was not worried that the odds against him were two to one. He knows that "God is with us; He is our leader" (2 Chron 13:12). This was correct, as verse 13:16 says, "God delivered them in their hands." (NIV) Over five hundred thousand casualties happen in this one battle (v 17). The sorrow had to have been oppressive.

Serenity

Among the dead was Jeroboam, the evil king (v 20). As often happens, a cataclysmic moment precedes peace. The storm before the calm. The tipping point. Just a few verses later, in 14:1, Abijah dies too. Asa, his son, follows him. Historians consider him a great king. First, he removed the foreign altars and high places (v 14:2). Then, he commanded Judah to seek the Lord (v 14:3).

Because of this, there is a rare event: the country was at peace for ten years (v 14:1). By driving out foreign idols and returning to God, they had lasting peace. God favored them and gave them rest (v 14:6).

This enabled them to prosper. They built up the towns and fortified their walls. The troops continued their training and improved their weapons supply. But the Spirit of God was with them. It came on their prophet, Azariah, son of Obed, who went to meet Asa. His name means "Yahweh has helped." He tells Asa, "The Lord is with you when you are with Him. If you seek Him, you will find him. But, if you forsake Him, He will forsake you (v 15:2)." This is what we must take from this storyline.

Salvation

Christian principles formed America. All thirteen of the colonies that formed the United

States required their governors to be religious, with nine specifying they must believe in Jesus. When we were with God, He was with us. He blessed us beyond measure. Our nation prospered. We would seek Him, and we would find Him. God does not hide from people. He wants His children to be around Him always.

But God warned Asa, just as He had warned Israel under Jeroboam. If Judah were to forsake God, He would forsake them. We have been forsaking God in our country since the middle of the 1960s. People have removed him from our schools, our courts, and even our public consciousness.

Before we found our home in our current church, we attended services at four others. We left without hearing about Jesus. That is why we didn't return. If they removed Jesus from their message, they weren't His church. Ours either.

Asa drove out all the idols, even the one his grandmother made (v 15:16). Because they sought God, they found Him. And "There was no more war until the thirty-fifth year of Asa's reign." (2 Chron 2:19, NIV)

Sin

Then Asa messes up. He seeks help from Aram instead of God. We do this today. We know who God is and how He is helping us. But we want something we know is outside of His will for us. So, we seek it through another means. Illness comes to Asa, and instead of seeking help from God, he looks for other cures. He looked for the physicians to treat him instead of repenting and letting God heal him. From that point on, they were always at war.

Opportunity only presents itself for small windows of time. We seize them, or we lose them. Time is short. We must not continue to forsake Him. Repent now and seek God. He is waiting for you to come home.

Tomorrow, we will read 2 Chronicles 18-20.

Day 126, 2 Chronicles 18-20:
Good vs. Evil: Choices and the Consequences

Hello, thank you for joining us as we read 2 Chronicles 18-20 today. Yesterday, at the end of our reading, we met Jehoshaphat, Asa's son.

Good People – Bad Choices

According to 2 Chron 17:3-4, he followed the ways of David and didn't consult idols. Instead, he sought the Lord, and verse 17:6 says his heart was in the right place. It also says he removed the high places. Therefore, I would group Jehoshaphat into the minority. He was a king who made good choices most of the time. Even those of us who strive to follow God and dedicate ourselves to His ways make mistakes.

When I was young, this did not describe me. I didn't know the Lord. But, I tried to make good life choices. Most of the time, I succeeded. I remember one night, however, when I was at Apache Lake, a popular waterskiing location in Arizona. There were thirty or forty people, all drinking beer and having a good time. My cousin and I liked to hang out together. We were close in age, a little younger than our brothers and their friends. On that night, we were also hanging out with a friend of theirs who didn't fit in with the others, so he was talking to us. He convinced us to go looking for girls, so we began walking around the campgrounds. As we passed by a tent, we could hear the people inside were having amorous activity. For reasons I will never know, this guy we're walking with decides it would be funny to pull up all the poles and make their tent fall on top of the inhabitants.

Our Choices Have Consequences

My cousin and I did not know what he was about to do, but when he took off running, we had to run with him. In the darkness, we did not see the barbed wire fence that ran across the wash we were running in. My cousin was a track star and was ahead of me. I could see as he hit the fence and flipped over it. There was a large gouge in his leg. Others can influence even "good" people to do foolish things.

King Jehoshaphat was doing right, when King Ahab reached out and asked him to go with him against Ramoth Gilead (v 18:3). Jehoshaphat tells him he must first check with the Lord (v 18:4). This was a wise response. Ahab, we may recall, had run off all the genuine prophets, and replaced them with his own people. He gathers all four hundred of those false prophets and asks them if he should go. They tell him what he wants to hear (v 18:5). Jehoshaphat knows this is a bad idea. He asks if there are no prophets of the Lord in Israel (v 18:6).

Listen to the Voice of Reason

There is one prophet, but Ahab knows he won't like his answer. We all have that one friend who would tell us not to jump off the bridge when everyone else was. When we get hurt or in trouble, we know we should have listened to him. After a while, when we are plotting misadventures, we contemplate leaving them out. We know they won't want to participate. That is how Ahab felt about Micaiah. He knows Micaiah will relay the Lord's message to him, and nothing else. Notice, even Ahab knew it was a lie (v 18:15). So, Micaiah tells him he will die. God has a spirit that mislead Ahab's prophets, because it is His will that Ahab fails. God's character would not allow Him to tell the lie, or even to tempt the spirit to do this evil thing. Evil is always around, working against the Lord. God allows the spirits to decide this on their own (v 18:21). Just as He lets Satan test Job; He allows this spirit to put this lie into all those prophets' mouths (v 18:22). Then, Micaiah tells Ahab the truth, that he will die (v 18:27).

The Price of Disobedience

You hear Ahab knows this is true but ignores it. If I were more mature that night at the lake, I would have admitted that I knew walking around with that guy at Apache Lake was a bad idea. It wasn't a matter of if we would get in trouble. The only questions were when and how.

Ahab tries to disguise himself, but you can't hide from God. An arrow hits the king with a lucky shot (v 18:33). He props himself up and watches the battle until sunset, then dies (v 18:24). When Jehoshaphat returns, Jehu, the seer, lets him know his actions are going to cost him (v 19:2). Because the king had done good deeds prior to making this poor alliance with Ahab, and has a heart set on God (v 19:3), God allows him to live.

We wish to believe our positive contributions far exceed our shortcomings. They don't. Think of every sinful thought, every lie, all the times we have malice in our hearts toward people who do things we disapprove of. Those are all sins. On a good day, I would say I sin a hundred times. It disgusts me, but it is that old nature. There is no amount of good I can do that would justify myself. Therefore, Jesus knew He had to die for me. He knew I could not pay that debt. He had no sin, so He took mine (2 Cor 5:21).

Jehoshaphat continues to do wise things throughout chapter 20. But that will never erase the mistakes he had made helping Ahab.

Judge yourself. Realize you cannot redeem yourself and seek Jesus today before the sun sets on you.

Tomorrow, we will read 2 Chronicles 21-24.

Day 127, 2 Chronicles 21-24: Bad Influences and Not Following Instructions

Following Instructions

Good morning. As I write this devotional, one of our cats pulled everything on our dining room table onto the floor. We have three cats, and they all look guilty. One was trying to jump onto the table, which they all know they should not do. Instead, he almost made it onto the table, but the tablecloth slid. We make a mess when we don't follow instructions.

I have been thinking about why I write these messages and why you should read them. God has given us instructions on how to live a life that is pleasing to Him. Following those instructions will draw us closer to God and enable us to experience His fullness.

People don't enjoy reading the instructions. Who among us has ever read the owner's manual to their car? We will pick through it when something is wrong, but that is as far as we get. Let's see, headlights not coming on, chapter 4 headlights, page 12 troubleshooting.

We often use our Bibles the same way. It would be much better if we knew all the rules and how to win the game before we started playing. I hope these forays into my experiences have kept you going. I pray you are growing in your knowledge and relationship with the Lord. That is what it is all about.

Today, we read 2 Chronicles 21-24.

The Problem with Wealth

We know Jehoshaphat was a righteous king, but death claimed him, and they buried him.

He had all the riches he inherited from Solomon, and he left these to all his sons (v 21:3). However, they gave the kingdom to his son

Jehoram, who was not righteous. One of the first acts was to have all his brothers slain (v 21:4). This leaves me with the question Jesus asked his disciples, "What good is it for someone to gain the whole world, yet forfeit their soul?" (Mark 8:36, NIV) Jehoram married Ahab's daughter and followed the ways of the kings of Israel (v 21:6). He caused the people of Judah to worship idols and foreign gods (v 21:11).

Whenever we are doing things we know are wrong, we like to get others to do them with us. If enough people are doing it, we hope they won't punish us all. Maybe it will even catch on and become the popular thing to do? Just because something is popular does not make it right.

What is Our Legacy?

Then, the prophet Elijah tells Jehoram he is going to die because of a bowel disease. This miserable and disgusting event happens in verses 21:18-19. Notice the people made no fire in his honor (v 21:19). No one regretted his passing (v 21:20).

I'm getting to the stage of my life where I think about the legacy I will leave. I don't want to cause anyone grief when I go to be with the Lord. There is no greater goal for one who serves the Lord. I would want no one feeling the world had lost anything great when I leave it.

Billy Graham was a legendary preacher, and I am certain many people came to know Jesus through his labors. I am sure his close friends and family miss him daily, the way I have missed my mother for three decades. But he was all about spreading the Gospel, and the infrastructure he built for his ministry continues to reach people for the Lord today. It was never about him but always centered on Jesus. That is the most any preacher could hope for. Through life or death, we will point others to Christ.

Poor Guidance

Speaking of mothers, I was lucky to have a wonderful mother. She struggled throughout life but always put her children first. She wanted the best for all her children and encouraged me to be anything I wanted to be in life. I honor her legacy by having the courage she instilled in me.

Then we look at Athaliah, the mother of Ahaziah. She epitomizes the image of the overbearing mother. She is always manipulating her son to do evil deeds. A vessel for the enemy of God, used to lead the people of Judah astray. In 2 Chron 22:10, she saw her favorite son had died. People respond to grief in various ways. Hers was vengeance.

Repairing the Temple

She tried to find the next in line for the throne and have him killed. So, they hid Joash in a bedroom. They kept him hidden for six years. In the seventh year, the priest set up security all around the young king, and introduced him as king. The people cheered and celebrated, but Athaliah screams, "Treason! Treason!" (v 23:13).

With her out of the way, the priest Jehoiada inspires everyone to return to the Lord (v 23:16). They tear down the idols and even kill the priests of Baal (v 23:17). But Athaliah's sons had already done a lot of damage to the temple (v 24:7). So, the king and Jehoiada collect the money, a temple tax, from the people and hire skilled craftsmen to do the repairs (v 24:1112).

Influences on Others

Unfortunately, Joash became king, and he did not follow the Lord. He turns people back to Baal and the Asherah. God's wrath burned against Judah again (v 24:18).

Yesterday, I wrote about protecting yourself from the influences of others. Today, let's flip that around and look at who we influence. For good or bad, we influence our children, coworkers, neighbors, families, and friends. It extends beyond that. If we raise a child that shows Christ in all they do, that influences their friends, who influence their families.

Like ripples in a pond. We must own our actions but realize we are not living in isolation. People will say, who is it hurting if I do whatever sinful thing they like to do? We all influence others. The hurt is happening, whether we accept the responsibility for it. Therefore, we must live intentionally. Realize you will affect the world around you. Decide what you want that legacy to be.

Tomorrow, we will read 2 Chronicles 25-28.

Day 128, 2 Chronicles 25-28:
The Struggle with Wholehearted Devotion

Good morning. Today, for the first time in decades, I am unemployed. Or I am now a professional writer. There are two ways to look at this transition in my life. I am not able to remain unemployed. I wish my book had been at the top of the Best Sellers list, but it was not. My intent was never to get rich from sharing the Word of God. Now, I must trust Him to provide. Today, we read 2 Chronicles 25-28.

God's Provision

It seems appropriate, under my circumstances, that we talk about Amaziah. This king "did what was right in the eyes of the Lord, but not wholeheartedly" (v 25:2). In his case, this meant he did not kill the children, but I know people who fit this description. We are people, more often than we would like to admit, that are not wholehearted. We want to be.

In our minds, we think we live to serve God. He is the first thing I think about when I awake. As I drink my morning coffee, I read His Word.

What Went Wrong?

When my wife brings me breakfast (I'm spoiled; she brings eggs and meat to me on the couch), I stop and pray. Thanking Him and asking for a good day before I eat. He always is faithful and gives us those good days. There was one of those days, a couple of weeks back, when I prayed for a good day, and within a few hours, I learned I was being laid off. Did He forget I asked for a good day? That was not feeling so good. I was feeling like Amaziah.

He had gathered his troops, but a man of God told him not to march with the men from Israel. God would overthrow him.

For decades, our old mobile home was a place of perfect contentment for my wife and me. We knew God was going to provide a way for us to survive the years when my legs would not work well and she might be too old to help me as much. Our income had increased, and we could have afforded more. But we waited. When the time came, we felt certain that God was telling us it was time to build. We had saved the money. We knew how many more years I would be working. All the plans pointed to go! Now, we have a beautiful home but not enough saved for retirement.

Not To Be Greedy

I think this is how Amaziah felt. He had paid these troops to go with him. Now the man of God is saying, send them home. He responds, "But what about the hundred talents I paid for these Israelite troops?" (v 25:9). I will take comfort in the answer he received. The man of God replied, "The Lord can give you much more than that."

We know God has already given us the life of His Only Son. When we deserved punishment, He gave us His righteousness. It feels inconceivable to ask for more. Amaziah did what I feel like doing. He sent the troops away; he was obedient to God. But then, he is furious and stomps out (v 25:10). God rewards his obedience; he wins the battle, and God gives him ten thousand more troops, whom they then throw off cliffs. I am not sure why they do this. It was a common practice with Romans and others doing it.

I think this shows that Amaziah, though obedient, was not wholehearted. He was still doing what he wanted to do, not what God wanted. That is what I see in the churches, and myself today. We follow God the best we can as long as we can do things our way. We have seen that our way leads to disaster, but the alternative is to do things God's way. This means giving Him complete lordship over our lives. While we like the sound of it, the practice of it eludes us.

It Always Escalates

When we start down that path of making our own rules, there is always a next step. Amaziah, as he returns from this slaughter, brings back the gods of the people of Sier. He had been seeking God. When told to send the troops away, He did. But after a small taste of rebellion, he falls into idolatry, like the kings before him. God sends a prophet who asks, "Why do you consult this people's gods, which could not save their own people?" (v 25:15). It is a good question, but we do foolish things all the time. We have seen God make the money we had cover our needs. Other times, we have seen Him provide more than we needed so we could share the blessings with others. Now, we are putting our faith back into the balance in our bank account. It could not save us before. Why are we not trusting in God?

Tomorrow, we will read 2 Chronicles 29-31.

Day 129, 2 Chronicles 29-31:
Revival Can Transform Our Nation

Changes in my life have felt like a dark cloud was hanging over me. I remember how God is the cloud the Israelites followed. We must praise Him for our victories and our defeats, in our joys and in our sorrows. The skies outside my office are overcast, and rain has been falling throughout the morning. We live in a desert, so rain is a blessing. Then, knowing God is always my comfort and my hope, today we read 2 Chronicles 29-31. What a great passage to focus on.

King Hezekiah

There are only five kings who did not either start out as evil, or fell and became evil. We have already discussed David, Asa, Jehosophat, and Josiah. Some lists will include Solomon, though he slipped up along the way. Today, we will talk about Hezekiah. History remains to be seen, but my hope for our current administration is that they will resemble Hezekiah when their days are over. Israel had been sinning, and Ahaz had hired the Assyrians to help them (2 Chron 28:16). The prophet Isaiah was active during this time, telling them of their past, their present mistakes, and foretelling the coming of Jesus.

Then Hezekiah becomes the king, and he isn't taking years to get started, like Solomon had done. This twenty-five-year-old opened the doors of the temple and had them repaired in his first month! (v 29:3). Then he gives orders to the Levites to consecrate themselves (v 29:5) and remove all the defilement from the sanctuary.

After I read my Bible verses today, I was looking at a list of all the sinful waste DOGE has found in our government. It isn't about the money savings, though that will help our country, but what they were funding. We cannot support activities or groups that are promoting sin. These agencies and organizations, both those in the United States and others overseas, have been doing the equivalent of "shutting the doors of the portico and putting out the lamps." Their actions, in direct conflict with the scripture, were causing God's anger to fall on our country (compare to v 29:7-8). By promoting deviant lifestyles, they have caused sin to proliferate. When they make sin seem mainstream and acceptable, it takes the innocent into captivity (v 29:9). In our country, the Administration cannot do this alone. They will need approvals from Congress. There will be challenges in the courts, and they will need the Supreme Court. For these changes, we see to take root and come to fruition, they will all have to assemble, as did the Levites (v 29:15) If God is with us, they will prevail to purify our country, the way the priests did the sanctuary in v 29:16. Removing everything that is unclean.

Not Only Sunday

After Hezekiah accomplished this, they had a feast. The king had them sacrifice seven bulls, as well as seven rams, goats, and lambs. A subdued sacrifice compared to the opulent spectacle Solomon had overseen. It was not about the size of the sacrifice but where their hearts were. They were seeking the Lord and following His commandments. Then they sang and prayed and worshiped the Lord (v 29:30). This lit the fire that started a revival. The people gave more to the offering without provocation. Six hundred bulls and three thousand sheep and goats (v 29:33). So many that the priests who were sacrificing them could not keep up. Their relatives consecrated themselves and joined the labor. (v 29:34)

It is my dream that righteousness catches fire in our land. That our churches can't hold all the people who want to praise the Lord. We will need to add preachers and music leaders and add service times. That would show God's acceptance of our repentance.

We read the people rejoiced because it happened so quickly (v 29:36). Change does not have to be slow. When God is behind it, miracles can happen. The king knew it was not the time of Passover, but it seemed right for them to have the feast. We can't wait for Sunday to decide in our hearts to worship God. Every day is the right day to praise Him.

Faith Grows

The celebration in Israel became a revival and everyone contributed. They could not praise God enough. So, King Hezekiah extended the celebration for another week (v 30:23). They were rejoicing because the "Lord heard Hezekiah and healed the people" (v 30:20).

People will come to church and worship the Lord, but before they get home, it's over. They return to living as if God didn't matter. Not these people. When genuine revival happens, the people keep it going. They went to the towns of Judah and smashed the idols (v 31:1). From there, they went to Benjamin and Ephraim. They were doing all of this in the third month, a hundred days into the reign of Hezekiah. They completed it within four months. (v 31:7). Because of this growth of righteousness, they needed more priests and we see them adding to those numbers throughout the rest of chapter 31. This was when God will speak to the prophets Isaiah and Micah. Those who will tell of the coming Messiah. Hezekiah was the fifth righteous king. Like the others, he had sins. But he did not cause God's people to sin.

The Sixth King

There was still one King remaining. The list of Old Testament kings omits him, although every page mentions him (Murray 2013). I am talking about the King of kings, the Lord of lords. The one who hung on a cross with signs written in three languages describing Him as King of the Jews. His name is Jesus. He is my King. Is He yours?

Tomorrow, we will read 2 Chronicles 32-34.

Day 130, 2 Chronicles 32-34:
Faith vs. Intimidation: A Biblical Showdown

Good morning, today we read 2 Chronicles 32-34. We're just about caught up. Remember, Chronicles is a recap of everything we have studied so far. Told from a different perspective. Just as the four different men wrote the Gospels, with different backgrounds and for unique audiences, that is what Chronicles is.

Intimidation

Here, in chapter 32, we encounter Sennacherib. You may recall from Kings, Sennacherib as brutal. He led the Assyrian army against the Babylonians and then conquered the northern kingdom of Israel. People also knew him as innovative in restoring Nineveh and overseeing the construction of the Hanging Gardens of Babylon. He has his aim set on the two tribes of Judah. Hezekiah is the king, and he is trusting in God for deliverance. Sennacherib mocks him and tries to wear down the resolve of the guards on the walls around Jerusalem. He asks why they think their God can protect them when the gods of all the other nations he had conquered could not.

People make this same mistake today. We see portrayals of gods in movies and in literature. We even read about God in the Bible, but without fully comprehending the difference. The God of Israel is the creator of all there is. He was outside of time and space and spoke everything into existence. When we dilute our understanding of what a god is, we come up with something like Loki, the god of mischief in Norse mythology. As the character The Hulk states in the movie "The Avengers," he's a puny god (Whedon 2012). We end up with a reduced fear of God.

Sennacherib is attempting to win over the hearts of the Israelite guards. Replacing the fear of the Lord with a fear of himself. Hezekiah and the prophet Isaiah are crying out in the streets. They're warning the people not to waver. As the troops with Sennacherib sleep, the Lord goes through their camp and slays them all. In the morning, there is nothing but death. Sennacherib rethinks his opposition to God and withdrawals. But the people's hearts are already affected.

When Hezekiah dies, his son Manasseh has no problem leading the people astray. They sin worse than they had before Hezekiah. Rebuilding the idols and desecrating the temple. In America, I have watched our morals continue to decline. I would say each generation gets worse, but I have seen some hope in the younger generations. Unfortunately, their schools instruct them to ignore their knowledge of God. We have made our own gods. Science, technology, wealth. These are like the gods Sennacherib had defeated. They could not protect the nations he subdued. They won't protect us.

Youthful Mistakes

There is hope in our youth, however. This is reminiscent of Josiah. He was only eight years old when he became king of Judah (v 34:1). Because of that, I always picture this brighteyed child seeing the Word of God when Hilkiah finds it. This was not the case. In verse 34:3, we read eight years had passed, which puts Josiah at sixteen, when he sought God. Four years later, he tells them to destroy the idols, tear down the high places, crush the Asherah poles and burn the bones of the priests of Baal.

We hear about God and He works in our lives. Though we did not believe in Him before, we are seeing Him move. The reality of His existence becomes clearer to us. It was around that time in my life I gave up smoking cigarettes and spending money on beer every day. These things had been a part of my life since I was a teenager, but I knew they didn't belong there anymore. I was standing in line at Walmart with a twelve-pack in the cart, knowing I needed to buy a carton of Marlboros. The pastor from the church we attended walked up behind me. There was an awkwardness, followed by guilt and embarrassment. He never said a word or even acted like he noticed what I was buying. There was no reason to. The Lord was convicting my heart. I had been praying for financial help and realized I was wasting the resources He was providing. I will have a drink one day a week now. The Bible teaches against drunkenness (Gal. 5:21). Because Jesus turned water into wine in Cana in John 2:9, I don't believe drinking is a sin in moderation. There was a time in my life I enjoyed getting drunk. I don't do that anymore.

Igniting a Fire

The Bible does not mention cigarettes, though it instructs us to glorify God with our bodies (1 Cor. 6:20). But, in that moment, I felt God say, for me, it was a sin. I had placed this habit at a level I should not have. I haven't smoked in over twenty years.

Around that time, I started desiring the Lord. He had been my enemy, became my Savior, and was now my Lord. I wanted to serve Him, and this was when I wanted to read through the Bible. I had to know every Word that it contained.

Then, for Josiah, in the eighteenth year of his reign (v 34:8), he sends Shaphan and Maaseiah with Joah to repair the temple. We read they worked diligently and went from job to job (v 34:13). Therefore, I am assuming some time had passed. The Bible doesn't specify what year Shaphan took the Book of the Law from Hilkiah (v 34:15). Josiah ruled for thirtyone years. Therefore, between the time he was twenty-six and forty-nine, he found the Word of God. It transforms him, and he inspires the nation to turn back to God.

Therefore, I read the Bible every day. It's why it matters that we let the whole Word of God speak to us, the way it did to Josiah. It's not enough to know who God is. Even the demons know that (Jam. 2:19). We should want more than God's knowledge of us. God wants a relationship with each of us. A relationship is a two-way situation. He hears our prayers. For us to hear His voice, we must let His Word speak to us. Interrupting someone midsentence is incredibly impolite. We must hear everything He has to say.

Tomorrow, we will read 2 Chronicles 35-36.

Day 131, 2 Chronicles 35-36:
Life Transitions: Plans and Purposes

Today, we will finish 2 Chronicles 35-36, then we will move into Ezra.

Transitions

There are major events that happen throughout our lives. We graduate, get married, and have children. In my part of the country, we begin our career and buy a house. Sometimes, things happen that you can't plan for. Thirty-nine years ago, my vehicle malfunctioned, and I rolled it. That resulted in a spinal cord injury and lifelong disability. Twenty-eight years ago, my mother died. She was a major part of my life. Six years ago, I had a heart attack. My employer laid me off two weeks ago. These are all normal moments of transition in people's lives. While reading chapter 35, I saw Josiah instructing the priests to "prepare themselves by families" (v 35:3). Because of what I am working through, that stood out to me. It's brilliant advice, even when taken out of context.

Plans and Purposes

In context, he is telling the priest to study all the instructions David and Solomon had provided. 2 Tim 2:15 says, "Study to shew thyself approved unto God, a workman that needeth not to be ashamed, rightly dividing the word of truth." (KJV). About eight years ago,

God inspired me to return to college and finish the computer science degree I started in 1981. I had worked in many industries, but sales was always what I returned to when I needed a job. Although I never considered myself a salesman, I was highly proficient at it. But I knew there were still fifteen years left in my career. I wanted to do something I enjoyed. Therefore, I enrolled at Liberty University and while maintaining my full-time job, I completed my degree in just over two years. One thing I have learned in life is everything we go through; God knew it before it happened. He had a purpose for us to experience it. Things I did simply because it was the only job I could find at the time turned out to be a skill I would need two decades later. He is efficient and does not waste our efforts. We may indulge in foolish pursuits, but God works everything out for the good of those who love Him and obey His commands (Rom 8:28). It's comforting to know that in hindsight, everything had a meaning. David and Solomon had written these instructions out. Josiah is having the priests recover the lost instructions. In verse 35:19, we find the answer to a question we had yesterday. Josiah was twenty-six years old when this all happened.

We then skip ahead thirteen years, since we know he reigned for thirty-one years, and Necho goes against him on the plains of Megiddo (v 35:22). There an arrow pierces Josiah, and then he dies (v 35:24). It is possible he lingered on in Jerusalem for some time, even years. The book of the kings of Israel and Judah records all the events of his life, as we read. The way these books—1 Kings, 2 Kings, 1 Chronicles, and 2 Chronicles—reference another object called the Books of the Kings of Israel and Judah, suggests the existence of a lost document. In them, we could learn of the detestable acts of Jehoiakim (v 36:8)

God Gives Up

The rest of chapter 36 is about a string of young, evil kings, which leads to God giving Israel and Judah over to their sins. Because of this, Nebuchadnezzar takes them captive and moves them to Babylon. They had mocked God's messengers, and scoffed at the words the prophets gave them (v 36:16), so he let the Babylonians burn Jerusalem down (v 36:19). We think it's alright to do whatever we want, as long as it isn't harming anyone other than ourselves. Jesus died for all sinners, wanting them all to repent. Therefore, those personal sins have hurt someone else. They also bleed over and influence evil in others. We must heed the warning of chapter 36. If we, like the people in Jerusalem, continue to resist God, He will turn us over to our sin (see Rom 1:24). I know people who believe He already has.

Tomorrow, we will read Ezra 1-3.

Conclusion of 2 Chronicles:

Now that you have read the fourteenth book of the Bible, take a moment to reflect. How have the events in 2 Chronicles mirrored lessons in your own life? Do you feel yourself growing in knowledge? Are you also growing in faith?

For fun, here are five questions I want you to answer (I will post some brief answers at the back of the book).

1. Who was the first king of Judah that 2 Chronicles primarily focuses on, and what special gift did he ask God for?

2. What magnificent building did Solomon construct in Jerusalem?

3. After Solomon's reign, the kingdom split. What was the name of the southern kingdom that 2 Chronicles mostly follows?

4. Many of the kings in 2 Chronicles are described as either doing "what was right in the eyes of the Lord" or "what was evil in the eyes of the Lord." What was usually the result for the kings who did what was right?

5. King Hezekiah is known for his great reforms. What major action did he take to restore proper worship in Judah?

Chapter 14: Footnotes

1. Ellicott, Charles John. *Ellicott's Commentary for English Readers.* s.v. "2 Chronicles 6:1." London: Cassell and Company, 1905.

Chapter 15:
EZRA

Day 132, Ezra 1-3:
God's Authority Transcends Limitations

Good morning. I hope this day brings you joy. Today, we will begin our fifteenth book. That is a nice accomplishment. Until now, the books have been long, except for Ruth. Now, things are going to move much faster. The challenge in that is we get accustomed to a writing style. The first five books were all penned by Moses. Now, they're going to change often. But not today. Scholars believe Ezra was the chronicler of Chronicles.[1] Today, we will read Ezra 1-3.

Respect Authority

The last paragraph in 2 Chronicles discussed how the Persians had taken control from Nebuchadnezzar, and now Cyrus is the king. This book opens in verse 1:1, with this being the first year of Cyrus. Though not a Jew, it says the Lord moved his heart.

God is the Lord of all creation. Our belief in Him does not change this immutable fact. Our lack of reverence does not diminish His authority. One day, we will all kneel before Him (Phi 2:10-11). Therefore, He places on Cyrus' heart the need to let the Israelites return to Jerusalem. What strikes me is the wording in Ezra 1:2. Cyrus states, "The Lord, the God of heaven, has given me all the kingdoms of the earth."

Avoid Satan

This is very close to the wording of Satan when he tempted Jesus. In Matthew 4:8-9, it says, "Again, the devil took him to a very high mountain and showed him all the kingdoms of the world and their splendor. 'All this I will give you,' he said, 'if you will bow down and worship me.'" I'm not saying Satan was directing Cyrus, but pointing out how Satan mimics God when he is trying to tempt us. Therefore, we must be careful not to follow false prophets and modern-day preachers who twist scripture. The enemy knows how to impersonate God and will fool us if we are not careful.

My wife and I enjoy the guilty pleasure of watching a television show called Ghosts. Whether the English version or the US version, it is hilarious. Last week, they had a character return from hell as a minion of the devil and trick Jay, the husband of the person who can interact with the ghosts. They make light of the fact that Jay wanted his restaurant to thrive, and he is getting everything he ever dreamt of. Then finds out he sold his soul.

We may laugh and think this only happens in fiction, but we know Satan tried to tempt Jesus. I know of a person who has been in ninety-five Hollywood productions, some popular movies, and television series.

He is an insider who knows of many famous people who have sold their souls to the devil. This is not a matter we should be laughing at.

Returning

Getting back to Cyrus, the Lord leads him to let the Israelites return and rebuild Jerusalem. He even provides the materials they will need. Then, he returns the items Nebuchadnezzar had taken from the temple.

When God changes a person's heart, even an enemy can become an ally. People may tire of fighting against someone and just let them go away. Three times, I ended my marriages because the effort wasn't worthwhile. We know this was a God-inspired, heartfelt action by Cyrus' generosity.

Take Inventory

Ezra then gives a count of the articles and the people that were returning. In verse 2:62, there are some priests who don't have records of their genealogy. Because the Levites consider them unclean, they prevent them from joining in the blessing until consecration. I also found it interesting that there were only about six Israelites to each slave (v 2:62-65). This tells me they must have treated them well; otherwise, a revolt would have been possible.

The numbering of the singers after the slaves and before the animals is also funny. Does that show their position in society? Not livestock, but less than a servant. There were one hundred twenty-eight musicians, the descendants of Asaph listed in v 2:41. They did not count the singers with the musicians.

Strength Isn't in Numbers

Israel came out of Egypt with two to three million people. Approaching towns and villages was intimidating, given their reputation for having God on their side. There was still a lot of fear. Remember, only Joshua and Caleb would enter Canaan, but they moved on with power.

Now, we have a tiny group moving back into an area their ancestors had left seventy years before. Their reputation is that of a group of people whom someone captured. Now, they had fear (v 3:3), but they worked past it. With danger all around them, they rebuilt the altar, offered sacrifices, and sang praise. The people now held those musicians in high regard. Some people remembered what it was like before they left. They wept to see the ruin. Other people did not remember or focused on the promise that the future held. They rejoiced. The noise of their worship was so loud it was impossible to distinguish the sounds of each (v 3:13). Even with danger on all sides, they made their presence known.

How many of us go to work and keep our faith hidden? Afraid that if people knew we were

Christians, they might not do business with us. We join them in celebrations and at company parties with drinking and carousing. Knowing we are out of place but keeping to ourselves because to do otherwise could jeopardize our career. Why has ensuring safety in our free country vanished when expressing our faith?

Tomorrow, we will read Ezra 4-7.

Day 133, Ezra 4-7:
Overcome Challenges and Grow Spiritually

Good morning. I am feeling inspired by Ezra. I hope you are as well. Today, we will read chapters 4-7.

Accept Responsibility

I have been involved in ministries now for twenty-five years. When you feel God calling you, it is intimidating. At first, I was eager to join in. I went to the pastor of the church we were attending and asked if I could teach a class. There was a shortage of teachers. I thought the answer would be an instant, "Thank you!" Instead, the pastor interrogated me. He questioned my beliefs, my conversion experience, and my qualifications to help. I was a little put off. I remember thinking, "Fine, I was just asking if you could use a hand." The pastor knew he had to protect his congregation. He was their shepherd and had to ensure anyone who was going to teach them was qualified. Many heresies have entered the church through apostates who teach incorrect doctrine. While we should all be willing to give an answer for our faith (1 Peter 3:15), to be given authority, to be permitted to teach, is a higher calling. We should not take it lightly. 2 Timothy 4:5 tells us you will have to be serious about how you conduct your life, and to expect hardship.

Not By Works

People will embrace this opportunity with wrong motives. My knowledge that I had been God's enemy most of my life (Rom 5:10) compelled me to make amends. We know how much sin we have in our ledger. If we can do enough good things, we reason, we can balance it out.

Salvation does not work this way. Let's say you were to be arrested for stealing a car and went before a judge. He will not care that you also do charity work for underprivileged children. Even if he wanted to give you a lighter sentence, his commitment is to the Law. He would have to judge you for the crime.

God is a perfect judge. He would refuse to pronounce one thief guilty because of his attitude and declare another innocent because of his generosity. That would not be justice. Therefore, Ephesians 2:8-9 says, "For it is by grace you have been saved, through faith—and this is not from yourselves, it is the gift of God — not by works, so that no one can boast". (NIV)

The Enemy

In verses 1-5, the Samaritans see the families of Judah have returned to Jerusalem. They can see they're rebuilding the temple and the walls of the city. Samaritans had always been enemies of Israel, but they had been in captivity for seventy years. Had this new generation forgotten past transgressions? Were they unfamiliar with their history? Their response was to offer to help. Were they trying to balance the scales? What was their motive? We don't know.

Zerubbabel's Responsibility

Zerubbabel had a decree from Cyrus, which did not include enlisting others to help. The leaders of Israel knew it was a sacred duty to rebuild the temple for their God. Therefore, they send them away. How we turn people away is important. We can deny them and still make them feel appreciated. "Thanks. We have some requirements, and King Cyrus will only let specific people work on this project, but we appreciate the offer." They might have responded, "No problem, we just had some time on our hands and wanted to be neighborly." Abrupt handling could cause the response to be taken as an insult. The Israelites flatly rejected the Samaritans' offer of help. They took offense. From that point on, they opposed the construction (v 4:5).

Seasons Changes

Cyrus died in battle, and Xerxes succeeded him. He had his own agenda. This is like a new administration no longer wanting to back the initiatives of its predecessor. He would have put in his own advisors and cabinet. They would want to drive their own initiatives. Artabanus assassinated Xerxes, and Artaxerxes replaced him. Therefore, anything Cyrus had in his heart, like allowing the Jews to return to Jerusalem, would no longer be a priority. The Samaritans exploit this and turn the Persians against the people of Judah. They dig up old records of what happened before the exile and convince King Artaxerxes to stop the building (v 4:19-23).

Expect Challenges

I have learned over the years whenever I am about to undertake a new ministry, the enemy will create opposition. He will attack my health or my finances. The enemy will create some diversion in my life, which will distract me. His goal is to prevent me from serving God. I had noticed this cycle, and it has caused me to hesitate before accepting other ministries. Even now, I wonder if there is a connection between publishing my second book and losing my job. This fits the pattern.

When you know it's for the Lord, not your ambitions, you push past the opposition. The advisors convinced Artaxerxes to consult the record books. There, he reads Cyrus had decreed to even provide funding for the Jews (v 6:8). He reinforces the edict, threatening to impale on a beam from their house anyone who hinders the construction. We will face challenges when we take a stand for the Lord. This is to be expected.

When God is For Us

Staying true to God always results in the situation, resulting in good for those who love God and keep His commands (Rom 8:28). With patience, prayer, and dedication to God's will, all things are possible. Artaxerxes sent Ezra, and they finished the temple's construction (v 7:6).

He has a thorough knowledge of the Law of Moses. God is with him, and the king gives him all he asks for. Ezra dedicated himself to studying, observing, and teaching the Law. When we devote ourselves to the Lord, we do not have to worry about the attacks of the enemy. God is stronger. When God is with us, who can stand against us (Rom 8:31)?

Tomorrow, we will read Ezra 8-10.

Day 134, Ezra 8-10:
Navigating Faith and Relationships

Good morning. Today is my wife's birthday. She has stood by me for over thirty-two years, so I need to remember this day. Our relationship is a good argument for and against what we read today in the final three chapters of Ezra.

Equally Yoked

2 Corinthians 6:14 warns, "Do not be yoked together with unbelievers. For what do righteousness and wickedness have in common? Or what fellowship can light have with darkness?" (NIV) A yoke is the wooden crossbeam, which connects two oxen to the plow.

You would not want to have one strong ox pulling on the right and a weaker one on the left. Your plow would pull to the right, and it would require more work for the farmer to keep his rows straight.

In modern use, yoked means strong. We consider a very muscular person to be yoked. Look at what Paul was asking the church at Corinth, "What do righteousness and wickedness have in common? "

Ezra 9:2 explains the answer and our connection between this verse and marriage. Like their ancestors, the people who were coming out of captivity in Babylon had taken foreign wives. We had read how God told the Israelites to kill all the men and women as they conquered the Canaanites and Amalekites, etc. He did this because they would marry these women and they would introduce their foreign gods, which would bring idolatry into their relationships.

This applies today. I was an atheist on our wedding day. My wife was a Christian. If she were following the commands of the Lord, she would have avoided me. The odds are my worldly lifestyle would have pulled her from the church. It did in the beginning. She did not attend church the first few years we were together. When our son was born, she was adamant about raising him in the church. This led to me attending and hearing the Gospel. God had planned this and, I believe, sent my wife into the world I was living in to bring me out of it. Thank you, Jesus.

God not Surprised

The strength of her faith pulled me in the right direction for my life. God did not take an inventory one day and realize, "Oh, we have a new believer! Maybe we will put him to work in the ministry." He knew, before creating the universe, that I was going to love and serve Him. Even as I was a prodigal wandering in the wilderness of sin, He was waiting for me to find my way home.

Here in Ezra, we have this small remnant that had been captive in Babylon. Whereas we had read of thousands, tens, even hundreds of thousands, in the exodus from Egypt. Now we are reading one hundred fifty (v 8:3), eighty (v 8:8) and even twenty-eight (v 8:11). A small group of people. Many of them were born in Babylon. They grew up as Babylonians. Then, married women from their towns, or Persians or Medes, who had moved into the area. They were more familiar with foreign gods than they were with the Lord. But God was gracious and brought them back to Jerusalem to possess the land they had inherited. Amidst this festive celebration, Ezra realized they were bringing their idols with them. He tears his robe and weeps. Pulling hair from his head and face (v 9:3), he prays for guidance (v 9:5).

Divorce

In Matthew 19:8, people asked Jesus about divorce, and he replied, "Moses permitted you to divorce your wives because your hearts were hard. But it was not this way from the beginning." (NIV) It was never God's intention for marriages to fail. We are to work through troubles and love our wives (Eph 5:25).

As the remnant was returning to Jerusalem, their hearts were open to the Lord. Before they became hardened, Ezra calls all the men together. As they stand in the rain, he tells them they must send away all their foreign wives. I cannot imagine the conflicting emotions. It would be devastating to lose my wife. They had built lives together. These women had left their families behind in Babylon. Now, the men are told to get rid of these partners.

We had seen how the women's beliefs had influenced earlier generations. I had seen this in my life. Therefore, the decision was correct. Though this would not make it any easier. They had families. The men, women and children all wept (v 10:1). Each of these families experienced disruption.

Sin, even unintentional sin, disrupts lives. Therefore, it is important for each of us to examine ourselves and assess what do we have in our lives that needs to be removed. What sin have we gotten comfortable with that needs to go? It may be a hard choice, but we see from Ezra that sometimes this needs to be done. Thankfully, God ordained my marriage. We have nothing to fear.

Tomorrow, we will read Nehemiah 1-4.

Questions for the Book of Ezra

Now that you have read the fifteenth book of the Bible, take a moment to reflect. How have the events in Ezra mirrored lessons in your own life? Do you feel yourself growing in knowledge? Are you also growing in faith?

For fun, here are five questions I want you to answer (I will post some brief answers at the back of the book).

1. What was the major construction project the returning exiles focused on in the first part of Ezra, despite opposition?

2. Who were the two prophets who encouraged the people to restart and complete the Temple rebuilding when they had stopped?

3. What important spiritual problem did Ezra discover among the Jews in Jerusalem that grieved him deeply?

4. What difficult but necessary action did the people agree to take under Ezra's leadership to correct their sin of intermarriage?

5. What was the ultimate purpose of Ezra's mission, as described in the book, beyond addressing the specific sin of intermarriage?

Chapter 15: Footnotes

1. James Strong and John McClintock, *The Cyclopædia of Biblical, Theological, and Ecclesiastical Literature* (New York: Harper & Brothers, 1880), s.v. "Ezra."

Chapter 16:
NEHEMIAH

Day 135, Nehemiah 1-4: Rebuilding More Than Walls

Good morning. I hope we are all ready to begin another book. Today, we will read Nehemiah 1-4. The book opens in the city of Susa. This is in the city of Shush in modern-day Iran. I believe it is important to understand where these events happened on our current world map. The Book of Revelation explains their relevance to the times to come.

City in Ruin

King Darius had a palace built in Susa, and the Persians would use that as their winter headquarters. This makes sense, since Kislev is around the end of November to the early part of December on our calendars. Nehemiah has heard reports about Jerusalem and the condition it is in. What was a beautiful city and the temple of God now is rubble and charred remains of walls and gates.

I spent a summer with my oldest sister in Daly City, California, when I was eleven years old. This is a suburb south of San Francisco. She would take my brother and me into the city to see Fisherman's Wharf, The Golden Gate Bridge, Telegraph Hill, and Lombard Street. It was so different from Tucson, Arizona, where we lived. It was beautiful. Today, in those same areas, people live on the streets, defecate and urinate in public. Addicts have scattered drug paraphernalia across the sidewalks.

Heart Broken

I was in the Bay Area just over a year ago, and it was depressing. Therefore, I can understand why Nehemiah sat down and wept in verse 1:4. Grief broke his heart. The people of Israel confessed their sins and repented. God hears our prayers when we do this. The people in California refuse to see their actions as sinful. If the Californians repented, verse 1:9 reminds us that God told Moses, "If you return to me and obey my commands...I will gather them from there and bring them to a place I have chosen as a dwelling place for my Name." That place is our hearts, where His Name, Jesus, will dwell when we confess our sins. In chapter 2, Nehemiah goes before King Artaxerxes, while in this depressed funk.

Teamwork

A servant had to appear joyful when they approached the king; otherwise, it could be dangerous. This could show they were ill and could infect the king. Therefore, just to expose the king to disease, they may have executed him. Instead, Artaxerxes asks why he has a long face. To assure the king he and his queen are in no danger, Nehemiah explains the trouble in his heart (v 2:17).

Then they get to Jerusalem and rebuild the wall. I love how, twenty-six hundred years later, we can read the names of those who were working on each section. First, it shows me that fixing a problem of this size is not something one person can do. They needed the edict from the rulers. Then, it took many people to accomplish the work.

They teach us in our society to be faceless, nameless data points on spreadsheets. The quality of our labor is irrelevant. Companies like this because it makes us replaceable (Godin 2010).

In Nehemiah 3, the heads of the family took pride in the work they did. Prizing their work immortalized their names. They may have been a perfume maker, like Hananiah in verse 3:8, but he didn't complain about being too busy. Nor did he claim it wasn't part of his job. He completed the work, and he will receive lasting credit for it. We might also say we aren't capable, and the work is too hard. In verse 3:12, we read that even Shallum's daughters helped. Their important work led to notice being given even to their grandfather, Hallohesh. Nehemiah, who was in charge of part of the district of Beth-Zur, got involved and helped with the repairs (v 3:16).

Facing Opposition

It is easy to be involved when everyone is cheering for you. I have seen celebrities and politicians pose for photo opportunities, holding shovels. That was not the case in Jerusalem. We have the Samaritans complaining and doing everything possible to frustrate their efforts (v 4:2). Because of this, the Jews had to have half their people stand guard while the other half did the work. They would trade off. Sometimes even keeping one hand on their sword while the other on a tool (v 4:21).

We have cities that were once treasures. San Francisco is not the only one. We took pride in them. Tourists would come just to look at them. Now they're an embarrassment. We want the government to fix them, but all they can do is approve the work. Everyone should take part in the repairs, not just provide funding. Instead of taking pride in our sins, we need to take pride if rebuilding America.

Tomorrow, we will read Nehemiah 5-7.

Day 136, Nehemiah 5-7: Breaking Free from Debt's Shackle

Good morning. As summer approaches, families turn their attention to vacations during prosperous times that may involve travel. These days have not been prosperous for everyone. One way to avoid being controlled by the economy is to distance yourself from debt. Today, as we read Nehemiah 5-8, we will be looking at three related topics: being a slave to debt, charging interest, and trying to earn salvation through works.

Avoid Slavery

The remnant of Israel that came back to Jerusalem was working on the wall, while being threatened by the Samaritans. With God's support, they will complete the repairs in only fifty-two days (v 6:15). Their needs went unmet while they were working. To keep going, they were borrowing from the wealthier people, including mortgaging their fields and homes (v 5:3). Moses had commanded them not to charge interest to a fellow Jew (Deut. 23:19). They were not following the commands.

Debt, like sin, is an escalating situation. They borrowed money to pay taxes to the king on their fields (v 5:4). The further they got in, the more they needed to borrow. In modern-day America, you need good credit. To develop good credit, borrow money and prove you can repay it.

Like most people I know, I overextended myself when I was younger. This allowed me to have nicer things than I could afford, including a brand new 1986 GMC Mini-Jimmy. When it rolled and injured my spine, I defaulted on those loans. The loans ruined my credit. This would affect our ability to buy a home later. We paid cash for years and re-established our credit.

There is a fine line that people must walk. Have and use credit, but exercise caution. When you are paying interest, you have fewer resources available. It is tempting to think you have room on a credit card. I encourage you to pray about this. Debt can make you its slave.

God Provides

Deuteronomy 28:12 states, "The Lord will open to you his good treasury, the heavens, to give the rain to your land in its season and to bless all the work of your hands. And you shall lend to many nations, but you shall not borrow" (NIV). God's timing should guide you when you trust Him for provision.

Taking on debt to avoid waiting makes money our master, and we become its servants. Look at how much interest most Americans pay on their mortgages, and how little comes off the principle. This is the problem.

This was happening to the Israelites. They returned to Jerusalem, but they found their homes ruined and their fields devastated. Instead of waiting for God to provide, they mortgaged themselves and were having trouble feeding their families (v 5:1).

The Problem with Interest

This would not have happened if the rich people had not violated the Law of Moses and had not charged interest. The sin of borrowing instead of waiting on God was being compounded by the sin of greed. Nehemiah steps in and gets the people to discontinue this sin, and their circumstances improve. He pushes back on the governors to remove the tax burdens as well. This is commendable. The people return to offering sacrifices to the Lord. This tells me that even while suffering, they prioritized following God's commands.

Not our works

For his hand in this turnaround, Nehemiah states, "Remember me with favor, my God, for all I have done for these people." (v 5:19, NIV). People like to think that God will bless us for doing good to others. If we are walking with God, we will want to help our brothers. When we do, He may bless us. Not for helping our brothers, but for seeking His will.

God will judge us all one day. God will judge the actions of those who trusted in Jesus as their savior. He will reward how we use our salvation to glorify God. But it won't get us into heaven. That is a different judgment. God will judge those whose names are not in the Book of Life because of their sins. We all have thousands, even millions, of sins on our ledger. It is not a balance sheet.

God will look at a sin we committed. Let's say we lusted after a person we see walking down the street, or coveted our neighbor's shiny sports car. God will not be looking in the credit column to see what will balance this. He will simply determine if you committed this sin. Sin cannot be in heaven, so if you are holding onto sin, you won't be. The only way to remove that sin is now, in this life, confess your sins, repent, and ask Jesus to save you. I urge you all to make sure you will be on the right line. But understand that if God saves you, he will judge how you used that salvation.

Tomorrow, we will read Nehemiah 8-10.

Day 137, Nehemiah 8-10:
Revival: A Week of Awakening

Good morning. I hope today's chapters encourage you as much as they encourage me. We will discuss Nehemiah chapters 8-10.

Opening God's Word

What a beautiful way to start out his morning. As I do daily, they come together and ask Ezra, the teacher of the Law, to grab the Book of the Law of Moses (v 8:1). The purpose of our reading through the Bible is to build that discipline. Even more so, it is to create the desire to hear the Word of God. That daily dose of vitamin G! Regardless of our circumstances, when we have God in our lives, we know we can face anything. There is no better way to know we are walking with God than to spend some time listening to Him. Praying is how we talk to God. Being quiet, we can hear His voice in our hearts. Reading the Word of God is how we hear that voice through even the most chaotic of times. Having someone read it to you helps you focus. This is one reason church attendance is vital.

I have had public engagements where I would sign my book Moving Ahead: How to Make America Godly Again. Even people wearing crosses or shirts with Christian-themed messages on them will see the word God and turn away. It is heartbreaking. Not because they reject my book but because they are avoiding God.

The situation in Jerusalem was different at the beginning of chapter eight. They came together, united in purpose. Yearning to hear the Word of the Law of Moses.

No Complaints

I have watched people in churches look at their watches. You know they are becoming impatient for the service to end. If you ask them about it, they have even mentioned that when they sit too long, their legs will fall asleep, or their back hurts.

Here we read Ezra preached from daybreak till noon (v 8:3). They were standing in the square (v 8:5). Not complaining but striving to understand all the teacher was saying.

At our church, we can get around one hundred people on a Sunday morning. Getting them to return on Wednesday night is more challenging. We are lucky to have fifteen people attend.

These Jewish people's hunger for God's word was so great that they came seven days in a row, from daybreak to dawn. We can assume Ezra was a captivating teacher. His purpose, like mine, is to help the people understand what the Word meant (v 8:8). They would share in a feast after the service (v 8:10), but this was not why they were there. They wanted to know God. As they heard the Words of the Law of Moses, they knew they were not following the commands. This convicted them, and they wept (v 8:9). The Law of Moses teaches us about sin and the commandments God gives us for righteous living.

People today want to hear about grace and prosperity. We want to hear about God's love. He hopes we find happiness and fulfillment. Many modern churches would reject Ezra's message. But these people wanted God. They didn't want what God could do for them or provide. They wanted His presence in their lives.

God is the only reward we need. Therefore, Ezra reminds them not to be sorrowful about their shame but to rejoice in having that relationship with God (v 8:10). They were not worried about their comforts. Their homes were in shambles, but they lived on the rooftops under palm branches (v 8:13-16).

Revival

They came every day for a solid week. The closest thing I have experienced was a three-day Peacekeepers event. To get people to gather for three days, they had to have a mix of different speakers broken up with praise bands and special guests. This was a transformative experience for me. I left feeling I had grown in my walk with the Lord.

These people were hearing Ezra preach somewhere around six hours a day, for a week! Half of that time, they were reading from the Book of the Law. The other half, they were confessing their sins (v 9:2-3). They were not hearing a new spin on anything. They were being reminded of all God had done for their ancestors and how He brought them out of bondage.

Then, they heard of their sins. How they acted wickedly (v 9:33). They remembered their relationship with God and admitted their failures. Then, they renewed their commitment (v 10:29). It was a genuine commitment. They would not even violate the Sabbath when merchants offered to sell merchandise or grain (v 10:31).

We get impatient if a sermon runs long, preventing us from going out to lunch or joining a friend to do some shopping. This had been their practice in Babylon. Now, they wanted to honor God and respect His Laws. This led them to give to their temple. Verse 10:39 says, "We will not neglect the house of our God."

Our churches today could be so much more than they are. We need to have a revival in our country. People need to recommit themselves to seeking God and following His ways. If we do, we can see the improvement in our land that followed this book of Nehemiah.

Tomorrow, we will read Nehemiah 11-13.

Day 138, Nehemiah 11-13:
The Ministry Unveiled – A Call to Service

Good morning. We have reached the end of another book. Thank you all for staying the course. Knowing you are reading is an encouragement. Today, we will look at Nehemiah 11-13.

The Ministry

I did not expect to find this message to be about types of ministry, but this is what God is showing me. Nehemiah 11:1 records that they chose people by lot to live in Jerusalem. This was a dangerous place to dwell. Foreigners all around the region had chosen Jerusalem as their favorite target.

Today, the nation of Israel remains surrounded by enemies. Because of the danger, people respected those who accepted that call (v 11:2). I equate this with people who accept the call to the ministry. We will read about various levels of ministers in these chapters. In verse 11:14, there is a select group of one hundred twenty-eight men of standing. This could include all preachers, but these men of valor could have been elsewhere.

Pastors

Their love for God dictated they would be in the temple where He dwells. Therefore, I see this to be the Pastors. They were the ones who would care for the city of God and would do the "outside work of the house of God" (v 11:16, NIV). This does not mean taking care of the landscape but going out to the community. Doing outreach.

My pastor is always in the hospital visiting sick members or even friends and family of members. He is performing the services at funerals, sometimes without a prior relationship with the deceased. In between this, he meets couples to discuss weddings and visits people who have shown interest in our church. I texted him in the middle of the night when heading to a hospital. He comes at any hour.

This is one aspect of ministry that the Lord has not put on my heart or equipped me for. Therefore, I remain an itinerant preacher with no desire to pastor a church. In our church, there are only a couple of paid staff members. Whatever they pay the pastor is not enough.

Music Director

The other employee of the church is our music director. He also takes care of administration duties and building maintenance. All of this corresponds with the writing in verse 13:5. This is fitting when we read in v 11:23, which says, "The musicians were under the king's orders, which regulated their daily activity."

I had aspired to that calling many years ago, but after praying, I could tell God had other plans for me. I was not like the musicians who had built villages for themselves around Jerusalem. Involved and available for everything, but not in the city. This resembles our deacons as well. The director of musicians, ordained for this task, leads "songs of praise and thanksgiving to God" (v 12:46). Some people desire these positions. That does not mean they are called by God. We must vet them. In verse 13:1, as they read the Book of

Moses, they find that Ammonites and Moabites should never be in the Assembly of God.

God brought their refusal to meet Israel while passing through the land to their attention.

Instead, they called on Balaam to curse them. God turned those curses into blessings. Then, we have priests who serve in daily activities. Not all denominations refer to their staff as priests. I would say in our church, this is my role as a preacher. It takes a well-rounded staff to keep a congregation going. In verse 13:10, we read the officials neglected the staff. Because of this oversight, they went back into their own fields. Therefore, they neglected God's house, and it showed signs of wear.

Nehemiah calls the officials who had caused this and rebukes them. He returned them to their posts to perform their duties.

Salvation

Then we see it is not just the staff members but even those outside the church. The merchants were trying to do business on the Sabbath instead of keeping it holy. Nehemiah rebuked this and forbade them from continuing to do so. To get around this, they tried to wait at the gates on the Sabbath to be the first into Jerusalem to conduct business. He rebuked them for this, because it still desecrated the Sabbath. Last, but not least, we see in Nehemiah saying, "Remember me for this, my God, and do not blot out what I have so faithfully done" (v 13:14). He added a list of his accomplishments and asked, "Remember me with favor, my God" (v 13:31).

I think Nehemiah had faith. He didn't know the name of Jesus, but he had faith in God.

Abraham was similar, and God accounted for his faith as righteousness (Rom 4:3). What

Nehemiah was doing in these verses, however, is not how anyone will enter the kingdom of God. This is a work-based religion. He was saying, keep my name in the Book of Life, because I did all these deeds. His name will not be in the Book of Life unless Jesus has accepted his faith. Ephesians 2:8-9 says, "For it is by grace you have been saved, through faith—and this is not from yourselves, it is the gift of God — not by works, so that no one can boast." That verse is in every Bible for the last two thousand years, and yet many try to earn their way into heaven.

No sinful person will be in heaven. It would be like letting a fish live on dry land. The environment would not be compatible. Heaven is holy, we must be holy to dwell there. The only way that can happen is to have all our sins forgiven. This happens when Jesus takes our sins and gives or imputes His righteousness to us. Which only happens when we place our faith in Christ (see Romans 3:22). Have you done this?

Tomorrow, we will read Esther 1-5.

Questions for the Book of Nehemiah

Now that you have read the sixteenth book of the Bible, take a moment to reflect. How have the events in Nehemiah mirrored lessons in your own life? Do you feel yourself growing in knowledge? Are you also growing in faith?

For fun, here are five questions I want you to answer (I will post some brief answers at the back of the book).

1. What was Nehemiah's job or position in the court of King Artaxerxes in Persia?

2. What news from Jerusalem made Nehemiah deeply sad and led him to mourn, fast, and pray?

3. How did Nehemiah organize the workers so they could both build the wall and protect themselves from attacks?

4. Besides external enemies, what internal problem arose among the Jews that Nehemiah had to address, involving debt and oppression?

5. How did the people react after hearing the Law of God read by Ezra, understanding its meaning for the first time in a long while?

Chapter 17:
ESTHER

Day 139, Esther 1-5:
Faith, Courage, and the Fight Against Hate

Good morning, and welcome to the next book in the Bible – Esther. Today, we will read the first five chapters. In the first half of this story, we will see how hatred can manifest itself against a nation. We will also learn some personal attributes that made Esther the hero she is. We can all show these noble traits if we seek God as she did.

Influential

According to BibleHub.org, a website I use for commentaries, Esther is the ninth most influential woman in the Bible.[1] This may not sound very significant, but it is one place ahead of the Virgin Mary, the mother of our Lord Jesus. What makes Esther so influential? We will look at several of these attributes and actions between today and tomorrow.

Preservation

The first is her pivotal role in preserving the Jewish people. In history, there have been several attempts to annihilate the Jewish people. The most obvious and famous, or infamous, would be Adolf Hitler. History does not record any direct mention that the book of Esther influenced Hilter. However, there are some strong links. He was familiar with some antisemitic tracts like the Protocols and Elders of Zion, which were popular in Germany. His vehemence toward the Jewish race parallels that of Haman. His actions are also very similar. Both men exploit their power to remove God's people. It is their hatred that fuels their actions and brings their demise. The second most notorious person who wanted to destroy the Jewish race was Haman. His personal animosity toward Mordecai caused him to issue an edict through the Persian empire to kill every Jewish person. He did this without being aware that Esther belonged to this group.

A Supreme Job Opening

Meanwhile, King Xerxes had a falling out with his wife, Queen Vashti (v 1:19). His solution was to replace her. Esther was the lucky girl who won the King's affection. He issued an edict, what today would be an executive order, to prevent all the wives throughout his kingdom from disrespecting their husbands. This document made every man the ruler of his household. God had already assigned this authority in Gen 3:16. To the woman, he said, "I will greatly increase your pains in childbearing; with pain, you will give birth to children. Your desire will be for your husband, and he will rule over you." (NIV) The King became quite fond of Esther. She was beautiful (v 2:9). He would give her anything she asked for (v 5:3). Meanwhile, Mordecai upset Haman because he would not kneel before him. This was a sign of worship. We are not to worship anyone other than God (Deut. 6:13). Therefore, Haman devises a plan to have gallows made to hang Mordecai on. In the NIV, it is described as a pole on which to impale him.

Finding Her Purpose

Though much of the action in these verses was between Mordecai and Haman, Esther takes center stage. She has access to the King. No one guaranteed this. If she approached King Xerxes uninvited, he could have her killed. Her bravery and courage to even risk her life was notable in verse 4:16. With the famous words, "If I perish, I perish," she gains his audience. If she had just asked the King, it would have created a conflict. His word was everything, and his officials had convinced him to issue the edict from Haman. To go back on it would damage his credibility.

Her Wisdom

She needed to create a way for King Xerxes to understand she would be at risk, because she was a Jew. Her strategic thinking enabled her to expose Haman. I prefer thinking of the apparatus as gallows, not a pole, because she gave Haman enough rope to hang himself.

Obedience and Faith

This required her unwavering faith that God would save her people. She trusted Him for their deliverance. Her obedience to her uncle Mordecai provides a great example to people across centuries. We can also learn from her humility. Even though she was queen and chosen from all the concubines, she knew this would not protect her or her people. Because of these actions, she has left a legacy. Jewish people still celebrate the story of Purim, which recalls her heroics. The festival of Purim commemorates the deliverance of the Jewish people from Haman's plot to exterminate them, as recorded in the Book of Esther (Esther 9:24-32).

Hate Continues

Today, there are countries throughout the Middle East that want Israel and the Jewish people annihilated again. Satan knows that God's salvation and deliverance come through the nation of Israel. Therefore, he continues to attack her. If he could eliminate the people, he feels the ending may change. It will not. God will complete His plan, which we will learn more about in the coming books. Tomorrow, we will see how this story of Esther concludes when we read chapters 6-10.

Day 140, Esther 6-10

A Story of Reward and Retribution

Hello, and thank you for joining us in wrapping up Esther. Today, we will discuss topics from chapters 6-10. We will see how God's absence causes people to struggle. Then, we learn how a sense of entitlement and misplaced pride can lead to disaster. Today's verses show us that the Lord rewards those who seek him.

Struggles

In the opening sentence of chapter 6, King Xerxes is having trouble sleeping. His trusted colleague, Haman, had led him astray. I would not want to be a king. The responsibilities of even a small kingdom would be enormous. King Xerxes ruled over the Persian empire, which reached from India to Cush (Est 1:1). For modern reference, that would reach from Pakistan to the border of Greece, up to the border with Russia, and include Egypt and parts of Libya. The tribes and peoples of that vast area were always at war with each other. They continue to fight today. A leader of such an extensive empire could not watch every detail. Therefore, he surrounded himself with advisors he could trust. His own actions did not trouble Xerxes, but God was preventing him from finding peace.

My mother always knew if I was out causing trouble. She had an inherent sense, which caused her uneasiness. I may have thought I was getting away with whatever action I was doing with my friends. She would question me in a way that always brought out the truth.

Part of what was bothering him was that he knew there were people trying to assassinate him, as stated in verse 6:1. This would be disturbing to any ruler.

Today, we have former FBI Director James Comey posting a message saying 8647. Bigthana and Teresh, two of King Xerxes' insiders, were supposed to be protecting him. Instead, they were plotting his demise. Mordecai exposed the plot, but Haman's anger meant he went unrewarded. This did not set well with the King.

Dangers of Pride

Haman had let his own pride go to his head. He felt entitled to be honored. He had done nothing of significance, but Haman felt the King was talking about him when Xerxes asked how he should honor someone (v 6:7). I love how this backfires on him, resulting in him being required to honor Mordecai. When we serve the Lord, it should be out of love. We should not be expecting the Lord to bless us. The Lord is our blessing. We must not want more. To say something is more implies it is greater than God. There is nothing greater than walking with God. Haman had access to Xerxes and everything that came with this honor. Instead, he wanted public notoriety.

Rewards

Mordecai was watching out for God's people. Knowing this, God orchestrated events, allowing Mordecai to gain respect. He also gave him the power to vanquish his enemies.

This included Haman, who would face impalement on the pole he had constructed for Mordecai (v 7:10). Esther describes him as "An adversary and enemy!" (v 7:5). Our adversary is the devil (see 1 Pet 5:8). Like Haman, he lurks around, scowling. Trying to get the King to accuse and destroy us. One cannot deceive God (see Gal 6:7). He knows what happens in the dark, when we think we have escaped detection (Matt 6:6). Not only was Mordecai rewarded, but his actions saved the Jewish race. Purim memorializes this every year. Acknowledging Esther's bravery and God's faithfulness toward his people, which we see in verses 9:20-28. This story teaches us that our actions will always come to light. We should avoid harboring hatred toward anyone. Our allegiance should always be in following God. God will reward this. There is nothing greater.

Questions for the Book of Esther

Now that you have read the seventeenth book of the Bible, take a moment to reflect. How have the events in Esther mirrored lessons in your own life? Do you feel yourself growing in knowledge? Are you also growing in faith?

For fun, here are five questions I want you to answer (I will post some brief answers at the back of the book).

1. In what vast empire and city does the story of Esther take place?
2. What courageous and dangerous action did Esther take to save her people, knowing it could mean her death?
3. How did Esther cleverly expose Haman's plot to the king without initially directly accusing him?
4. What was Haman's fate after the King discovered his plot and grew angry?
5. At the end of the book of Esther, which Jewish holiday establishes to commemorate the deliverance of the Jews from Haman's plot?

Chapter 17: Footnotes

1. https://biblehub.com/top10/most_influential_women_in_the_bible.htm
2. "Top 10 Most Influential Women in the Bible," Bible Hub, accessed July 1, 2025, https://biblehub.com/top10/most_influential_women_in_the_bible.htm.

A Final Word

Thank you for reading the first seventeen books of the Bible with me. This is a good start.

We have talked about how few people read the entire Bible.

The Bible is important but should not be worshiped. Only God deserves our praise.

Reading the Bible is how we come to know God better.

This book covered seventeen of sixty-six books. They are longer books, and we have covered a third of the scripture.

In my next book, we will start Job and look at the books of Poetry. The Psalms will provide more context on how the people we've already met, worshipped God.

Then, we meet all the prophets, major and minor. This will set the stage for the coming Christ.

As you have seen, Jesus was present throughout the Bible. He is the overriding theme of all sixty-six books.

The prophets will help us see how we can trust that Jesus is the Son of God. They will also tell us what our future contains.

Now that you have built this habit, don't lose momentum.

Join me in my next book.

Final Bibliography

The Holy Bible, New International Version. Grand Rapids, MI: Zondervan, 2011.

"Americans Are Fond of the Bible, Don't Actually Read It." Lifeway Research. April 25, 2017. https://research.lifeway.com/2017/04/25/americans-are-fond-of-the-bible-dont-actuallyread-it/.

Barnes, Albert. *Barnes' Notes on the Old and New Testaments*. London: Blackie & Son, 1884.

Benson, Joseph. *Benson Commentary on the Old and New Testaments*. London: Thomas Tegg and Son, 1854.

Blackaby, Henry T., Richard Blackaby, and Claude V. King. *Experiencing God: Knowing and Doing the Will of God*. Nashville: B&H Publishing Group, 2008.

Boretti, Alberto. "mRNA Vaccine Boosters and Impaired Immune System Response in Immune Compromised Individuals: A Narrative Review." *Clinical and Experimental Medicine* 24 (2024). https://link.springer.com/article/10.1007/s10238-023-01264-1.

The Breakfast Club. Directed by John Hughes. 1985; Universal Pictures.

Carnegie, Dale. *How to Win Friends and Influence People*. New York: Simon and Schuster, 1936.

Children's Hospital of Philadelphia. "Immune System and Vaccines." Accessed July 1, 2025. https://www.chop.edu.

"Chronicles: Not Just a Repeat." The Bible Project. Accessed June 1, 2025. https://bibleproject.com/articles/chronicles-not-just-repeat/.

"Did the Author of Chronicles Also Write the Books of Ezra and Nehemiah?." Biblical Archaeology Society Library. Accessed June 1,

2025. https://library.biblicalarchaeology.org/article/did-the-author-of-chronicles-also-write-thebooks-of-ezra-and-nehemiah/.

"Does the COVID-19 Vaccine Weaken the Immune System? What to Know." *Medical News Today.* Last modified April 2023. https://www.medicalnewstoday.com/articles/is-yourimmune-system-weak-after-covid-vaccine.

Ellicott, Charles John. *Ellicott's Commentary for English Readers.* London: Cassell and Company, 1905.

Finding Nemo. Directed by Andrew Stanton and Lee Unkrich. Burbank, CA: Walt Disney Pictures, 2003.

"General Conference Prayer Length." *Zelophehad's Daughters* (blog), July 13, 2020. https://zelophehadsdaughters.com/2020/07/13/general-conference-prayer-length/.

Gibson, Mel, director. *The Passion of the Christ.* 2004; Newmarket Films.

Godin, Seth. *Linchpin: Are You Indispensable?* New York: Portfolio, 2010.

Harvard Business School Online. "6 Characteristics of an Effective Leader." Accessed July 1, 2025. https://online.hbs.edu/blog/post/characteristics-of-an-effective-leader.

Henry, Matthew. *Matthew Henry's Concise Commentary on the Bible.* Grand Rapids, MI: Christian Classics Ethereal Library, n.d.

Hughes, John, director. *The Breakfast Club.* 1985; Universal Pictures.

Jamieson, Robert, A. R. Fausset, and David Brown. *Commentary Critical and Explanatory on the Whole Bible.* Hartford, CT: S.S. Scranton Company, 1871.

Keil, C. F., and F. Delitzsch. *Commentary on the Old Testament.* Vol. 1. Accessed via Bible Hub.

Kirkpatrick, A. F., ed. *The Cambridge Bible for Schools and Colleges.* Cambridge: Cambridge University Press, 1907.

Knowlton, Scott. "8 Mind-Blowing Stats About Church Invites." *Scott knowlton* (blog). Accessed June 30, 2025. https://scottknowlton.com/8-mind-blowing-stats-about-churchinvites/.

Kramer, Stephanie. "Polygamy is rare around the world and mostly confined to a few regions." Pew Research Center. December 7, 2020. https://www.pewresearch.org/shortreads/2020/12/07/polygamy-is-rare-around-the-world-and-mostly-confined-to-a-fewregions/.

Linders, Thom. *Moving Ahead: How to Make America Godly Again*. Tucson, AZ: Book Writing Pioneer, 2025.

"List of Religions and Spiritual Traditions." Wikipedia. Last modified June 30, 2025. https://en.wikipedia.org/wiki/List_of_religions_and_spiritual_traditions.

Murray, D. P. *Jesus on Every Page: 10 Simple Ways to Seek and Find Christ in the Old Testament*. Thomas Nelson, 2013.

Nie, Cody. "When Do Most Crimes Happen?" Deep Sentinel. February 16, 2024. https://www.deepsentinel.com/blogs/home-security/when-do-most-crimes-happen.

Orwell, George. *Animal Farm*. London: Secker & Warburg, 1945.

Orwell, George. *Nineteen Eighty-Four*. London: Secker & Warburg, 1949.

The Personal Growth Project. "The Role of Isolation in Abuse." Accessed July 1, 2025. https://www.thepersonalgrowthproject.com/blog/the-role-of-isolation-in-abuse.

Piper, John. *Desiring God: Meditations of a Christian Hedonist*. Sisters, OR: Multnomah Publishers, 1986.

The Princess Bride. Directed by Rob Reiner. 1987; Twentieth Century Fox.

Russell, Adrian. "Lamenting the Days When Boxing Was the Sport of Kings." *Irish Examiner*, September 23, 2011.

"The Story Behind Turkey's Underground Cities." The Culture Trip. Last modified March 8, 2021. https://theculturetrip.com/europe/turkey/articles/the-story-behind-turkeysunderground-cities.

Strong, James, and John McClintock. *The Cyclopædia of Biblical, Theological, and Ecclesiastical Literature*. New York: Harper & Brothers, 1880.

Sun Tzu. *The Art of War*. Translated by Lionel Giles. Boston: Shambhala, 2005.

"Top 10 Most Influential Women in the Bible." Bible Hub. Accessed July 1, 2025. https://biblehub.com/top10/most_influential_women_in_the_bible.htm.

U.S. Food and Drug Administration. "Antibacterial Soap? You Can Skip It, Use Plain Soap and Water." Last modified December 1, 2021. https://www.fda.gov/consumers/consumerupdates/antibacterial-soap-you-can-skip-it-use-plain-soap-and-water.

The Wizard of Oz. Directed by Victor Fleming, et al. 1939; Metro-Goldwyn-Mayer.

Whedon, Joss, director. *The Avengers*. 2012; Walt Disney Studios Motion Pictures.

"Why Do Cain's Descendants Show After the Flood?." The Bible Project Podcast. Accessed June 1, 2025. https://bibleproject.com/podcast/why-do-cains-descendants-show-afterflood/.

Answer Key

Section 1: Genesis

1. Their disobedience and sin.

2. To save Noah, his family, and animals from a worldwide flood; the flood destroyed the wicked, and Noah and his family repopulated the earth.

3. Abraham was a patriarch of faith; God promised him descendants as numerous as the stars, land in Canaan, and that through his lineage, all nations would be blessed.

4. Sodom and Gomorrah were cities filled with wickedness and sexual immorality; God destroyed them because of their extreme sin.

5. Joseph's brothers sell him into slavery, but he rose to a position of power in Egypt; his experiences show how God can use demanding situations to bring about His good purposes.

Section 2: Exodus

1. The ten plagues that God sent upon Egypt, culminating in the death of the firstborn, forced Pharaoh to release the Israelites.

2. God parted the Red Sea, allowing the Israelites to walk through on dry land, while Pharaoh's army was subsequently drowned.

3. The Ten Commandments, which are a foundation of Jewish and Christian morality.

4. The Passover was a celebration commemorating God's deliverance of the Israelites from slavery in Egypt. It involved a special meal and the marking of doorways to protect against the death of the firstborn.

5. A long and difficult journey through the wilderness, guided by God, towards the Promised Land of Canaan.

Section 3: Leviticus

1. Leviticus primarily focuses on the laws and regulations God gave to the Israelites concerning worship, sacrifice, and holiness.

2. Leviticus describes types of sacrifices, including burnt offerings (completely consumed by fire), grain offerings (food offerings), peace offerings (communion meals), sin offerings (atonement for unintentional sins), and guilt offerings (atonement for intentional wrongs).

3. Yom Kippur was the most sacred day of the year, where the high priest would make atonement for the sins of the people by performing special rituals in the Tabernacle.

4. The laws in Leviticus covered aspects of daily life, including food laws (kosher), cleanliness rituals, and social conduct, teaching the Israelites how to live a life pleasing to God.

5. The main message of Leviticus is the importance of holiness and the need to live a life set apart for God, demonstrating reverence and obedience to His laws.

Section 4: Numbers

1. The census was to count the fighting men of Israel, to determine the number of tribes and their military strength. This was important for organizing the Israelites and for making sure that each tribe contributed their fair share of the work and the fighting.

2. The Israelites wandered in the wilderness for 40 years after God rescued them from Egypt. Their journey was long and difficult, marked by rebellion, testing by God, and miraculous provision. They moved from Mount Sinai towards the Promised Land, but their disobedience delayed them.

3. Numbers contains laws and instructions from God, including laws related to camp organization, sacrifices, vows, and the

treatment of others. There are also instructions related to the role of the priests and Levites in leading the people.

4. The bronze serpent, lifted on a pole by Moses, was a symbol of healing and salvation for those bitten by poisonous snakes. It served as a physical representation of God's ability to heal and rescue. It also foreshadowed Jesus on the cross.

5. Their frequent complaints, rebellions, and lack of faith often resulted in punishment, delays, and hardship. God gave them trials throughout their journey, and their repeated disobedience made the journey 40 years instead of the much shorter journey it should have been.

Section 5: Deuteronomy

1. Deuteronomy is a retelling of the Law given to Moses on Mount Sinai, but this time it focuses on how the Israelites should live once they enter the Promised Land. It's a reminder of their covenant with God and a guide for their future.

2. The Ten Commandments are ten important rules given by God to Moses. They're super important in Deuteronomy because they show the basics of how the Israelites should live to keep their agreement with God. Following them is key to their success and relationship with God.

3. If the Israelites followed God's laws, Deuteronomy says they'd have good harvests, win battles, and live happily in the Promised Land. Obedience meant a good life.

4. Deuteronomy also talks about terrible things that would happen if they disobeyed. These include losing wars, suffering from drought and famine, and getting sick. It makes it clear that going against God has dire consequences.

5. Deuteronomy explains how a king in Israel should rule fairly, humbly, and always follow God's laws. It warns against kings

who might be mean or forget about God. It emphasizes a king's responsibility to God and his people.

Section 6: Joshua

1. Joshua led the Israelites into the Promised Land of Canaan after Moses died, conquering the land and dividing it among the tribes.

2. The battle of Jericho was the first major victory for the Israelites in Canaan. God miraculously caused the walls of Jericho to fall, demonstrating his power and support for his people. This victory gave the Israelites courage and momentum to continue their conquest.

3. The crossing of the Jordan River is a significant miracle. The river's waters miraculously parted, allowing the Israelites to pass through on dry ground, mirroring the parting of the Red Sea and emphasizing God's power and protection.

4. After conquering Canaan, God divided the land into different areas for each of the twelve tribes of Israel. The division wasn't always equal or easy and sometimes led to disputes. The land division represented the fulfillment of God's promise to give his people a home.

5. Joshua emphasizes God's faithfulness to his promises and his power to help his people overcome obstacles. The book shows the importance of obedience to God and the consequences of disobedience, demonstrating God's guidance and support for those who follow him.

Section 7: Judges

1. The Israelites would sin by disobeying God and turning to idolatry. This resulted in oppression from their enemies. Then, they would cry out to God, and God would raise up a judge to deliver them. This cycle repeated throughout the book.

2. Deborah was a prophetess and judge who led the Israelites to victory against Sisera and the Canaanites. She is significant because she is one of the few female judges in the Bible and her leadership highlights God's ability to use anyone, he chooses to lead his people.

3. Gideon initially doubted his ability to lead the Israelites against the Midianites. Despite his fear, God gave him victory through a smaller army, demonstrating that God's power is greater than any human army. His story teaches about trusting in God's power even when facing overwhelming odds.

4. Samson was a powerful judge with incredible strength. But disobedience and weakness characterized his life. His story serves as a cautionary tale about the importance of obedience and faithfulness to God. It demonstrates that strength and power are not enough without faith.

5. The book of Judges highlights the consequences of disobedience and the importance of faith and reliance on God. It shows that despite repeated cycles of sin and redemption, God always remained faithful to his people. It emphasizes the need to follow God's commands for strength and peace.

Section 8: Ruth

1. The story takes place in the land of Moab, and later in Bethlehem in ancient Israel, during a time when the Israelites were harvesting barley and gleaning.

2. Gleaning was a custom where the poor could collect leftover grain in the fields after the harvest. Ruth's gleaning in Boaz's fields set the stage for her meeting Boaz and their eventual marriage.

3. The kinsman-redeemer law required a close relative to take responsibility for a deceased relative's property and family. Boaz

fulfilled this role for Naomi, marrying Ruth and providing for her and Naomi.

4. Obed, the son of Ruth and Boaz, is an ancestor of King David, connecting Ruth's story to the royal lineage of Israel.

5. Ruth's story celebrates themes of loyalty, kindness, faithfulness to God, and redemption. It shows how God works through ordinary people to accomplish his purposes and bless those who trust him.

Section 9: 1 Samuel

1. Samuel was a prophet and judge who anointed Saul and David as kings of Israel. He played a crucial role in guiding the Israelites and establishing the monarchy.

2. Saul's disobedience to God was his fatal flaw. He repeatedly failed to follow God's commands, leading to his downfall. He also showed signs of pride and insecurity.

3. David was known for his faith, courage, skill as a warrior, and musical talents. He also had an ability to connect with people and inspire loyalty.

4. Their relationship was complex. It started as one of respect and friendship, but turned into a rivalry and conflict, as Saul grew jealous of David's growing popularity and favor with God.

5. 1 Samuel traces the transition of leadership from a decentralized system of judges to a centralized monarchy in Israel. It emphasizes the importance of obedience to God, the consequences of disobedience, and God's choice of leaders based on His plan, not human expectations.

Section 10: 2 Samuel

1. David became king after Saul's death.

2. David committed adultery with Bathsheba and had her husband killed, a significant moral failing in his life.

3. Bringing the Ark to Jerusalem established Jerusalem as the central location of worship and symbolized the unification of Israel under David's rule.

4. Nathan was a prophet who confronted David about his sin with Bathsheba, prompting repentance and highlighting God's justice and mercy.

5. 2 Samuel shows the complexities of leadership and the consequences of both good and bad choices. It shows God's faithfulness despite human failings and highlights the importance of repentance and the establishment of a lasting dynasty through David.

Section 11: 1 Kings

1. It was a symbolic victory demonstrating David's faith and God's power over the Philistines. It established David's reputation for courage and faith.

2. Solomon was David's son and successor. He was known for his wisdom and for building the Temple in Jerusalem.

3. The Temple became the main place of worship for the Israelites. It represented God's presence among his people and the fulfillment of a long-held promise.

4. Solomon's wisdom was legendary, renowned throughout the ancient world. He was known for his ability to solve difficult problems and to make wise decisions.

5. While David was a warrior king who expanded Israel's territory, Solomon focused on establishing a strong central government, building the Temple, and promoting trade and prosperity. His reign was more peaceful than David's.

Section 12: 2 Kings

1. Jeroboam's action was an act of idolatry, leading to the division and spiritual decline of the northern kingdom of Israel. It caused the people to turn away from worshiping God in Jerusalem.

2. Elijah challenged the prophets of Baal to a contest to demonstrate the true God's power. Elijah's God answered with fire, proving the supremacy of Yahweh over Baal.

3. The Assyrian invasions led to the downfall of the northern kingdom of Israel, highlighting the consequences of the people's persistent disobedience and idolatry.

4. The prophets, like Elijah and Elisha, served as messengers of God, warning the kings and people about the consequences of sin and encouraging them to return to God. Their actions demonstrated the necessity of following God's guidance.

5. 2 Kings shows the consequences of disobedience and the importance of faithfulness to God. It demonstrates God's judgment on sin but also shows his mercy and compassion towards those who repent. The book highlights the rise and fall of kingdoms and the ongoing relationship between God and His people.

Section 13: 1 Chronicles

1. King David brought the Ark of the Covenant to Jerusalem.

2. David intended to build the Temple for God.

3. The tribe of Levi was emphasized for worship and service.

4. David provided materials, treasures, and detailed plans for the Temple.

5. It emphasizes the importance of proper worship and a centralized place for it, highlighting God's presence among His people.

Section 14: 2 Chronicles

1. Solomon; he asked for wisdom and knowledge to govern God's people.

2. Solomon constructed the magnificent Temple in Jerusalem.

3. The southern kingdom was called Judah.

4. Kings who did what was right generally experienced success, prosperity, and peace.

5. Hezekiah repaired and cleansed the Temple, reinstituted the Passover, and destroyed idols and high places.

Section 15: Ezra

1. Rebuilding the Temple of the Lord in Jerusalem.

2. The prophets Haggai and Zechariah.

3. They had intermarried with foreign people from the surrounding lands, violating God's commands.

4. They agreed to send away their foreign wives, and the children born from those marriages.

5. His purpose was to teach God's Law to Israel, enforce it, and lead the people back to obedience and spiritual purity.

Section 16: Nehemiah

1. He was the cupbearer to the king.

2. He heard that someone had broken down Jerusalem's walls and burned its gates.

3. He had them work with one hand and hold a weapon with the other, and ordered them to stay overnight in Jerusalem.

4. The wealthier Jews were charging excessive interest to their poorer brothers, leading them into slavery and loss of property.

5. They wept when they heard the words of the Law, realizing their disobedience.

Section 17: Esther

1. The Persian Empire, in the citadel of Susa.

2. She approached King Ahasuerus without being summoned (which was punishable by death).

3. She invited the king and Haman to two separate banquets, where she revealed Haman's wickedness at the second one.

4. They hanged him on the gallows he had prepared for Mordecai.

5. The festival of Purim.

Appendix: Daily Bible Reading Plan

Day	Book	Chapters
Day 1	Genesis	1, 2, 3
Day 2	Genesis	4, 5, 6
Day 3	Genesis	7, 8, 9, 10
Day 4	Genesis	11, 12, 13, 14
Day 5	Genesis	15, 16, 17, 18
Day 6	Genesis	19, 20, 21
Day 7	Genesis	22, 23, 24
Day 8	Genesis	25, 26, 27
Day 9	Genesis	28, 29, 30
Day 10	Genesis	31, 32
Day 11	Genesis	33, 34, 35
Day 12	Genesis	36, 37, 38
Day 13	Genesis	39, 40, 41
Day 14	Genesis	42, 43, 44

Day 15	Genesis	45, 46, 47
Day 16	Genesis	48, 49, 50
Day 17	Exodus	1, 2, 3, 4
Day 18	Exodus	5, 6, 7
Day 19	Exodus	8, 9, 10, 11
Day 20	Exodus	12, 13, 14
Day 21	Exodus	15, 16, 17, 18
Day 22	Exodus	19, 20, 21
Day 23	Exodus	22, 23, 24
Day 24	Exodus	25, 26, 27
Day 25	Exodus	28, 29
Day 26	Exodus	30, 31, 32
Day 27	Exodus	33, 34, 35
Day 28	Exodus	36, 37, 38
Day 29	Exodus	39, 40
Day 30	Leviticus	1, 2, 3, 4
Day 31	Leviticus	5, 6, 7
Day 32	Leviticus	8, 9, 10

Day 33	Leviticus	11, 12, 13
Day 34	Leviticus	14, 15
Day 35	Leviticus	16, 17, 18, 19
Day 36	Leviticus	20, 21, 22
Day 37	Leviticus	23, 24, 25
Day 38	Leviticus	26, 27
Day 39	Numbers	1, 2
Day 40	Numbers	3, 4
Day 41	Numbers	5, 6
Day 42	Numbers	7, 8
Day 43	Numbers	9, 10, 11
Day 44	Numbers	12, 13, 14
Day 45	Numbers	15, 16
Day 46	Numbers	17, 18, 19, 20
Day 47	Numbers	21, 22, 23
Day 48	Numbers	24, 25, 26
Day 49	Numbers	27, 28, 29
Day 50	Numbers	30, 31, 32

Day 51	Numbers	33, 34
Day 52	Numbers	35, 36
Day 53	Deuteronomy	1, 2
Day 54	Deuteronomy	3, 4, 5
Day 55	Deuteronomy	6, 7, 8, 9
Day 56	Deuteronomy	10, 11, 12, 13
Day 57	Deuteronomy	14, 15, 16, 17
Day 58	Deuteronomy	18, 19, 20, 21
Day 59	Deuteronomy	22, 23, 24, 25
Day 60	Deuteronomy	26, 27, 28
Day 61	Deuteronomy	29, 30, 31
Day 62	Deuteronomy	32, 33, 34
Day 63	Joshua	1, 2, 3, 4, 5
Day 64	Joshua	6, 7, 8
Day 65	Joshua	9, 10, 11
Day 66	Joshua	12, 13, 14
Day 67	Joshua	15, 16, 17, 18
Day 68	Joshua	19, 20, 21

Day 69	Joshua	22, 23, 24
Day 70	Judges	1, 2
Day 71	Judges	3, 4, 5
Day 72	Judges	6, 7, 8
Day 73	Judges	9, 10, 11
Day 74	Judges	12, 13, 14, 15
Day 75	Judges	16, 17, 18
Day 76	Judges	19, 20, 21
Day 77	Ruth	1, 2, 3, 4
Day 78	1 Samuel	1, 2, 3
Day 79	1 Samuel	4, 5, 6, 7
Day 80	1 Samuel	8, 9, 10, 11
Day 81	1 Samuel	12, 13, 14
Day 82	1 Samuel	15, 16, 17
Day 83	1 Samuel	18, 19, 20
Day 84	1 Samuel	21, 22, 23, 24
Day 85	1 Samuel	25, 26, 27
Day 86	1 Samuel	28, 29, 30, 31

Day 87	2 Samuel	1, 2, 3
Day 88	2 Samuel	4, 5, 6, 7
Day 89	2 Samuel	8, 9, 10, 11
Day 90	2 Samuel	12, 13, 14
Day 91	2 Samuel	15, 16, 17
Day 92	2 Samuel	18, 19
Day 93	2 Samuel	20, 21, 22
Day 94	2 Samuel	23, 24
Day 95	1 Kings	1, 2
Day 96	1 Kings	3, 4, 5
Day 97	1 Kings	6, 7
Day 98	1 Kings	8, 9
Day 99	1 Kings	10, 11
Day 100	1 Kings	12, 13, 14
Day 101	1 Kings	15, 16, 17
Day 102	1 Kings	18, 19, 20
Day 103	1 Kings	21, 22
Day 104	2 Kings	1, 2, 3, 4

Day 105	2 Kings	5, 6, 7
Day 106	2 Kings	8, 9, 10
Day 107	2 Kings	11, 12, 13, 14
Day 108	2 Kings	15, 16, 17
Day 109	2 Kings	18, 19, 20
Day 110	2 Kings	21, 22, 23
Day 111	2 Kings	24, 25
Day 112	1 Chronicles	1, 2
Day 113	1 Chronicles	3, 4, 5
Day 114	1 Chronicles	6
Day 115	1 Chronicles	7, 8
Day 116	1 Chronicles	9, 10, 11
Day 117	1 Chronicles	12, 13, 14, 15
Day 118	1 Chronicles	16, 17, 18, 19
Day 119	1 Chronicles	20, 21, 22, 23
Day 120	1 Chronicles	24, 25, 26
Day 121	1 Chronicles	27, 28, 29
Day 122	2 Chronicles	1, 2, 3, 4, 5

Day 123	2 Chronicles	6, 7, 8
Day 124	2 Chronicles	9, 10, 11, 12
Day 125	2 Chronicles	13, 14, 15, 16, 17
Day 126	2 Chronicles	18, 19, 20
Day 127	2 Chronicles	21, 22, 23, 24
Day 128	2 Chronicles	25, 26, 27, 28
Day 129	2 Chronicles	29, 30, 31
Day 130	2 Chronicles	32, 33, 34
Day 131	2 Chronicles	35, 36
Day 132	Ezra	1, 2, 3
Day 133	Ezra	4, 5, 6, 7
Day 134	Ezra	8, 9, 10
Day 135	Nehemiah	1, 2, 3, 4
Day 136	Nehemiah	5, 6, 7
Day 137	Nehemiah	8, 9, 10
Day 138	Nehemiah	11, 12, 13
Day 139	Esther	1, 2, 3, 4, 5
Day 140	Esther	6, 7, 8, 9, 10

www.ingramcontent.com/pod-product-compliance
Lightning Source LLC
Chambersburg PA
CBHW052005070526
44584CB00016B/1630